Import Marketing

Import Marketing

A Management Guide to
Profitable Operations

Jerry Haar
Florida International University

and

Marta Ortiz-Buonafina
Florida International University

Lexington Books
D.C. Heath and Company/Lexington, Massachusetts/Toronto

Library of Congress Cataloging-in-Publication Data

Haar, Jerry.
    Import marketing.

    Includes index.
    1. Imports—United States. 2. Foreign trade promotion—United States.
3. Foreign trade regulation—United States. I. Ortiz-Buonafina, Marta. II. Title.
HF3031.H23   1989   658.8′48   86-46350
ISBN 0-669-15692-2 (alk. paper)

Published simultaneously in Canada
Printed in the United States of America
International Standard Book Number: 0-669-15692-2
Library of Congress Catalog Card Number: 86-46350

The paper used in this publication meets the minimum requirements of American National
Standard for Information Sciences—Permanence of Paper for Printed Library Materials,
ANSI Z39.48-1984. ∞™

Year and number of this printing:

89 90 91 92 8 7 6 5 4 3 2 1

To my wonderful son Eric.

—*Jerry Haar*

*To M.T. Hernandez, as a special thank you
to a special friend.*

—*Marta Ortiz-Buonafina*

Contents

List of Figures, Tables, and Exhibits

Figures

Tables

Exhibits

Preface

International trade has undergone a dramatic transformation since the mid-1970s. The United States in particular has been affected profoundly by changes in the global economy. Notable among these changes are:

the maturation and decline of many sectors of the manufacturing base in industrial nations and the gradual shift to service-oriented economies,

the fluctuation and realignment of exchange rates,

high levels of consumer, public, and external debt among developed as well as developing nations,

the aggressive and extensive export drive (in both industrial and consumer goods) not only of Japan, but of a number of other Asian and Latin American newly industrializing nations.

The marked change in the U.S. merchandise-trade position from surplus to deficit and the accompanying calls by many for increased protectionism are testimony to these significant developments in the world economy. In consumer goods, import penetration of U.S. markets rose to 11.6 percent in 1987 and up from 6.9 percent in 1980. As for capital goods, foreign producers captured a whopping 37.7 percent of the U.S. market in 1987, up from 14.6 percent in 1980 according to the U.S. Department of Commerce.

The impetus for this book came from two sources: First,

1. There is a dual recognition that in spite of all the rhetoric, posturing and positioning (such as the need for an "industrial policy"), the United States, for structural reasons, will continue to be the final destination for massive amounts of foreign exports, and that this reality will continue to permeate U.S. trade, regardless of U.S.-government or private-sector export-promotion policies and programs.

2. Despite the tremendous demand and absorptive capacity of the U.S. market for imports, there currently does not exist, as far as we know, an up-to-date handbook, guide, or ready-reference for business people engaged in, or considering, importing. Information on importing is usually found as part of a larger, generally academic volume on marketing, often specifically on

international marketing. Also, there are smaller technical pamphlets that focus on one or two aspects of importing such as customs valuation or the new U.S. harmonized system of tariff classification. While these sources of information may be useful to their respective constituencies, students and specialists (attorneys and customs brokers), they are of limited use to the practitioner who needs a hands-on, advanced primer on the context, process, and operation of importing. The authors have attempted to fill that void, while at the same time providing business students and technical specialists with both an overview and a concise, systematic approach to import marketing.

This book is divided into three parts. The first analyzes the import-marketing environment, beginning with a brief discussion of the importance of trade, the roles of the International Monetary Fund (IMF) and General Agreement on Tariffs and Trade (GATT), the reasons nations trade, and sources of supply in the world economy. The domestic environment of import activities is discussed, including the political, legal, economic, demographic, and sociocultural aspects of import activities. The U.S. market, the size of the current import market, and the benefits of importing into the United States are covered as well. In analyzing import markets, detailed attention is given to finding attractive opportunities and the workings of consumer, producer, and reseller markets, with accompanying vignettes or cases.

Part II of the book discusses the import-marketing strategy. Factors affecting import-product decisions as well as the sources and production are presented. This is followed by a discussion of import channels of distribution: what they are, their function, factors affecting them, retailing, wholesaling and physical distribution. The chapter on import-promotion strategy covers the significance of marketing communication, cross-cultural influences, and the strategic relevance of advertising, promotion, and personal selling. The last chapter in part II highlights import-pricing strategy, including factors affecting import-price decisions, government regulations, foreign-exchange movements, competition, and buyer reactions.

The final part of the book examines in depth the import function and covers the various features of the import process:

searching for supplies,

negotiating the import purchase,

completing the invoices, contracts, and financing arrangements necessary to carry out the transaction.

Traffic, insurance and documentation, along with import procedures (such as customs) and other legal requirements, are fully discussed.

We hope this book will advance the understanding of importing into the United States and be of practical use to those who actually import or aspire to do so.

Acknowledgments

This book is the outgrowth of experience and frustration. In the first instance, the authors' extensive experience in teaching, research, and consulting in importing prompted the desire to share this knowledge with others in a systematic and useful fashion. In the second instance, we found ourselves frustrated in our professional lives due to the lack of a practical, import marketing guide and reference book.

We hope this book will alleviate some of the concerns and frustrations of others who travail in importing *and* exporting. It is intended as a useful guide to U.S. importers and foreign exporters who wish to understand the complex and dynamic nature of the U.S. market, the implications and role of the marketing strategy in the import process, and the basic fundamentals of importing.

We wish to express our gratitude to all the people who worked with us in this project: from those who helped prepare the manuscript to those who assisted in typing it and those who helped with their candid assessment and critique.

We wish to acknowledge in particular: Ludvik Jakopin, American Express Corporation (Canada), who provided invaluable research assistance and helped in the preparation of manuscript drafts; the World Trade Center, Miami; the U.S. Department of Commerce, Miami District Office; the Florida Department of Commerce, International Trade Office; Florida International Bankers Association; Florida Exporter and Importer Association; Armando Martinez, President of Avian Services; Edgar Bravo, President, Bravo Trading Company; Paul Simons, Simons and Rose Insurance Agency; Penny Willis, Sun Bank; Saturnino E. Lucio, II, law firm of Weil, Lucio, Mandler, and Croland; Samuel L. Hayden, Q.D.A. Investment Corporation; and Ruth Chapman, Melissa Rodriguez, and Irene Young, all of Florida International University.

Part I
Analysis of the Import-marketing Environment

1
An Introduction to Import-maketing Management

The Importance of Trade

The decade of the '80s has been marked by worldwide conflict between the forces of protectionism and those of free trade. Not since 1930, a date associated with the Smoot-Hawley Tariff, and the decade thereafter has international trade—and the world economy—been so vulnerable and so wracked by political demagoguery and market turmoil.

The United States has not escaped the global urge to establish barricades at the border. Addressing Congress in 1962, President John F. Kennedy proclaimed: "Trading one brick at a time off our respective tariff walls will not suffice. We must talk instead in terms of trading whole layers at a time in exchange for other layers."

Nonetheless, under both Democratic and Republican administrations, protectionist concessions have been granted to a number of powerful domestic industries: steel, lumber, automobiles, semiconductors, textiles, and machine tools, to name but a few. These resulting trade restraints have caused consumers to pay as much as twice the price as before the imposition of these controls. Not surprisingly, the United States's trading partners have erected barriers of their own prior to, as well as in response to, U.S. trade restrictions: Japan in agriculture, Brazil in informatics, and the Andean Pact countries in financial services.

In an even more foolhardy economic move, a number of nations have consciously manipulated their money supplies and exchange rates and expanded local subsidies (adding to their debt burden) to enhance their export competitiveness and resuscitate fossilized industries (such as the U.S. shoe industry).

Where reason has prevailed in international trade—overall the patient's vital signs do remain intact—it is due to the simple recognition by government, business, and consumers that the standard of living of a country can be enhanced by its trading with foreign countries. Numerous useful goods originate in other countries and provide the consumer with a greater diversity of products from which to select. These products range from simple household items to sophisticated videocassette recorders.

And trade *is* a two-way street. The Japanese may well be producing a huge share of the exported compact-disk players on the market today, but it is the music of American performers Michael Jackson, Madonna, and the Miami Sound Machine that Japanese young people are buying. Along with Levi's, bubble gum, toothpaste, and fast food, many other made-in-the-U.S.A. products are having their own special success in Japan and other Asian markets perceived as "export-only" trading partners. The same is true in the industrial-goods sector, where the notable performance of Toyota, Honda, and Nissan in automobiles is matched by Boeing, Lockheed, and McDonnell Douglas in aerospace.

Despite the mercantilist posturing of many newly industrialized nations—and a number of older industrialized countries as well—no nation can produce everything efficiently, effectively, and competitively. The United States is no exception. American consumers possess a wide range of needs and desires, and it is simply not possible to manufacture or grow domestically all the products to satisfy these buyers. The purchase of products from abroad can fill present needs, create new ones, and supplement the domestic product base. These products have three competitive advantages.

1. Imported goods may carry competitive prices relative to domestic prices. This may be due to the exporting country's weaker currency and lower wage levels (as in the case of U.S. imports of Mexican furniture) or more efficient production technology and higher worker productivity, even where a stronger currency and comparable wage levels exist (as with electronic goods exported from Japan). One must also not overlook government subsidization and other fiscal and regulatory policies (many of which are unfair, illegal, and trade-distorting) that falsely create an impression of competitiveness.

2. One often finds consumer preference for imported products over domestic ones. There are a myriad of reasons for this choice. Quality (as with the Volvo automobile from Sweden) ranks highest in many cases. However, there are aesthetic reasons as well, in the case of furniture (Roche-Bobois) and clothing (Giorgio Armani); taste, in the case of food (Droste cocoa from Holland, canned plum tomatoes from Italy); and panache or "status," as found in Corona beer from Mexico and the Rolex watch from Switzerland.

3. Competitiveness may be achieved due to the lack of availability of similar products in the domestic market. Portable radiocassette recorders from Japan and tomato paste in a tube from Italy are examples of products that achieved initial success due to the absence of domestic competition in the U.S. market.

All of these fundamental reasons motivate countries to trade.

In today's world economy, there are 161 independent nation-states that want to trade and improve their standard of living. Each country has the objective of gaining advantages in trade with other countries, and each nation wants to "play" in the international "arena" to pursue economic and political goals. Trade is unquestionably an economic activity that is complex, ever-changing, and permeated with regulations. These complexities are a result of interrelationships between trading nations, as goods and services are distributed to fulfill those nations' economic, political, and social goals.[1] The pursuit of these goals may be complementary and mutually beneficial in the case of trade between a country rich in raw materials and modest in the production of consumer electronics (such as Canada) and one poor in natural resources and wealthy in consumer-product manufacturing (Japan, for example). However, when economic and political objectives supersede the market-driven laws of free trade, conflict in the foreign relations among nations often results. Such is the case between the United States and Brazil regarding informatics. The former seeks open market access while the latter restricts or "reserves" the domestic market for its own infant industries of microcomputers, minicomputers, software, and dozens of others that employ digital technology.

International and Domestic Trade

International trade differs from domestic trade in four significant ways:

1. Goods and services travel across national boundaries.
2. In international trade, at least two currencies are involved in every transaction.
3. The countries engaged in international trade often differ in geography and physical features.
4. The physical spaces separating buyers and sellers, along with the regulatory structures and processes of nations engaged in trade, create an unavoidable time lag.

Goods and services travel across national boundaries. This flow exposes those involved in international business—exporters and importers—to the policies and regulations of each country. For a variety of reasons—political, economic, social, national security—nations may choose to intervene in the free flow of goods and services. Although the freest trade market in the world, the United States does possess, and enforces, regulations that restrict or impede imported products. Primarily, these pertain to health, safety, and the environment. The U.S. Food and Drug Administration and the U.S. Department of Agriculture keep a careful and tight vigil over products seeking entry into the United States, such as pharmaceuticals, pesticides, and live animals. Restrictions on the free access of goods from countries inimical to U.S. interests (Cuban cigars, Iranian pistachio nuts) also apply. However, the most common and widest set of limitations governs products that actually or potentially could disrupt specific sectors and industries in the U.S. economy. The U.S. government regulates these products through tariffs, quotas, orderly marketing arrangements, voluntary restraint agreements, and a host of other unilateral trade mechanisms. For the importer, it is crucial to understand how foreign-trade policies can affect import activities. The presence of these policies, as well as the part played by the countries in shaping the flow, composition, and volume of trade, presents political variables as a factor in the development of an international marketing strategy.

In international trade, at least two currencies are involved in every transaction. Even if the U.S. importer pays for supplies with U.S. dollars as the paying currency, sellers must translate the export/import transaction to their own currencies. Further complicating the exchange process, other currency units have varying prices vis-à-vis one another.

Moreover, exchange rates vary, not only with respect to one another, but also day to day. This affects the price of the goods as well as other export/import costs such as transportation, insurance, and duties.

From 1985 to the present, foreign-exchange rates have fluctuated dramatically. Between 1985 and 1987, the U.S. dollar used to be worth 45 percent more than a yen, but is now worth 45 percent less than a yen. Luckily for the U.S. importer of Japanese goods, the yen's strength has not resulted in a corresponding increase in prices. Defending their U.S. market position, the Japanese have chosen to raise merchandise prices modestly in order to keep their principal objectives (sales volume and market share) on track. To illustrate, a 1987 Toyota Corolla retailed for $8,178, up 14 percent from $7,148 for a 1986 model. Sony's average price increase for its products made in Japan was 18 percent during that period.

In recent years, voluntary multilateral arrangements have been established as a means of coping with the volatile foreign-exchange movements. Most notable has been the Louvre Accord (composed of the United States, United Kingdom, Japan, Germany, Canada, France, and Italy), in which government officials (usually the finance ministers) meet periodically to attempt to balance or smooth out the foreign-exchange markets. Although target ranges or bands have not been firmly established, member nations coordinate policies with particular guidelines in mind.

The countries engaged in international trade often differ in geography and physical features. This leads to various levels of economic development as well as different cultural, legal, political, economic, and commercial structures. This affects sources of supply, the types of goods each country can produce, quality levels, prices, and, hence, market opportunity for products from different countries, resulting in an extremely complex environment for trade activities. One need look no further than Hong Kong versus the People's Republic of China (PRC). Although the cultures are quite similar, that is probably the only similarity. Hong Kong—a tiny island enclave and British crown colony, devoid of natural resources, yet possessing a hard-working and capitalist-minded labor force—has succeeded in producing large volumes of quality goods at competitive prices and in a reliable manner. The PRC, on the other hand, lacks that tradition and is just now beginning the long and arduous task of attempting to become a major supplier of goods other than low-end products.

The physical spaces separating buyers and sellers, along with the regulatory structures and processes of nations engaged in trade, create an unavoidable time lag. The time factor affects import practices such as financing, form of transportation, costs of transportation, and inventory-holding costs. This has a definite and strong effect on competitive aspects in the import market.[2] Far Eastern exporters are well aware of this. For this reason, Asian nations have organized their merchant shipping and established freight-rate schedules to compete in the lucrative North American market. At the same time, government regulations have been set up to expedite exports, while banking and financial institutions have been geared to facilitate exports. Therefore, U.S. importers of Asian goods, for the most part, do not regard spatial separation as a great impediment to their merchandise sales.

On the other hand, a number of South American nations, such as Venezuela and Argentina, have been unable to use physical proximity to the U.S. market to their advantage. Their regulatory systems and operations governing exports are extremely bureaucratic, cumbersome, and slow. Transportation costs are relatively high and schedules often limited and inconvenient. Access to financing is not always available in the quantity and terms necessary. In the case of Venezuela, the exchange-rate system is structured in a way that actually *discourages* exports.

The IMF and the International Monetary Environment

Role of IMF

The International Monetary Fund (IMF) was created at the Bretton Woods monetary conference in 1944 and originally represented forty-four countries. Controlled by industrial nations, it attempts to foster stability in the world economy by cajoling prosperous nations to follow policies of growth without inflation and helping ailing economies with short-term loans. The fundamental objective of the IMF was to realize the benefits of the gold standard without its disadvantages. Every member country must subscribe to the Fund's capital according to a quota. The quota is determined by the member's monetary reserves, foreign-trade volume, and national income. Members must pay 25 percent of their quota in gold or 10 percent of their net official holdings in gold and U.S. dollars, whichever is the lesser amount. The rest of the quota is paid in the member country's currency.

The International Monetary fund has three major functions that attempt to circumvent problems in international financial relations that arose prior to the second World War:

1. Provision of short-term credit,
2. Coordination of economic policies,
3. Adjustment of exchange rates.

Provision of Short-Term Credit. A major function of the IMF is to provide member nations with foreign-exchange funds on a temporary basis. In the event that a country has a temporary imbalance caused by the liability for imports, short-term credit can prevent this short-term imbalance from becoming a major imbalance. This credit facility is available to all members, subject to restrictions. The limit on foreign currency purchased is 200 percent of the quota (amount paid into the Fund for membership). When a balance has been reached, the member nation can repurchase with its improved foreign-exchange reserves the local currencies that have been deposited with the Fund. Thus, the IMF provides a means for short-term disequilibrium to be balanced.

Short-term credit facilities can be extremely helpful in cases where unforeseen events beyond the control of the individual nation disrupt a country's foreign-currency–reserve situation. For example, the steep fall in world prices of a commodity (such as copper, which may be a significant export of a country) or a food shortage due to a drought or other natural disaster will require large expenditures of foreign exchange: in the first instance, to provide relief to the nation's producer of the affected commodity and to purchase essential goods and services budgeted previously based on anticipated export revenue, in the second, to import foodstuffs needed for domestic consumption. It is important to note that the short-term–credit facility is clearly intended to be temporary, based on the assumption that it will be.

Coordination of Economic Policies. A second function of the IMF is that of monitoring countries' transactions to ascertain excessive indebtedness. In addition, the economic policies of countries are analyzed to maintain that transactions do not make an imbalance. Should a member-nation develop a surplus in the balance of payment, the counsel will propose to the nation that import barriers and export subsidies be reduced. Further recommendations would be to lend these surplus funds abroad. However, if a country is suffering excessive domestic inflation, the counsel may suggest that government programs be reduced and that the rate of monetary growth be moderated. Essentially, the objective of the counsel is to develop international economic cooperation.

Adjustment of Exchange Rates. Finally, the IMF provides for regulated fluctuation in exchange rates. A member-nation may appreciate/depreciate its currency by some percentage. To prevent speculators from causing imbalance in the system, the IMF provides the member-nation that will devalue with significant loans from its own holdings and from individual countries. The major function here is to facilitate orderly change in exchange rates.

Since the global debt crisis began in late 1982, the IMF has come to center stage in providing funds and technical assistance. Its influence has grown tremendously since multinational commercial banks and governments take their cue from the IMF in rescheduling and new lending to debtor nations. The IMF "seal of approval" has become *the* prerequisite for debt relief. In counseling debtor nations, the IMF insists that spending and development projects be scaled back to levels that can be financed increasingly from domestic savings along with lower and more manageable levels of foreign borrowing. However, in carrying out an adjustment program, debtor nations must bite the bullet and remove the major impediments to economic health. These include:

rigid, overvalued exchange rates,

costly subsidies,

non–market-determined consumer and producer prices,

inefficient state-controlled enterprises,

uncontrolled government spending and large fiscal deficits,

inefficient tax systems,

excessive and inflationary monetary growth,

interest-rate controls that discourage savings and distort investment flows,

disincentives to private-sector development.[3]

The IMF's adjustment regimes are not without their critics. Leftists, nationalists, industrialists, the poor, and supply-side economists all believe that the Fund's inflation-fighting austerity program is a prescription for social misery, political upheaval, and economic hardship. According to them, the deep spending cuts slow economic growth, resulting in unemployment and higher prices for basic goods and services, while the tax-increase component chokes off production, dries up capital for expansion, and raises business-financing costs.

Nevertheless, the Fund maintains that austerity and reform measures do result in an improved economy, and that this benefits everyone. According to IMF officials, the experience of debtor countries in the 1980s suggests that nations that have restrained monetary, credit, and fiscal expansion on a consistent basis have succeeded in improving their international competitiveness. Moreover, these countries have also made real progress in managing their current-account positions and in maintaining or improving growth in their economies.[4]

Trade Policy

Following the second World War, the United States became the undisputed leading economic power in the world. The central bankers of the West designated the dollar as the base in restructuring the world's monetary system. The Bretton Woods conference in 1944 established a new system of international monetary cooperation whereby stability was sought without returning to an international gold standard, abolished ten years earlier, or infringing upon a sovereign nation's monetary and fiscal independence. The IMF gave impetus to a multination accord establishing exchange rates governing both public- and private-sector transactions. Changes in a currency's par value were permitted only when necessary to correct a basic disequilibrium in a country's balance of payments.

The dollar played a major role in structuring the international monetary system. It provided a practical base for setting international exchange rates, since it has been the one currency most widely used in international trade and financial transactions. In 1949, the United States agreed to keep the international value of the dollar on a steady course: the government would buy and sell gold at the fixed price of $35 per ounce. Other nations agreed to stand by their currencies' values, in consort with the IMF agreements, and to buy or sell dollars in international-exchange markets. While the dollar's value was tied to gold, other currencies were pegged to the dollar. The dollar thereby became an intervention currency, used by other nations (along with gold) as a currency reserve. Soon after, however, volatile dollars kept offshore brought about a great degree of instability in the international monetary system. The U.S. government responded with a package of measures to stem the balance-of-payments deficit that had resulted—namely, from dollar outflows not matched by an inflow of dollars from overseas. Government action included linking foreign aid to the recipient's purchase of U.S. goods and services and the creation of a gold pool with other industrial nations' central banks to intervene in the London gold market to maintain a gold price more or less equal to the official one. In 1965, the U.S. Congress eliminated the 1913 requirement that Federal Reserve banks maintain a reserve of gold certificates to back at least 25 percent of commercial-bank–deposit holdings by the Reserve bank. Congress intervened again in 1968 by releasing more of the gold supply from currency reserves via legislation abolishing the remaining gold backing from the dollar.

In spite of these measures, the deficit grew to the point that in 1971, the United States ran its first trade deficit since 1893. Successive balance-of-payments deficits prompted major congressional and executive-branch actions in the early 1970s. As imports exceeded exports, the deteriorating balance-of-payments situation led to the dollar's first devaluation since 1934. The Joint Economic Subcommittee on International Exchange and Payments of the U.S. Congress acknowledged the overvalued dollar, claiming that its foreign currency value in reality was overstated. This overvaluation was said to impede the sale of U.S. goods and services abroad, significantly increase imports, drive U.S. business investment to other countries, and slow down foreign direct investment in the United States.

However, due to the international role of the dollar, the United States could not move to correct its overvaluation without causing upheaval of far-reaching impact in the world monetary system. On August 15, 1971, President Nixon proclaimed a sweeping new economic program to curtail inflation, expand employment, and protect the dollar. To attain the last objective, he suspended the convertibility of the dollar into gold, allowing the dollar to float. Soon after, the finance ministers of the six Common Market countries and Great Britain met and subsequently issued a joint statement accepting the U.S. position that it was time to restructure the world monetary system. At a historic meeting of the finance ministers at Washington's Smithsonian Institution that December, the United States consented to devalue the dollar 8.57 percent by lifting the price of gold to $38 from the $35-per-ounce level maintained since 1934. The immediate impact was a decline in the U.S. balance-of-payments deficit. Less than one year later, however, it became clear that a second devaluation of the dollar was imminent. President Nixon subsequently asked Congress to devalue the dollar by 10 percent. Congress acted and approved the dollar devaluation. As in the previous devaluation, the adjustment of the dollar's value vis-à-vis other countries' currencies attempted to establish the U.S. currency at a level that more accurately reflected the nation's true economic strength.

International economic instability marked the period from 1973 to 1976 as a series of severe economic shocks—mainly, shortfalls in the grain harvests, major commodity shortages, and large oil-price hikes—ignited a global epidemic of inflation from 1972 to 1973. Things worsened as the major trading nations of the world stimulated their economies at the same time. The negative effects of huge price rises combined with deflationary actions by government policymakers produced a recession in 1974–75. The oil-price increases were devastating in their impact, and the industrial nations of the West had to make very difficult adjustments from 1973 to 1976 to protect their countries from the fourfold increase in crude-oil prices imposed in stages by the OPEC cartel. Severe energy shortages along with inflation played major roles in the recession.

The financial crunch that resulted forced a cutback in domestic economic programs in a number of countries, while petroleum price increases sparked inflation in all countries and had a negative effect on investment. Following the February 1973 dollar devaluation, the forces of inflation and wild exchange-rate movements along industrialized nations led governments to abandon efforts to maintain fixed exchange rates through market intervention. The Bretton Woods structure was discarded, and in its place the world witnessed a de facto system of floating exchange rates. Under these conditions, supply and demand factors were the prime shapers of the relative values of currencies. These floating rates produced a great many problems, however. Wide-ranging currency fluctuations were caused by differentials in inflation rates. Countries whose currencies had depreciated, such as Great Britain and Italy, found it impossible to hold onto their export market shares following the expansion of world trade after the 1973 recession. On the other hand, West Germany and Japan, whose currencies were significantly stronger, expanded their exports—in no small measure due to low inflation rates, higher levels of savings, and cooperative relations between management and labor than in the United States.

Opponents of the floating-rate system (notably those urging a return to the gold standard) claimed that exchange-rate movements worsened the pressure on prices in inflation-ravaged countries because currency depreciation made imports more costly. Proponents of the system, on the other hand, asserted that exchange could be maintained only if a nation's government took the tough steps required to curtail structural inflationary pressures at home.

The debate rages today as proponents of the floating-rate system, those who seek a return to the gold standard, and those who support some kind of modified system between a float and a target (narrow-range "bands" within a basket of currencies) prescribe and urge nations to adopt a less volatile system for managing international monetary policy. These "bands" reflect levels *within* ranges where currencies relate to one another.

Bretton Woods Amendments

An agreement in 1975 between France and the United States authorized the IMF to construct international monetary agreements that made the floating system a permanent reality. In 1976, Congress approved the U.S. government's ratification of the agreement, the centerpiece of which stipulated that IMF signatories would engage in the manipulation of exchange rates *only* to stave off disorderly conditions. It also provided for the possible readoption of fixed rates at some future date, substituted IMF Special Drawing Rights for gold in

IMF transactions, and authorized the IMF to sell some of its gold reserves to capitalize a special trust fund for poor nations struggling with high oil-import bills.

These amendments to the Bretton Woods agreement also included formal recognition of currency exchange rates' "floating" to differing values according to market forces, IMF quota reallocation (cutting the U.S. share vis-à-vis other member-nations'), and greater authority for disposing of the IMF's gold stock.

Special Drawing Rights (SDRs)

A viable solution to the need for expansion in world monetary reserves was Special Drawing Rights (SDRs) as created by the IMF. An agreement signed in Rio de Janeiro in 1967 empowered the IMF to create these new reserves and parcel them out to each member country in proportion to the nation's quota. Referred to as "paper gold," these reserves would be in a quantity sufficient to satisfy the basic reserve requirements for world trade. Exchanged only among central banks, SDRs could be converted to other currencies, but not into gold. By 1985, fifteen years after first issuance, 14 billion SDRs (equal to U.S. $15 billion) were in circulation, almost 5 percent of nongold international reserves.

Initially, the value of the SDR was calculated from the average value of a basket of currencies—those of the major trading nations. These currencies were weighted according to their relative importance in world trade. While the first SDR was equal to one U.S. dollar, the SDR does fluctuate in value relative to the dollar, given the relative performance of the currencies of each of the trading nations. In 1981, the basket of currencies was reduced to five: the U.S. dollar, the deutsche mark, the French franc, the pound sterling, and the Japanese yen. Once the U.S. dollar/SDR exchange rate is established, other currency values in terms of the SDR are determined by applying their market rates with respect of the dollar and then, using the U.S. dollar/SDR rate, converting it. The IMF announces daily SDR rates for over fifty currencies.[5]

The Role of GATT in Trade Liberalization

The General Agreement on Tariffs and Trade (GATT) is of key importance to the liberalization of trade among nations. The GATT is the principal international forum for countries to resolve trade disputes and disagreements between one another. Additionally, it serves as the arena for conducting multilateral trade negotiations. Long series or "rounds" of negotiations (such as the Kennedy, Tokyo, and Uruguay Rounds) strive to reduce tariff as well as nontariff barriers within a multilateral framework.

The GATT became effective on January 1, 1948, in an agreement among the United States and seven other major trading powers to freeze tariffs at their then-current levels and establish multilateral trading rules—most notably the principle of "most-favored–nation" status. As of late 1988, eighty-seven governments, accounting for four-fifths of world trade, belong to GATT and, therefore, subscribe to its basic mission: the liberalization of world trade and its establishment on a firm basis, thereby promoting economic growth and development worldwide.

In its role as mediator of trade disputes between member countries and occasional enforcer of disciplinary actions against members who fail to honor the trading rules, the GATT seeks to assure that its credibility as an active agent of trade liberalization is maintained. The GATT's principal activity, however, is the multilateral trade negotiations. These discussions aim to achieve a balance around the world through which every nation that benefits from the many tariff concessions granted by other nations provides tariff concessions of approximately the same value to the other countries.

During the first twenty-five years of the GATT, it successfully concluded six major trade negotiations aimed at reducing tariffs among trading nations. Thousands of items involved in world commerce saw their rates reduced or frozen against any increase. The result was a tremendous upswing in world trade. The trade negotiations also produced far-reaching reductions of the quantitative restrictions countries place on importable items.

The GATT's framework of rules for trade relations, although presented in a lengthy and complicated document, is grounded on only a few principles and objectives. The centerpiece of the framework is the most-favored–nation clause, which specifies that trade must operate on a nondiscriminatory basis. All parties are required to grant one another trade treatment as favorable as that granted to any other nation in setting and administering import and export duties. In essence, all trading nations are on an equal basis; no country grants special favor to another, except in special circumstances.

Another GATT principle is that protection to domestic industries should be executed only via customs tariffs—not through other commercial provisions. Clearly defined measures and a competitive trading environment are the intent of this rule.

The binding of tariff levels negotiated among contracting parties assures a stable and predictable basis for trade. The bound items are listed for all countries in the GATT's tariff schedules. However, "waiver" procedures are provided whenever economic or trade circumstances present critical problems for signatory countries. Additionally, there are escape provisions for emergency actions in a limited number of situations.

GATT also prohibits quantitative restrictions. Although they are less significant today than when the GATT was established, they do remain numerous, mainly affecting trade in agricultural products, textiles, and other products of key export importance to *less* developed countries, such as Brazil, South Korea, Mexico, and Taiwan.

Whenever possible, the GATT encourages members to consult with one another on trade matters. If a nation feels that its benefits under the GATT are being voided or restricted, it may seek to work out the difficulty through direct consultation with the party or parties concerned. In serious disputes, the parties may seek to avail themselves of the GATT's Panel of Experts, which will investigate and make recommendations. The panel members are selected from countries having no direct interest in the issue being disputed.

Regional trading arrangements aimed at reducing import barriers, such as the Andean Pact Accord, have been increasing in recent years. The GATT allows these groupings as an exception to the general rule of most-favored–nation treatment, provided the contracting parties do not raise barriers to trade with nations outside the regional trading agreement. To assure that the negotiated removal or reduction of tariffs remains in force, the GATT prohibits compensatory domestic taxes, such as the imposition of higher excise taxes on imported products than on the same goods produced domestically.

In recent years, a number of industrial nations—notably the United States—have sought relief from certain categories of imports. Under the GATT, when imports are shown to threaten domestic industries manufacturing the same products, member countries may impose antidumping or countervailing duties to offset the damage. According to the provisions of Article VI of the GATT:

Antidumping duties are to be imposed only if goods are sold for export at a price below that at which they are sold for domestic consumption.

Antidumping duties may not be greater than the amount by which the domestic price exceeds the export price.

Countervailing duties may not exceed the amount of the subsidy or bounty.

Duties may be imposed only if there is a threat of injury to industry in the importing country.

Import quotas are allowed only for agricultural and fishery products in cases where domestic production-control programs are threatened and when a country is faced with a balance-of-payments crisis.

The Tokyo Round of Negotiations (1973–79) was a benchmark in the GATT. The negotiations were structured not only to reduce or phase out tariff and nontariff barriers to agricultural and industrial trade, but also to design a multilateral trading system and set the course for international-trade relations through the next decade and beyond. Agreement was reached on a "codes of conduct" approach since it permitted negotiators to tackle the barriers to trade without having to confront one another over the rationale or justification for these kinds of trade-policy measures. The results of the Tokyo Round produced major tariff cuts, a series of international codes of conduct, and dispute-settlement procedures to enforce trade-agreement rights and obligations.

The three-hundred–member GATT Secretariat, based in Geneva, Switzerland, continues to provide an international forum for contracting nations to air their disputes, enabling the GATT to carry out its mediating role in world trade.[6]

Why Nations Trade

Although a nation may be capable of producing all the goods it needs, it simply cannot do so with equal efficiency among industries. No one country can be number one in everything. Therefore, as has been demonstrated time and time again, a nation benefits and profits from trade as long as it has some advantage in the production of particular goods and services. The fundamental tenets for comprehending the process of trade between nations are provided by the "theory of comparative advantage." The theory holds that a country should strive to specialize in producing goods in which it is comparatively more efficient and export these to the rest of the world. Similarly, the country should import those products in which it is comparatively less efficient. To illustrate, the United States has lost, for the most part, its comparative advantage in producing shoes and machine tools; however, it does maintain a competitive position in manufacturing (and exporting) advanced technologies and processes used in producing footwear and machine tools. The reasons for comparative-efficiency differences lie in the nature of production. Each country possesses different factors and resources, such as raw materials, skill levels of workers, infrastructure, and installed industrial base. Different goods require different factors of production; and since the supply of factors differs, so will production costs. As different mixes and resource quality lead to different cost/price structures, different efficiency levels arise—hence, comparative advantage.

The United States provides an excellent illustration. The U.S. economy has three main economic strengths: advanced technology, large markets, and low ratio of population to arable land. These factors combine to give the United States comparative advantage in the production of certain goods. First, the combination of farmland and technology allows the U.S. agricultural sector to be highly productive. In fact, many of the problems presently besetting U.S. agriculture are due to this sector's success. Fewer and fewer workers are required as agriculture becomes more capital-intensive and machines replace most farm-workers. Additionally and most strikingly, the agribusiness sector is becoming increasingly more efficient as fewer inputs of labor and capital are producing both a larger and higher-quality agricultural output. The downside to this is a growing number of small-farm bankruptcies, increasing unemployment and underemployment in the agricultural sector, plus organized protests demanding higher subsidies and/or higher prices, protection from foreign agricultural imports, and other relief measures. Second, large markets and advanced technology facilitate the production of large volumes of goods and low-cost methods of manufacturing. In high tech and capital-intensive industries such as capital equipment, electrical machinery, and industrial electronics, the United States has witnessed steady improvements in productivity. The large domestic market and the development of new technologies and processes of manufacturing, such as computer-assisted design/computer-assisted manufacturing and robotics, have resulted in greater economies of scale and unit-cost reductions while improving quality control at the same time. The United States has been able, therefore, to maintain, and in a number of instances widen, its comparative advantage in certain industrial subsectors of the economy.

Imports, on the other hand, indicate a nation's economic liabilities. For example, the United States is the higher-cost source of many primary materials; it is a nation deficient in tropical agriculture; and it pays relatively high wages in its agricultural and natural-resources sectors. Therefore, the United States imports tropical agricultural products such as coffee, bananas, and rubber—products with high labor value added, unlike mass-produced capital-intensive merchandise such as computer chips, aircraft parts, and customized industrial products.[7]

The Balance of Payments

Trade transactions that occur globally are summarized in the balance of payments. These statistics can be an extremely useful indicator of economic activity and an aid to importers in scanning worldwide courses of supply. The balance of payments are divided into three parts:

1. *Current account.* This account records the sum total of goods and services of a nation with all of its trading partners. Merchandise trade is the export and import of goods, such as heavy machinery, consumer electronics, and apparel. The export and import of services are known as invisible trade. Included in this are management consulting, legal counsel, tourism, and transportation. The balance of trade is the net between exports and imports.

2. *Capital account.* The flow of capital, both short- and long-term movements, between a nation and its trading partners comprises the capital account. Short-term loans and payments are included in short-term capital movements. Long-term capital movements involve foreign direct investment (such as a U.S. chemical plant in Egypt or a Danish furniture operation in the United States) as well as portfolio investment (such as bonds, equities, and government paper).

3. *Official reserve account.* This section of the balance of payments entails the accounting of the inflows and outflows of reserve currencies (for the most part, U.S. dollars and other currencies of trading partners) to harmonize the flows of both the current and capital accounts. The net account position reflects the country's asset situation to balance its trade and investment activities with its trading partners.

Surpluses or deficits are periodic and usually short-term imbalances in either the nation's balance of trade or balance of payments. When exports exceed imports, a surplus situation arises. A deficit occurs when the reverse takes place. Problems arise when imbalances persist. A nation that habitually achieves trade surpluses with its trading partners is, in essence, financing the buyer nation's purchases. West Germany vis-à-vis the United States in the early 1980s is a prime example. Very often this type of situation puts pressure on a nation's economic system, resulting in a country's having to revalue its currency. As its exports become more expensive and its imports cheaper, the impact shows up in its foreign-trade activities. Also, while the surplus country is, in fact, financing the importing country's deficits, it runs the risk of the surplus producing an inflationary impact on the domestic economy. Deficits, on the other hand, produce an effect on a country's ability to finance its imports; consequently, pressure arises for a currency devaluation. The result of such an action is a decrease in the nation's ability to buy in world markets. Unless the nation can influence prices in world markets, a devaluation can result in losses in foreign-exchange earnings and a subsequent disruption in the nation's economy, particularly if export dependence is significant.

For the importer, the balance of payments can be a very useful source of marketing information. Providing an indication of the economic health of a nation, the balance of payments can furnish the importer with data on the importing country's trade activities, goods traded in the market, the country's principal sources of supply, and share of supply vis-à-vis other exporting countries. Assessing the composition of trade can also reveal insights into the priorities, strengths, and weaknesses of both the importing and exporting economies. Moreover, it can help the importer select importable products that are allowed favorable terms of entry into the country (such as special tariff reductions, as in the case of selected products entering the United States from Caribbean Basin Initiative countries). The extent of trade imbalances can also be ascertained from analyzing trade relationships. Moreover, one can evaluate government actions to remedy the imbalances, revealing key information on a nation's foreign-trade and commercial policies.[8]

The World Economy: Sources of Supply

The U.S. manufacturing sector has seen its share of world markets decline since the end of the World War II. The war wrecked the economies of most of America's chief competitors, leaving them with little productive capacity.

As the number-one developed nation to survive with its industrial base untouched, it was not surprising that the United States became the world's chief source of supply. Rebuilding Europe and Japan created a short-term upswing in world demand for manufactured goods beyond what "normal" growth in demand should have been. Much of that demand was channeled to the United States and was reflected in U.S. trade surpluses. Europe and Japan, during the 1950s and 1960s, basically rebuilt their economies from scratch. Where plants had been destroyed, the most modern equipment available was installed. The United States helped through such programs as the Marshall Plan. The rebuilding process was largely completed by the late 1960s.

However, the consequences of the world's postwar economic recovery for the United States have been many and varied. Since Europe and Japan can now meet many of their domestic economic needs, a major cause of postwar U.S. export growth has ended. Although prosperity has created new markets for U.S. exports, Europe and Japan now compete with the United States in global markets. In many cases, their output comes from plants as technologically advanced or more so than their U.S. competitors'. As these countries began to produce increasing amounts of manufactured goods, the U.S. share of world manufactures production declined. Out of fifteen major industrial countries, the U.S. share of total manufactures production dropped 27.8 percent in two decades—from 54.7 percent in 1960 to 39.5 percent in 1982. If U.S. competitiveness had really fallen, America's share of world export markets for manufactures should have fallen by at least as much as its share of total production. However, when compared with these countries, the U.S. share of total manufactured exports decreased only from 25.3 percent in 1960 to 19.8 percent in 1982.

This also holds true for total world production and exports of manufactures. The share of U.S. manufactured exports has decreased less than the U.S. share of world production. The indication in either case is that the United States is not undergoing a significant loss of long-term competitiveness. Moreover, the debate over aggregate market-share statistics ignores important differences among various manufacturing industries. Certain basic industries within U.S. sectors have been particularly affected by shifts in comparative advantage, and including these firms skews overall statistical totals. In 1984, for example, the trade deficits in iron and steel, textiles, clothing, and automobiles combined accounted for 52 percent of the total trade deficit and 72 percent of the manufactured-goods deficit. Although the United States is no longer the economic powerhouse it was in the 1950s, much of the recent decline in the U.S. trading position overseas is mainly due to the macroeconomic factors causing the U.S. trade deficit. However, America's current economic competition increasingly comes from the newly industrialized countries (NICs) in Asia. Compared to their economic growth, America's does not seem as robust. Between 1965 and 1985, for example, U.S. per capita GNP rose at a 1.7 percent annual rate compared to 7.6 percent in Singapore, 6.1 percent in Hong Kong, 6.6 percent in Korea, 4.3 percent in Brazil, and 2.7 percent in Mexico.

To cite another example, the United States increased its exports from 6.9 percent annually from 1965 to 1980, but witnessed a decline of −2.7 percent from 1980 to 1986. On the other hand NICs such as Brazil, Mexico, and Hong Kong averaged close to 10 percent during the mid-sixties to the mid-eighties. Korea scored an astounding 27.3 percent rate from 1965 to 1980 and 13.1 percent from 1980 to 1986. Moreover, the composition of their trade has shifted from exporting fuels, metals, and other primary commodities toward manufactured products including machinery and transportation equipment. The newly industrialized countries have made tremendous progress on the road to development. But certain key points must be noted when evaluating their record. First, NIC growth rates reflect their infrastructure development. A good chunk of their growth can be attributed to constructing the roads, communication systems, and industrial plant and equipment that the United States and other industrialized countries had already built during the nineteenth and early twentieth centuries. When U.S. industrial development blossomed in the late nineteenth century, its growth rate exceeded that of the period's economic leaders in Europe. Between 1870 and 1913, U.S. per capita GNP rose at a 2.2 percent annual average rate compared to 2 percent in Canada, 1.7 percent in Germany, 1.4 percent in France, and 1.2 percent in the United Kingdom. The growth and development of new manufacturing technologies and methods of innovation and their dissemination and transfer to developing nations are the principal reasons for the quantum leap these nations have made in industrialization and in export performance.

Less-developed countries today also have an advantage in the development process that Europe and the United States did not: the industrialized world. Europe and the United States had no advanced nations to provide technological and developmental short cuts. Due to the progress of Western industrialized nations, developing nations can avoid some of the learning costs associated with pioneering any particular area.

Furthermore, developing nations routinely receive development assistance from a host of foreign governments and international organizations. They have the opportunity to obtain the industrialized world's technological know-how (via technology transfer) without incurring the full cost of acquiring these skills. By purchasing turnkey plants and attracting foreign direct investment, developing countries are able to leapfrog at least some of industrialization's early stages. All of this has led to an abundance of world supplies in an enormous number of products, manufactured as well as agricultural. The reasons are many and varied.

Since the early 1980s, commodity prices have declined, particularly for foodstuffs. Most commodity exporters have experienced significant deterioration in their terms of trade since 1981. The decline has been due generally to sluggish demand caused by lower economic growth globally and an abundant supply of raw materials. This has impacted developing countries particularly severely. Less developed countries are affected most because of their lack of product diversification and their heavy reliance on a single good for export. For example, Nicaragua obtains 25 percent of its export income from cotton; Zambia depends on copper for 85 percent of export income; and one Filipino in four relies on coconut products for his or her income. These countries are vulnerable to fluctuations in price.

A number of nations have not sat still, but have continued to diversify into more exotic items. New Zealand has developed a large export of kiwi fruit, the Philippines is farming mangoes and shipping shrimp raised on water farms. Developing countries have learned their lesson the hard way—dependence on a few exports is dangerous. With the glut of food commodities preventing any price increases, exotic foods and processed foods continue to be a successful export strategy for developing countries.

Diversification within the agricultural sector has been impressive, but not nearly as striking—even radical—among nations that have been so dependent on imported manufactured goods, and, finding themselves unable to afford them as imports, have come to produce them domestically.

There is no better example of this phenomenon than Venezuela, an oil-export monoculture that has been faced with a declining world oil market, a devaluing currency, and a high debt burden. In 1983, it relied on imports for more than 60 percent of its food consumption and at least 50 percent of its textile needs. Today, the percentages have dropped to 20 percent and 5 percent, respectively according to an unpublished report by the U.N. Food and Agriculture Organization. In the past, Venezuela imported pharmaceutical syringes in packages. Now, it makes the syringes' plastic tubes, rubber components, and paper packages, while Venezuelan firms are planning to set up plants to produce their own needles. Exporting will follow. Venezuela has the highest-quality toys in Latin America, is beginning to export construction materials, and has seen dozens of other nontraditional exports such as ceramic products, mattresses, and beer join the ranks of the world supply of exports to industrial as well as less developed countries. Many factors such as high exchange rates in industrial nations, devaluing currencies in less developed countries, and growth and diversification of agricultural and industrial manufactures have resulted in increases in the volume, quality, and price-competitiveness of imported goods. For developing countries experiencing high debt burdens, the need to export is expecially pressing as these nations see hard currency to pay for the debt they have accumulated.

Sources of supply have been affected by developments in industrialized nations as well. Industrial countries too have been undergoing social and cultural changes. High economic growth has been met with higher levels of disposable income (lower overall savings), resulting in greater expenditure on goods. This fundamental shift in consumer behavior has changed the buying habits and the attitudes of consumers; namely, there is a growing disregard for the future with greater emphasis for spending and living today.

Regardless of the shifts in the economy of the United States, the budget and trade deficits, major corrections in the stock market, exchange-rate movements, and "deindustrialization," the United States will continue to import certain products it no longer makes (such as black and white TV sets), certain products it continues to manufacture but that compete with imports (automobiles, for example) and still other products it manufactures domestically *and* offshore (such as electronics and clothing).

Technology transfer and efficiency in production of both agricultural and industrial goods combined with a growing determination and sophistication on the part of offshore suppliers to penetrate, expand, and diversify their product offerings in the U.S. market have created an unstoppable momentum of foreign exports. Partly due to the shift to a services-oriented economy in the United States, a more productive manufacturing sector in specialty areas (such as aerospace, computers, and biotechnology), high levels of disposable income (and spending), and a growing number of employed workers, American consumers and industrial buyers will increasingly look to a wide array of imports to fill their needs and satisfy their desires.[9]

Summary

Foreign trade is a reality that all nations must address. Import goods may be price-competitive, be preferred by consumers, or fill a void in the market. Still, importers need to consider the impact of protectionist pressures from domestic manufacturers; dealing in at least two currencies; geographic and physical differences among nations; and time lags due to international travel, distance, and governments' regulatory structures and foreign-trade processes.

Reducing trade barriers has long been a goal of governments. The International Monetary Fund furthers this aim by providing short-term credit, coordinating economic policies, and adjusting exchange rates. Also noteworthy over the years have been the Bretton Woods agreement and its subsequent amendments, the General Agreement on Tariffs and Trade, and the Tokyo Round of Negotiations.

International transactions are summarized in the Balance of Payments (broken down into current account, capital account, and official reserve account). As the U.S. share of global manufactures falls, fast-growing newly industrialized countries are becoming a significant source of supply for advanced industrial nations, though substantial differences among sectors remain.

Notes

1. Marta Ortiz-Buonafina, *Profitable Export Marketing: A Strategy for U.S. Business,* © 1984 (Englewood Cliffs, N.J.: Prentice-Hall, 1984), pp. 21–22. Reprinted by permission

2. Adapted from ibid., op cit., pp. 27–28.

3. Jerry Haar, "Private Investment, Taxes, and Economic Growth," in Michael Novak and Michael P. Johnson, eds., *Latin America: Dependency or Interdependency?* (Washington, D.C.: American Enterprise Institute, 1985), p. 60.

4. Excerpted from *World Economic Outlook* (Washington, D.C.: International Monetary Fund, 1984), p. 50.

5. *Trade: U.S. Policy since 1945.* (Washington, D.C.: Congressional Quarterly, 1984), pp. 76, 80.

6. See also Eugene T. Rossides, *U.S. Import Trade Regulation* (Washington, D.C.: Bureau of National Affairs, 1985), pp. 416–22; and *Trade: U.S. Policy since 1945,* pp. 36–38.

7. John Fayerweather, *International Marketing,* 2nd ed. (Englewood Cliffs, New Jersey: Prentice-Hall, 1970), pp. 6–7. For a comprehensive discussion of trade theories, see Franklin Root, *International Trade and Investment* (Cincinnati: Southwestern, 1978); and Charles P. Kindleberger, *Foreign Trade and National Economy* (Westport, Conn.: Greenwood, 1975).

8. Ortiz-Buonafina, *Profitable Export Marketing,* pp. 37–38.

9. Nicholas D. Kristof, "Raw Material Prices Recover," *New York Times* (September 15, 1987), pp. D1, D10.

2
The Domestic Environment of Import Activities

Size of the U.S. Import Market

The U.S. is the single largest importer of manufactured goods. Its total imports amounted to $424.1 billion in 1987. U.S. imports were 180 percent greater than those of the second-ranking importer in the world, West Germany. The dominant role of manufactured goods among U.S. imports points to the fact that the United States is a vast, affluent market. As shown in table 2–1, imports of merchandise trade have grown from $42.4 billion in 1970 to $424.1 billion in 1987, an increase of 890 percent. Consumer goods accounted for 16.3 percent, automobile vehicles and parts 14.7 percent, and food and beverages 5.6 percent of total merchandise trade in 1986. Overall, manufactured products accounted approximately for 79 percent of total U.S. imports.[1]

It can be seen that the U.S. imports have been growing steadily in the 1970s and 1980s. This can be attributed to the affluence and life-styles of American consumers, which make the United States the highest consuming nation in the world, opening up significant opportunities for imported products in consumer as well as industrial and institutional markets.

There has been a long-held assumption that in the U.S. market, low-technology manufacturers produce the most competitive imports.[2] In fact, foreign imports are making inroads in practically every sector, with the exception of wood, natural gas, inorganic chemicals, and some food categories. In table 2–2, the examination of U.S. merchandise imports by principal product groups provides us with an overview of this fact. The largest percentage change in the 1986–87 period as compared to the 1984–85 period occurred in mineral fuels and lubricants (a 17.3 percent change in 1986–87 as compared to – 11.8 percent in the 1984–85 period). Similarly, manufactures classified by material increased by 9.0 percent between 1986 and 1987, compared to a 1.0 percent increase during the 1984–85 period. In more technical products such as specialized industrial machinery and parts, imports increased by 15.4 percent in the 1986–87 period, as compared to 7.9 percent in the previous period. Telecommunications apparatus, however, declined to a 0.5 percent increase in the 1986–87 period, down from 16.4 percent in the 1984–85 period.

Table 2–1
U.S. Merchandise Trade, General Imports, 1970–1987
(millions of dollars)

Year	Imports	Year	Imports
1970	$ 42,806	1979	$222,228
1971	48,970	1980	256,984
1972	59,667	1981	273,352
1973	74,231	1982	254,885
1974	110,407	1983	269,878
1975	105,880	1984	346,364
1976	132,498	1985	352,463
1977	160,411	1986	382,964
1978	186,045	1987	424,082

Source: *United States Trade: Performance in 1987* (Washington, D.C.: U.S. Department of Commerce, 1988), p. 84.

Note: Dollar values are CIF (cost, insurance, freight, named point of destination).

As shown in tables 2–3 and 2–4, the most important U.S. trading partners were Japan and Canada, together accounting for 37.7 percent of the total U.S. imports in 1987 and 45.4 percent of total merchandise imports. These nations, with the industrial European countries (primarily West Germany, United Kingdom, Italy, and France) and the newly industrialized countries were by far the leading foreign suppliers of manufactured goods to the United States. Let us now examine the five largest manufactures-import categories in order to highlight the nature of their demand and the magnitude and composition of each product group.[3]

Road Vehicles. This group includes passenger cars, trucks, tractors, motorcycles, special-purpose vehicles, and parts. By far the single largest category in the U.S. import component, road vehicles and parts amounted to $78.8 billion in imports and generated $53.3 billion in deficits in 1987. In spite of slowed down U.S. economic growth, imports of passenger cars rose rapidly in 1985 and continued growing in the 1986–87 period, albeit at a slower pace. The number of passenger vehicles increased by 838,000 in 1985 compared to an increase of 421,000 in 1984. Of the 4.4 million cars imported into the United States in 1985, Japan supplied 57 percent, Canada 26 percent, and Germany 11 percent. The same suppliers continued to be the main foreign sources of these products in the next few years, while some NICs such as South Korea are beginning to make inroads in the passenger-car category. The Japanese and European automakers have an established reputation for quality and style. This is the competitive advantage they enjoy in the U.S. market. Other players that have entered the industry, such as Yugoslavia and South Korea, are becoming new factors in the U.S. market. Included in this category are parts and components, which grew at a rate of 14.5 percent during the 1986–87 period.

Table 2–2
Selected U.S. Imports by Principal Product Group, 1984–1987
(in millions of dollars)

	Total 1985	% Change 1984–85	Total 1987	% Change 1986–87
Food and live animals	20,292	4.4	22,224	− 0.8
Fish	4,202	8.9	5,872	19.0
Coffee	3,492	1.5	3,061	− 34.9
Vegetables and fruits	4,619	3.8	5,133	6.4
Beverages and tobacco	4,124	2.9	4,461	5.6
Alcoholic beverages	3,298	4.8	3,554	5.7
Crude materials, excluding fuels	11,167	− 6.8	12,299	10.0
Wood	3,279	6.7	2,228	− 33.2
Pulp	1,569	− 17.2	2,129	29.0
Ores, concentrate, scrap	2,564	− 19.1	2,666	12.9
Mineral fuels and lubricants	55,843	− 11.8	46,723	17.3
Petroleum, crude	34,123	− 10.1	30,840	27.5
Gas (natural and manufactured)	4,176	− 15.9	2,581	− 16.5
Oils and fats	730	− 1.6	630	8.6
Chemicals and related products	15,321	6.4	17,036	7.8
Organic chemicals	4,833	7.7	5,686	14.5
Inorganic chemicals	3,554	− 1.4	3,199	− 6.6
Manufactures classified by material	49,499	1.0	56,364	9.0
Paper and manufactures	6,248	7.3	7,613	14.0
Textiles excluding clothing	5,274	8.2	6,927	12.6
Iron and steel products	11,223	− 5.3	9,844	3.0
Machinery and transportation equipment	141,721	15.1	182,807	10.0
Power-generating machinery	9,051	21.2	11,068	10.7
Industrial machinery and parts	8,032	7.9	11,168	15.4
General industrial machinery	8,527	17.6	11,547	14.8
Telecommunications apparatus	19,114	16.4	21,272	0.5
Passenger cars, new	37,617	24.5	49,134	5.5
Automotive parts	9,801	16.4	13,125	14.8
Miscellaneous manufactures	51,684	13.9	69,037	14.9
Clothing	16,056	10.6	21,960	18.4
Footwear	6,104	12.5	7,654	11.6
Toys and sporting equipment	4,451	20.3	6,438	26.5

Source: Summarized from *United States Trade; Performance in 1987* (Washington, D.C.: U.S. Department of Commerce, 1988), p. 107.
Note: Dollar values are CIF (cost, insurance, freight, named point of destination).

Apparel Articles and Accessories. The apparel trade deficit—$20.8 billion in 1987—was second only to the road-vehicles deficit. The East Asian NICs— the number-one supplier of labor-intensive apparel imports—have a clear labor-cost advantage, with hourly pay levels in Taiwan and South Korea in 1987 estimated at no more than 15 percent of U.S. levels, U.S. bilateral quotas

Table 2–3
Total U.S. Imports, 1985–1987
(in billions of dollars)

	1985	1986	1987	Percentage of 1987 Imports
Japan	72,380	85,547	88,074	20.8
Canada	69,427	68,662	71,510	16.9
West Germany	21,232	26,128	28,029	6.6
Taiwan	17,761	21,251	26,406	6.2
Mexico	19,392	17,558	20,520	4.8
United Kingdom	15,573	16,033	17,998	4.2
South Korea	10,713	13,497	17,991	4.2
Italy	10,381	11,312	11,698	2.8
France	9,959	10,586	11,177	2.6
Hong Kong	8,994	9,474	10,490	2.5

Source: *United States Trade: Performance in 1987* (Washington, D.C.: U.S. Department of Commerce, 1988), p. 84.

negotiated with some countries under the Multi-Fiber Arrangement encouraged an expansion in the number of countries exporting to the United States and an upscaling and diversification of their shipments. U.S. clothing imports have been growing at an average of 18 percent a year since 1981. This trend is expected to continue as U.S. firms are making increasing use of foreign assembly plants taking advantage of the Caribbean Basin Initiative (CBI), which allows duty-free import of products manufactured or processed in the group of countries benefited by the CBI.

Table 2–4
Manufactures Imports into the United States, 1985–1987
(in millions of dollars)

	1985	1986	1987	Percentage of 1987 Imports
Japan	71,628	84,736	87,354	25.9
Canada	50,626	53,041	54,538	16.1
West Germany	20,356	25,253	27,240	8.1
Taiwan	17,293	20,709	25,769	7.6
South Korea	10,463	13,237	17,605	5.2
United Kingdom	11,268	12,963	14,610	4.3
Mexico	9,163	10,625	13,861	4.1
Italy	8,868	9,966	10,384	3.1
Hong Kong	8,885	9,348	10,349	3.1
France	8,636	9,256	9,896	2.9

Source: *United States Trade: Performance in 1987* (Washington, D.C.: U.S. Department of Commerce, 1988), p. 113.

Telecommunications and Sound-reproducing Equipment. Many of the consumer products that make up this group, (such as VCRs) are now produced outside the United States. Production facilities have been established in Japan, the Asian NICs, and, more so, Latin America, especially Mexico. The trade deficit for this product classification—$15.5 billion in 1987—is the third-largest group deficit. This deficit is expected to slow down due to saturation of the import markets in this product category, especially consumer markets. The United States exports semifinished goods predominantly for assembly; goods are then reshipped back to the United States assembled, often in the finished-product state. The United States has deregulated the telcommunications market, which has reduced barriers to entry. Japanese and Western European suppliers should benefit in particular from this policy change.

Miscellaneous Consumer Manufactures. Imports of toys and games, rubber and plastic articles, artworks, jewelry, sound recordings, and sporting goods come mostly from the East Asian NICs and increased at an average yearly rate of 17.1 percent in the early 1980s. Between 1984 and 1985, however, this product category increased by 20.3 percent and continued growing at a rate of 26 percent in the 1986–87 period. A significant growth of this import category has been due to the movement of production facilities to offshore locations in Taiwan, South Korea, and Hong Kong. U.S. consumption of leisure products such as toys and sporting goods is rising. The advantage to the offshore production facilities is the foreign labor cost. Also, these production facilities are poised and ready to alter their production line to keep in tune with shifts in American consumer tastes and preferences. U.S. producers have lost that competitive advantage of quality and style differences to their foreign producers.

Iron and Steel. U.S. steel exports have historically been low. Import growth averaged 7.5 percent per year during the 1980–85 period and through 1990 is expected to be moderated by negotiated bilateral trade agreements, limiting future growth in the steel trade deficit which, in fact, already declined by about $500 million in 1985. During the early part of the 1980s, dollar appreciation hurt the competitiveness of the U.S. steel industry significantly. Global overcapacity, foreign-government subsidies aiding exports and strong competition from Canada and Mexico indicate that U.S. producers face major obstacles in their competitive efforts both at home and abroad.

Future Scenario

Overall, U.S. imports have been growing at a rate of 2 percent for each 1 percent of GNP growth. Thus, the expected 4 percent GNP growth rate expected in the later part of the 1980s could increase U.S. imports by $8–10 billion annually. Similarly, it is expected that merchandise trade will continue to dominate the U.S. current account and that manufactures will be the main component of merchandise trade.

The trade and capital flow trends from 1985 to 1989 reflected very large U.S. trade and current-account deficits cannot be sustained indefinitely. The shrinkage of U.S. capital inflows and the trade deficits that must ultimately take place pose significant long-term problems for both the United States and its trading partners. The result of the large capital inflows in recent years has quickly converted the United States from the world's largest creditor nation to a debtor nation.

Debt growth in excess of GNP growth cannot continue indefinitely. The 1985 current-account deficit of $118 billion is equal to about 3 percent of U.S. GNP; the ratio of U.S. international debt to GNP is also increasing. The cumulative effects of increasing debt costs are significant. As debts grow, so do interest payments on foreign-held U.S. securities and dividends and profit remittances on foreign direct investments in the United States. The net debt-servicing outflows will make the United States more dependent on improvements in the merchandise trade if it is to improve its current-account position.

Manufactures trade will necessarily be the principal factor in a U.S. trade- and current-account–performance improvement. Manufacturing output and employment will receive a boost from increased exports. To attain a balance in current account will require a substantial manufactures-trade surplus if a large international U.S. debt generates large debt-service payments. Over the long haul, the United States must export about the same amount of manufactures that it imports.

Undoubtedly, the inroads made by developing countries in U.S. import markets have helped expand their productive capabilities and, in many instances, have helped avoid financial disaster. The U.S. market, with its size and affluence, has been an inviting target for expansion of exports. With special incentives (described later in this chapter) such as the Generalized System of Preferences and the Caribbean Basin Initiative, the United States has made clear its policy to help developing countries in their endeavor to expand their export capabilities by providing preferential access to the U.S. market. Clearly, efforts to reduce U.S. trade deficits must take this into account. Moreover, imports from industrial countries are not likely to decline significantly as there is a very strong domestic demand for such products.[4]

The importer must keep in mind that, even with America's vast size, and the affluence that a significant percentage of its population enjoys, the American consumer is demanding, critical, and highly discriminating in the marketplace. Research has indicated that a significant preference for imported goods exists. However, U.S. as a target for consumer- and industrial-goods producers, the United States offers a highly competitive market. Consequently, the importer must face strong competition from domestic- as well as imported-goods merchandisers who woo American consumers with a vast assortment of consumer and industrial products. While the market's size and affluence may appear to be a bonanza, it is this same size and affluence that make it difficult to serve. The importer must be able to put together a proper marketing strategy to meet consumer needs in the particular segment(s) served. The marketing strategy must be effective and efficient. Understanding the marketplace and consumer behavior is a must to provide the marketing utilities:

time: to get the product to the consumer on a timely basis when the consumer wants it,

place: to get the product where the consumer wants it and in the style, sizes, and specifications that the consumer wants,

possession: to provide for the efficient transfer of title to the consumer so that he or she can take possession of the product.

The U.S. Macromarketing Environment

The United States is a dynamic, fast-changing society that requires progressive marketing strategies to serve its market needs. Marketers need to evaluate the macromarketing environment in order to identify trends that may be sources of opportunities or pose threats to the importing firm. These are the uncontrollable factors that help determine a marketing strategy. The importing firm must monitor and respond to these forces and trends. John Naisbitt, a noted futurist, identified ten major forces or "megatrends" that are transforming the U.S. society.

1. The Information-Based Society—The American economy is undergoing a "megashift" from an industrial to an information-based society. In the United States 13 percent of the total work force is employed in manufacturing, while 60 percent produce or process information. Information "crunchers" include teachers, clerks, secretaries, accountants, stockbrokers, lawyers and insurance people. In the timespan 1970 to 1980 the total labor force increased 18 percent. Managers and administrators rose by 58 percent, health administrators by 118 percent, systems analysts increased 84 percent, and bankers increased 83 percent. To recap, definitely a deemphasis from the production line developed during the industrial revolution, to an information and service revolution.

2. High-Tech Is Where It's At Indeed!—High-touch is being added to the high-tech to increase the latter's acceptance. The Apple Computer Co. chose a bitten apple (that IBM bit into) and a rainbow as its logo to symbolize its "user-friendly" nature. These efforts are thwarted toward making the technology more down-to-earth and less complex.

3. Global Marketing—The U.S. is moving away from isolation and self sufficiency and recognizing its global interdependence. The change of emphasis is to global thinking and acting locally. Illinois and Florida, for instance, are trading with countries around the globe.

4. Long-Term Corporate Strategy—U.S. corporate managers are beginning to think about the long term rather than the short term. The emphasis by management was on the short term because of the pressure from stockholders and managers to attain profitable results in the short term. Short-term performance is evaluated and rewarded. This reduces the importance of long-term planning because if productivity is poor in the short term there may not be a long term! American auto makers are suffering because of short-term behavior, which led to cutting costs at the expense of quality and durability. Japanese management is the perfect example of long term corporate strategy.

5. Decentralized Structure—Companies are moving away from a centralized structure toward a decentralized structure. In an information society, all one needs is a telephone and a typewriter (or keyboard).

6. Entrepreneurial Explosion—We are returning to an emphasis on self-reliance and deemphasizing help from institutions. No longer are people content to devote their lives to corporations and be a good company man. In the 1950s, 93,000 new businesses were commenced, today in the 1980s, 600,000 new businesses are forming per year.

7. Workers and consumers are demanding and getting a greater voice in government, business, and in the marketplace. People today want to have a say in decisions that affect their lives. With the increase in information available to voters, it is possible for the average voter to know as much or more than his or her representatives.

8. Moving from Hierarchies to Networks—Information is power and people who have good access to information can increase their influence in organizations. People are forming networks across organizational charts and depleting the value of traditional organizational hierarchies. Networks are being formed where ideas, information and resources are being shared. The computer is reformulating organizational charts, particularly the formal structure with greater emphasis on the informal structure.

9. From the North and Northeast to the South and Southwest—There has been a shift in the geographic location of the population. The movement from the North to the Sun Belt has been prevalent for some years now. During the 1970s, Buffalo, Cleveland, and St. Louis lost almost 25 percent of their populations. The cities showing the greatest opportunity are Albuquerque, Austin, Dallas, Denver, Phoenix, Salt Lake City, San Antonio, San Diego, San Jose, Tampa, and Tucson.

10. Variety Instead of "One Size Fits All"—The family over the years has changed considerably from the traditional family of profile; ie., working father, mother at home, two children. With the rise in single parent households and

fewer children the market is more varied and complex than it was years ago when there was more uniformity in family structures. Today there are 752 different models of cars and trucks, 2500 types of light bulbs, and 200 different TV channels on cable networks.[5]

The macromarketing environment is of interest to the importing firm and is broken down into the following components:

demographic environment,

economic environment,

legal/political environment,

sociocultural environment.

The Demographic Environment

Markets are people with purchasing power. Consequently, the demographic structure of the American population provides useful descriptions of the U.S. markets that can serve as the basis for quantifying markets and market segments. The picture that emerged from the 1980 census shows some significant changes in the demographic composition of the U.S. population that have strong implications for the formulation of marketing strategy and can provide breakdowns for segmenting dimensions.

The United States is undergoing some alterations in the age structure of its population, racial composition, and family life-styles. Accompanying geographic shifts also have marketing implications. The U.S. population grew at an average rate of 1.1 percent during the 1970s, a higher rate of growth than the precensus estimate of .8 percent, in part because of a large influx of refugees plus other legal and illegal immigration. The following are some of the major demographic trends uncovered by the 1980 census.

Slowdown in the U.S. Birthrate

The U.S. population in 1987 numbered close to 240 million with projections estimating growth to 267 million by the year 2000. But despite the increase, the rate of increase is declining compared to the 1950s and 1960s. Annual births reached a peak in 1960 at 4.3 million and tailed off to under 3.2 million by the mid-1970s. Recent trends show an improvement with a slight gain to 3.6 million births. The population is forecasted to grow less than 1 percent per year in the '80s. The factors that have caused this trend are numerous, such as smaller families having a desire to improve their living standards, the rising number of women in the workplace outside the home, and the improved technology and knowledge of birth control. (See figure 2–1.)

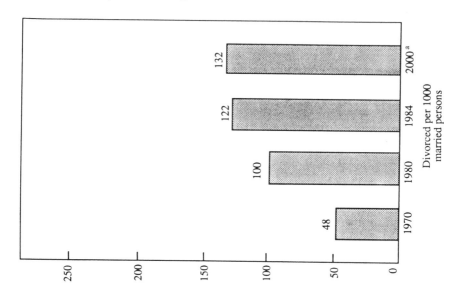

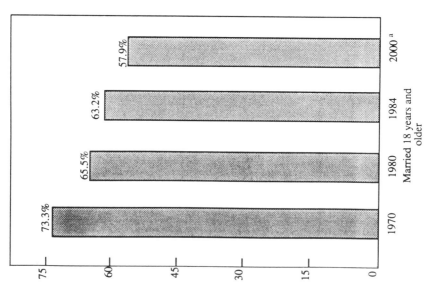

Source: *Statistical Abstract of the United States.*
[a]Estimated.

Figure 2–1. Marriage and Divorces: 1970–1984

With declining birthrates, many industries that cater to the children market will be suffering a loss of market and financial difficulty unless they are able to refocus their strategy. The flip side of the coin is also true—new markets will emerge with new needs to be fulfilled. For many years, the Gerber Company had as its slogan "Babies are our business—our only business" but quietly dropped this slogan some time ago. Gerber now sells life insurance to older folks, using the theme "Gerber now babies the over-50's." In a similar maneuver, Johnson & Johnson took action in view of the declining birthrate by promoting its line of baby products such as baby powder, baby oil, and baby shampoo to adults. The new enterprises that have emerged (such as hotels, airlines, and restaurants) have cashed in on young, childless couples who have the time and income to travel abroad and dine out more frequently.[6]

Rising Average Age of the U.S. Population

Recent generations have been blessed with a declining death rate and a growing number of consumers age 65 and over. Average life expectancy is 74 years with a breakdown of 70 for men and 78 for women. The rise in life expectancy combined with a declining birthrate is producing the "graying of America."[7] The median age in 1984 was 31 and forecasts estimate the median to reach 37 by the turn of the century. (See tables 2–5 and 2–6.)

Age-group populations show different rates of growth:

Ages 15–24: A decrease of 17 percent, or 7.1 million in the 1980s, implies a reduction in sales growth of motorcycles, most sporting equipment, denim clothing, and records as well as in college enrollment.

Ages 25–34: A healthy increase of 14 percent in this age group in the 1980s will raise demand for furniture, vacations, life insurance, and tennis and golf equipment.

Ages 35–54: This age group will undergo the greatest increase of all age groups in the 1990s, namely 25 percent. Members of this group are well established in their work life and are a major market for large homes, new automobiles, and clothing.

Ages 55–64: A drop of 2 percent will shrink this classification. They are often termed "empty-nesters," whose children have left home, leaving the parent(s) with plenty of time and income to allocate to various forms of recreation such as eating out, travel, expensive clothing, and golf.

Ages 65 and over: This group will experience the second-largest increase in the 1980s (20 percent). Their demand will be for products and services such as retirement homes and communities, campers, comparatively quiet forms of recreation (fishing, golf), single-portion food packages, and

Table 2–5
Median Age of the U.S. Population, 1970–2000
(*years*)

	Total	*Male*	*Female*
1970	28.0	26.8	29.3
1980	30.0	28.8	31.3
1984	31.3	30.0	32.5
2000	37.0[a]		

Source: *Statistical Abstract of the United States*, 106th edition
(Washington, D.C.: U.S. Department of Commerce, Bureau of
the Census, 1986).
[a]Estimated.

medical goods and services (medicine, eye glasses, canes, hearing aids, and
convalescent homes). This group is becoming more self-centered, active,
and leisure-oriented than comparable groups in past generations. They are
willing to spend more money on themselves and not worry about in-
heritances for their children.

The Changing American Family

The character of the American family is changing as a result of such factors
as later marriage, fewer chldren, a higher divorce rate, and more working wives.
We shall take a closer look at each of these factors.

Later Marriage. The vast majority (96 percent) of all Americans will marry
in their lifetime. However, the mean age of marrying couples making their first
attempt has been rising over the years and in 1986 stood at 23.4 years for males
and 21.6 for females. By the end of the 1980s, over half of the 20–24-year-old
women and one third of those in the 25–29 age category will never have married according to the U.S. Census Bureau. These statistics will have dramatic
impact on industries such as wedding paraphernalia that serve this transition
period for newlyweds.

Fewer Children. The average size of families has been falling, particularly when
we consider that almost 50 percent of all families have no children under 18
years of age. Newlyweds are postponing childbearing longer to pursue careers,
leisure, and greater income in two-income households. Those who have children
have on average 1.07 children, a significant decrease from 3.5 in 1955. Demand for infants' and children's products is thus diminishing.

Higher Divorce Rate. The United States has the highest divorce rate in the
world, with about 50 percent of all marriages ending in divorce. This has created

Table 2–6
Percent Distribution of the U.S. Population, 1970, 1984, 2000

	1970	1984	2000[a]
Under 5 years	8.4%	7.5%	6.9%
5–14	20.0	14.3	13.5
17–24	17.5	16.9	15.7
25–34	12.2	17.3	13.2
35–44	11.4	13.3	15.9
45–54	11.5	9.5	13.8
55–64	9.1	9.4	8.9
65 and over	9.9	11.8	12.1
Total	100.0	100.0	100.0

Source: *U.S. Bureau of the Census, unpublished data and Statistical Abstract of the United States* (106th and 108th editions, 1986 and 1988).
[a]Estimated.

over a million single-parent families, which is altering the structure of the family and its needs. The type of household products demanded is changing along with the rising number of small housing units. The family no longer has the profile of families of just a couple of decades ago. Statistics indicate that of these divorced persons, 79 percent will remarry, with about 69 percent of all males and 63 percent of all females presently married according to 1986 U.S. Census data.

More Working Wives. Over 50 percent of all married women hold some form of position outside of the home. Women have become more accepted in the workplace, resulting in more opportunities for them than ever before. Since their earnings comprise about 40 percent of total household income and permit the purchase of higher-quality goods and services, markets have developed to cater to their needs and wants (such as good clothing, child-care services, and convenience foods). Even marketers of tires, automobiles, insurance, and travel services are increasingly targeting their promotions toward working women.

For example, the Spiegel Corporation refocused its strategy to upscale working women who do not have time to shop for clothes but want fashion and quality. Its business grew through catalog shopping and has been enhanced by the efficiency of its service.

With more women working outside the home, less time is devoted to watching television soap operas and reading such women's magazines as *Good Housekeeping* and *Ladies' Home Journal.* The growing female work force has also resulted in changes in roles between husbands and wives. Men are assuming more domestic functions, so marketers of food and household appliances are targeting some of their promotions toward them.

*The Growing Number of Single-Member and
Nontraditional Households*

The number of single-member households is increasing, going from 19 percent of all households in 1970 to 26 percent in 1980. Single-member households are forecasted by the Census Bureau to be 30 percent in 1990. With the increase in single-member and nontraditional households, greater market segmentation is needed by the marketers to meet their special needs.

Single-Adult Households. Many young adults leave home when they gain employment and move into an apartment. Separated and divorced people tend

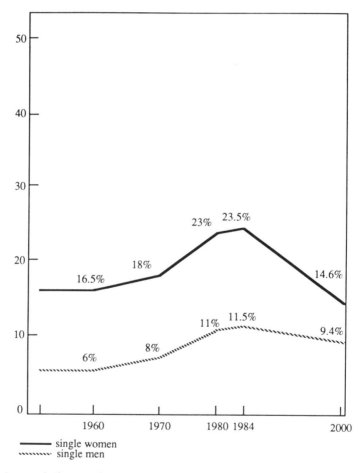

Source: *Statistical Abstract of the United States.*

Figure 2–2. Single-member Households (As a Percentage of the Adult Population)

to live alone. About 18 million people live alone, which accounts for 23 percent of all households. Predictions for 1990 indicate that 45 percent of households will be single-person or single-parent households. This segment of the market is the fastest-growing category of urban home seekers. This group of adults (single, separated, divorced, and widowed) needs smaller apartments; inexpensive and smaller appliances, furniture, and furnishings; and food that is packaged in small sizes. They tend to purchase small cars as well.

Two-Person Cohabitor Households. A growing trend is unmarried persons of the opposite sex sharing living quarters. There are many households made up of two or more persons of the same sex sharing living quarters. Since their arrangements tend to be of a temporary nature, they create a market for inexpensive or rental furniture and furnishings.

Group Households. This entails households of three or more people of the same or opposite sex that share expenses by living together. This would include college students and religious groups that live in communes.

In summary, importers must keep single-member and nontraditional households in mind when formulating their strategy because they have special needs and are growing more rapidly than family households.

Continued Geographical Shifts in the Population

Residents of the United States are a mobile people. About 20 percent (46 million) move in a single year. Major mobility trends include:

Movement to the Sunbelt states,

Movement from rural to urban areas,

Movement from city to suburbs.

Movement to the Sunbelt States. In the decade of the '80s, the West will experience an increase in population growth of 17 percent, with the South increasing 14 percent. From the early 1970s to the '80s, these two areas increased from 45 to 51 percent of the U.S. population. The cities of the Northeast experienced a reduction in population. With this exodus to the Sunbelt states, there will continue to be an increased demand for air conditioning and decreased demand for heavy clothing and home heating equipment. Of interest to the importer, the Western consumer tends to spend more on automobiles and less on food when compared to the Northeastern consumer.

Movement from Rural to Urban Areas. For over one hundred years, people have been moving from rural to urban areas. In the 1980s, about 75 percent of the American population resides in urban settings. The city provides a different

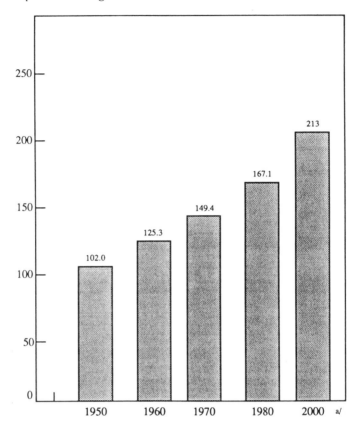

Source: *Statistical Abstract of the United States.*
ªEstimated.

Figure 2–3. Absolute Number of Persons Living in Urban Areas 1950–1980

life-style, a faster pace of living, more commuting, higher incomes, and greater variety of goods and services than are available in small towns and rural areas. The largest cities (New York, Chicago, and Los Angeles) account for a major portion of the sales of expensive furs, perfumes, luggage, and works of art. These cities also support the opera, ballet, and other forms of "high culture." Recently, however, there has been a slight return of population to the small towns and rural areas.

Movement from City to Suburbs. With the development of rapid transit, highways, and automobiles, people travel further distances to their employment. This commute is primarily to the city for employment and back to the suburbs, where people have increasingly been residing. Approximately 60 percent of the total metropolitan population now lives in suburbs. Suburbs are associated with a more casual life-style, outdoor living, greater neighbor interaction, higher incomes, and younger families. Suburbanites' purchase habits include station wagons, home workshop equipment, garden furniture, lawn and gardening tools and supplies, and outdoor cooking equipment. The purchasing volume is significant as displayed by the massive suburban shopping centers that cater to the suburbanites.

As was mentioned, there has been a recent migration back to the city where urban renewal has been successful. These residents tend to be younger and older adults who have no children and can enjoy the superior cultural and recreational opportunities. This has resulted in new high-rise apartment developments and retail outlets in the city.

Legal and Illegal Immigration Changing the Ethnic and Racial Population Distribution

The U.S. population in 1987 is 79 percent white, 10 percent black, and 7 percent Hispanic with the largest subgroups being Mexicans, Puerto Ricans, and Cubans. The Asian population has been growing, with the Chinese having the largest representation, followed by the Japanese, Filipinos, Koreans, and Vietnamese. Hispanic and Asians are predominantly in the Far West (California), South (South Florida), and Southwest (Texas), with dispersal slowing taking place to other parts of the country. Each population group has unique wants and buying habits. Importers can segment the market and serve these groups specifically with their foods, clothing, and furniture.

A Better-Educated and White-Collar Population

About 69 percent of Americans over 25 years old have high school degrees, while 16 percent have college degrees. These statistics are on the rise. With more educated persons, there will be an increase in demand for quality products, books, magazines, and travel.

From 1960 to 1980, white-collar workers increased from 43 to 52 percent, and blue-collar workers declined from 37 to 32 percent. The service industry work force increased from 12 to 13 percent, while farm workers fell from 8 to 3 percent. These shifts in employment bring out the shift in emphasis in the United States from a production-oriented society to one that is information- and service-driven.

Rising Income for the Average Household

U.S. family income has been increasing steadily for the past century. The middle- and upper-income brackets have been experiencing growth, particularly the former. Table 2–7 shows the growth of the median family income in the 1970s.

Table 2–7
Median Family Income   1960–1986
(in current and constant dollars)

Year	Current Dollars	1986 Constant Dollars
1960	$ 5,620	$20,807
1965	6,957	24,176
1970	9,867	27,862
1975	13,719	27,948
1980	21,023	27,974
1986	29,458	29,458

Source: U.S. Bureau of the Census, *Statistical Abstract of the United States: 1988*, (108th edition) (Washington, D.C.: U.S. Department of Commerce, 1987), p. 421.

The breakdown is as follows: 61 percent of the households receive 86 percent of all income paid out to households. Thus, 39 percent of the households are left with 14 percent of the income. This represents a fairly good distribution of income among the population.

In summary, there has been a shift from mass marketing to target marketing. The result of all the changes that have taken place in the United States has resulted in an environment of smaller families, more single-family housholds, an aging population, and high growth rates of Hispanic, Oriental, and black markets, transforming the U.S. marketplace from a mass market into more fragmented micromarkets, differentiated by age, sex, geography, life-style, ethnic background, education, and so on. Each group has strong preferences and consumer characteristics and is reached through increasingly differentiated media. Companies are abandoning the "shotgun" approach that aimed at a mythical "average" consumer and are increasingly designing their products and marketing programs for specific micromarkets.

The Economic Environment

Markets require purchasing power as well as people. Changes in real income, inflationary pressures, and consumer expenditures can be a source of opportunities and threats to marketers of domestic and imported products alike.

Slowdown of Real-Income Growth

The decade of the '70s saw money income rise to a median of approximately $20,000 per houshold. This rise is deceiving because real income per capita has stagnated, being hurt by an inflation rate exceeding the money-income

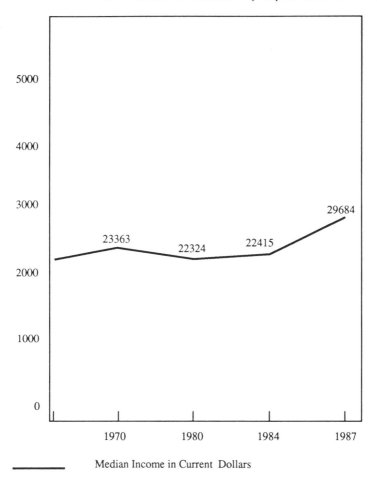

Source: *Statistical Abstract of the United States.*

Figure 2–4. Median Family Income

growth rate, an unemployment rate between 6 and 10 percent, and increase in tax burden. These developments have reduced disposable personal income (after-tax money available for spending). There has also been a fall in discretionary income (funds available after necessities such as food, clothing, and shelter have been purchased). On the other side, there has been a rise in the number of two-income families, with the result being increased average family income.

The implications of these trends are significant to importers. With the decline in real income, many Americans have become more cautious in making purchases. To save money, fewer name brands are purchased and more store brands and generics are bought as substitutes. To compensate for these buying habits, companies are adjusting their packaging strategies and moving to economy sizes along with price appeals in their advertising messages. As for durable goods, some consumers are postponing purchases while others purchase out of fear of future price increases in the short term. The American dream of possessing the material wealth of this world is slipping away along with the sunset on the horizon.

Inflationary Pressures

Inflation has declined from a peak 13.5 percent in 1980 to 2.8 percent in 1986. It is projected to continue at a rate of 3.4 percent a year in the next few years. After inflation remained relatively stable during the mid-1980s, wholesale prices began to accelerate in 1988 as producer prices rose at a yearly rate of 4.0 percent. However, by the end of the year, wholesale prices rose by a modest 0.4 percent. The Bureau of Labor Statistics estimates that inflation will continue at levels of 0.2 percent to 0.3 percent throughout most of 1989.[8] Although the inflation rate is now modest, there are still several sources of continued inflationary pressure:

cartel price fixing of several commodities, including oil

the lack of competition in certain sectors of the economy

the demands of several labor unions for wage increases that exceed productivity gains

the unfavorable balance of trade

high expenditures on public services and nonproductive capital investment

a psychology of inflationary expectation, which in turn feeds the inflation

The results of these inflationary pressures are clear. Consumers search for ways to save money, such as buying cheaper brands in economy sizes, buying from discount stores, attempting do-it-yourself projects, and bartering for services with others.

Consumer Expenditures

Consumer credit has enabled consumers to purchase in excess of their earnings and savings. Purchasing power is increased through borrowing. In 1986, outstanding consumer credit stood at $723.6 billion. The ratio of consumer credit (not including mortgages) to disposable personal income stood at 24 percent in 1986. The cost of credit is high also, with credit-card companies charging interest rates between 12 and 20 percent. This retards the ongoing growth of housing and other durable-goods markets that are heavily dependent on credit.

Over the years, there have been fluctuations in consumption of major goods and services. Food, housing, household operations, and transportation use up two-thirds of household income. However, over time, the food, clothing and personal-care bills of household have been declining percentage-wise while housing, transportation, medical-care, and recreation bills have been increasing.

Thus it can be said that changes in such major economic variables as money income, cost of living, interest rates, and savings and borrowing patterns have an immediate impact on the marketplace. Importers working with products that are particularly income-sensitive should be advised to invest in economic forecasting. Businesses do not have to be wiped out by a downturn in economic activity. With adequate forewarning, they can take the necessary steps to reduce their costs and ride out an economic storm.

The Legal/Political Environment

U.S. businesses today face an environment of government regulation. Of concern to the importer are the laws, government agencies, and pressure groups that affect or constrain import activities. Areas with implications to importers are (1) laws that regulate business, (2) laws that protect consumers from unfair business practices, and (3) foreign-trade legislation, especially import laws. Public-interest groups' efforts must also be taken into account.

Laws That Protect Businesses from
Unfair Business Practices

These laws were developed to protect companies from each other and regulate competition. They address any business behavior aimed at unfair competition and efforts to create a monopoly.

The *Sherman Antitrust Act* (1890) prohibits "monopolies or attempts to monopolize" and "contracts, combinations, or conspiracies in restraint of trade" in interstate and foreign commerce.

The *Federal Trade Commission Act* (1914) establishes the commission, a body of specialists with broad powers to investigate and to issue cease-and-desist orders to enforce Section 5, which declares that "unfair methods of competition in commerce are unlawful."

The *Clayton Act* (1914) supplements the Sherman Act by prohibiting specific practices (certain types of price discrimination, tying clauses and exclusive dealing, intercorporate stockholdings, and interlocking directorates) "where the effect . . . may be to substantially lessen competition or tend to create a monopoly in any line of commerce." It provides that violating corporate officials could be held individually responsible. The act exempts labor and agricultural organizations from its provisions.

The *Robinson-Patman Act* (1936) amends the Clayton Act, adding the phrase "to injure, destroy, or prevent competition." It defines price discrimination as unlawful (subject to certain defenses) and provides the FTC with the right to establish limits on quantity discounts, to forbid brokerage allowances except to independent brokers, and to prohibit promotional allowances or the furnishing of services or facilities except where they are made available to all "on proportionately equal terms."

The *Miller-Tydings Act* (1937) amends the Sherman Act to exempt interstate fair-trade (price-fixing) agreements from antitrust prosecution. (The *McGuire Act* of 1952 reinstates the legality of the nonsignor clause. "Nonsignor" clauses adopted in most states say price-fixing acts bind persons who are not parties to the contract to control resale prices and provides that a violation is unfair competition and actionable by law. Most states, however, have abandoned Fair Trade Laws due to the changing nature of discount retailing.)

The *Wheeler-Lea Act* (1938) prohibits unfair and deceptive acts and practices regardless of whether comptition is injured. It places advertising of foods and drugs under the Federal Trade Commission's (FTC's) jurisdiction.

The *Antimerger Act* (1950) amends Section 7 of the Clayton Act by broadening the power to prevent intercorporate acquisitions where the acquisition may have a substantially adverse effect on competition.

Laws That Protect Consumers from
Unfair Business Practices

This second group of laws is of considerable importance to importers as they affect many aspects of the marketing strategy. These laws are aimed at making products safer and at controlling deceptive and unfair advertising, pricing, and other business practices that can injure consumers in the marketplace.

The *Federal Food and Drug Act* (1906) forbids the manufacture, sale, or transport of adulterated or fraudulently labeled foods and drugs in interstate commerce. It was supplanted by the *Food, Drug, and Cosmetic Act* (1938) and amended by the *Food Additives Amendment* (1958) and the *Kefauver-Harris Amendment* (1962). The 1962 amendment deals with pretesting of drugs for safety and effectiveness and labeling of drugs by generic name.

The *Meat Inspection Act* (1906) provides for the enforcement of sanitary regulations in meat-packing establishments and for federal inspection of all companies selling meats in interstate commerce.

The *Automobile Information Disclosure Act* (1958) prohibits car dealers from inflating the factory price of new cars.

The *National Traffic and Safety Act* (1958) provides for the creation of compulsory safety standards for automobiles and tires.

The *Fair Packaging and Labeling Act* (1966) provides for the regulation of the packaging and labeling of consumer goods. It requires manufacturers to state what the package contains, who made it, and how much it contains. It permits industries' voluntary adoption of uniform packaging standards.

The *Child Protection Act* (1966) bans sale of hazardous toys and articles. It was amended in 1969 to include articles that pose electrical, mechanical, or thermal hazards.

The *Federal Cigarette Labeling and Advertising Act* (1967) requires that cigarette packages contain the statement "Warning: The Surgeon General Has Determined that Cigarette Smoking is Dangerous to Your Health."

The *Truth-in-Lending Act* (1968) requires lenders to state the true costs of a credit transaction, outlaws the use of actual or threatened violence in collecting loans, and restricts the amount of garnishments. It establishes a National Commission on Consumer Finance.

The *Fair Credit Reporting Act* (1970) insures that a consumer's credit report contain only accurate, relevant, and up-to-date information and be confidential unless requested for an appropriate reason by a proper party.

The *Consumer Product Safety Act* (1972) establishes the Consumer Product Safety Commission and authorizes it to set safety standards for consumer products as well as exact penalties to uphold the standards.

The *Consumer Goods Pricing Act* (1975) prohibits the use of price-maintenance agreements among manufacturers and resellers in interstate commerce.

The *Magnuson-Moss Warranty/FTC Improvement Act* (1975) authorizes the FTC to determine rules concerning consumer warranties and provides for consumer access to means of redress, such as the class-action suit. It also expands FTC regulatory powers over unfair or deceptive acts or practices.

The *Equal Credit Opportunity Act* (1975) prohibits discrimination in a credit transaction because of sex, marital status, race, national origin, religion, age, or receipt of public assistance.

The *Fair Debt Collection Practice Act* (1978) makes it illegal to harass or abuse any person, make false statements, or use unfair methods when collecting a debt.

Public-Interest Groups' Efforts

Also noteworthy are the public-interest groups that have increased in number and power since the 1960s lobbying government officials and putting pressure on corporate executives to allocate more resources to consumer rights, women's rights, and other public interest issues. Many larger corporations have established public-affairs departments to work with these groups to maintain a favorable image in the minds of the public. New laws, stronger enforcement, and growing numbers of pressure groups together impact importers and the products they market. Importers must clear their plans with their corporate legal counsel. In this regard, the consumer may not be king or queen as he or she is just one voice among many.

The organization of interest will vary with the type of corporation and product. For example, minority activist groups affect the design of dolls by requesting representative figures. The impact of interest groups require the importer to incorporate not only the question of what the consumer wants but what the consumer can have, as well.

Foreign-Trade Legislation

U.S. trade policy has been founded on the premise that a free exchange of goods among nations benefits not only this country but others as well. The body of import laws addresses two issues that are important to U.S. trade concerns: the control of the nation's borders and defense against unfair import competition. Thus, U.S. trade laws are designed either

To alleviate on a temporary basis the dislocations of U.S. industries caused by unfair competition of imports or

To eliminate the effects of import competition in the United States from certain foreign practices that the international community recognizes as unfair and injurious.[9]

U.S. Customs Service Offices

Goods arriving from a foreign country must go through a customs port of entry to the United States. These ports of entry are located in every state as well as Puerto Rico and the Virgin Islands. The headquarters of the U.S. Customs Service is in Washington, D.C. The nine regional Customs offices are located in:

Region I	Boston
Region II	New York
Region III	Baltimore
Region IV	Miami/Puerto Rico/Virgin Islands
Region V	New Orleans
Region VI	Houston
Region VII	Los Angeles/Long Beach
Region VIII	San Francisco/Oakland/Alaska/Hawaii
Region IX	Chicago

Foreign Trade Zones. U.S. laws permit establishing, operating, and maintaining foreign trade zones in or near ports of entry under the jurisdiction of the United States. The purpose of foreign trade zones is to permit foreign merchandise of every description, except such as prohibited by law, to enter the United States without paying duties (that is, without being subject to customs laws).

The merchandise can be stored, sold, exhibited, broken up, repacked, assembled, distributed, sorted, graded, cleaned, mixed with domestic or foreign merchandise, manipulated, or manufactured without being subject to laws and regulations that affect imported merchandise. Only until such time as the merchandise is removed from the foreign trade zone is it deemed to be imported into the United States and subject to U.S. Customs laws, unless it is reexported.[10]

The Trade Act of 1930. The Tariff Act of 1930 provides the basis of U.S. trade and tariff law and customs administration. The act contains guidelines for:

marking of articles and containers,

bonded warehouses,

drawback,

unfair practices in import trade,

countervailing and antidumping duties.[11]

Marking of Articles and Containers. Every article of foreign origin imported into the United States must be marked in a conspicuous place as legibly and permanently as the nature of the article and container permit. The purpose is to indicate to an ultimate purchaser in the United States the English name of the item's country of origin. Articles that would be excepted from meeting these criteria include:

those incapable of being marked,

those that cannot be marked prior to shipment without injury,

those that cannot be marked prior to shipment to the United States except at an expense economically prohibitive of its importation,

those whose containers' markings reasonably indicate their origin.

If at the time of importation any article is not marked, there shall be levied, collected, and paid upon such a duty of 10 per centum ad valorem, which shall be deemed to have accrued at the time of importation, shall not be construed to be penal, and shall not be remitted wholly or in part nor shall payment thereof be avoidable for any cause. Such duty shall be levied, collected, and paid in addition to any other duty imposed by law.

Bonded Warehouses. The Trade Act provides for exemption from customs duties and internal revenue tax for articles that are intended for exportation and that are manufactured in whole or in part of imported materials, to be manufactured and then exported from bonded warehouses. The manufacturer must first give satisfactory bond and observe the provisions of the law faithfully and satisfactorily.

Drawback and Refunds. Upon the exportation of articles manufactured or produced in the United States with the use of imported merchandise, the full amount of the duties paid upon the merchandise so used shall be refunded as drawback, less 1 per centum of such duties. Where two or more products result from the manipulation of imported merchandise, the drawback shall be distributed to the several products in accordance with their relative values at the time of separation.

Unfair Practices in Import Trade. Unfair methods of competition and unfair acts in the importation of articles into the United States, or in their sale by the owner, importer, consignee, or agent of either, the effect or tendency of which is to destroy or substantially injure an industry, efficiently and economically operated, in the United States, or to prevent the establishment of such an industry, or to restrain or monopolize trade and commerce in the United States, are declared unlawful. If the International Trade Commission determines, as a result of an investigation that there is violation, it shall direct that the articles concerned be excluded from entry into the United States.

Countervailing and Antidumping Duties. Under the Trade Act, imports from countries that pay or bestow, directly or indirectly, any bounty or grant to any organization, public or private, that engages in export activities and thus provides an unfair advantage in the import trade are subject to countervailing and antidumping duties. These are discussed more thoroughly in chapter 7.

The Trade Fair Program. The purpose of the program is to allow articles imported or brought into the United States to be displayed at an exhibition. The articles specified are in the custody of customs covered by a customs-exhibition bond or in a foreign trade zone. Though, no duty or internal revenue tax has been paid on these articles, but this does not preclude exhibition at a fair.

Upon payment of duties and taxes (within a three-month period), any article entered for such a fair may be sold or removed from the fair. If such duties or any due taxes are not paid within the three-month period, any articles entered for such a fair may be reexported, transferred to another location under customs custody, placed in a foreign trade zone, destroyed, or abandoned by the U.S. government.[12]

The Trade Expansion Program. The purpose of this program is to attain trade agreements through mutual trade benefits. The objectives are twofold:

To stimulate the economic growth of the United States and to maintain and enlarge foreign markets for the products of U.S. agriculture, industry, mining, and commerce and

To strengthen economic relations with foreign countries through the development of open and nondiscriminatory trading in the free world.

Countries classified under the most-favored–nation principle are subject to duty or other import restriction or duty-free treatment proclaimed in carrying out any trade agreement that applies to products of all foreign countries, whether imported directly or indirectly. The president may at any time terminate, in whole or in part, any proclamation made in the trade agreements. The opposite is also true—increases or imposition of duty or other import restrictions on any articles that may cause or threaten to cause serious injury to an industry may be imposed.

In industries where duties have been imposed, the U.S. International Trade Commission shall monitor developments with respect to the industry concerned. The economic effects are analyzed to determine the impact of an imposition of a duty or restriction. Also, the effects of a reduction in duty or restrictions are analyzed. The economic factors reviewed include idling of productive facilities, inability to operate at a level of reasonable profit, unemployment or underemployment, and all other economic factors that it considers relevant.[13]

The Trade Act of 1974. The Trade Act of 1974 was a broad reform of U.S. law pertaining to international trade. It was the only comprehensive trade legislation since the Trade Expansion Act of 1962 that authorized the president to negotiate and enter into trade agreements with foreign governments. The Trade Act of 1974 is divided into five major titles:

Negotiating Authority,

Import Relief,

Adjustment Assistance,

Retaliatory Powers,

General System of Preferences.[14]

Negotiating Authority. The president was authorized to enter into trade agreements with other countries for the purpose of harmonizing, reducing, or eliminating tariff and nontariff trade barriers.

Import Relief. It relaxed criteria for industries to be eligible for relief from injuries caused by import competition by requiring the U.S. International Trade Commission (ITC) to make a finding that increased imports were a substantial cause of serious injury, rather than a major cause as in previous law. The president is required to provide some form of import relief within sixty days where the ITC finds serious injury. If this action is not in the national interest, then alternate action is needed.

Adjustment Assistance. This enactment eased the criteria for workers who suffered displacement due to imports to qualify for adjustment programs by requiring that imports "contribute importantly" rather than be the major cause as in the past. Workers would be eligible for weekly benefits of 70 percent of their average weekly wage for fifty-two weeks. In addition, they could qualify for training, job search, and relocation allowances. Aid was also available for communities adversely affected by imports with loans and grants.

Retaliatory Powers. It authorized the president to take retaliatory actions against unjustifiable or unreasonable import tariff restrictions imposed by foreign countries against U.S. goods, services, and access to supplies, including antidumping measures, countervailing duties, and actions against unfair import practices.

General System of Preferences. The president was granted the authority to administer this program, which extends duty-free treatment to certain products imported from eligible beneficiary developing countries, up to certain dollar-value or percentage limits. The president was prohibited from designing an article for duty-free treatment if the article fell within specific categories of import-sensitive articles. Further details on the General System of Preferences appear in chapters 7 and 10.

The Trade Agreements Act of 1979. The Trade Agreements Act of 1979 approved and implemented the trade agreements negotiated by the United States under the Trade Act of 1974. The act also fosters the growth and maintenance of an open world-trading system; seeks to expand opportunities for the commerce of the United States in international trade; and attempts to improve the rules of international trade and to provide for enforcement of such rules.

The act incorporated into U.S. law the multilateral trade negotiations on countervailing and antidumping duties, customs valuation, government procurement, product standards, tariffs, civil aircraft, meat and dairy products, and liquor. In addition, it extended the president's authority to negotiate trade agreements with foreign countries and to reduce or eliminate nontariff barriers, and it required the president to reorganize executive-agency trade functions and responsibilities.[15]

Countervailing and Antidumping Duties. The act allowed countervailing duties to offset export business subsidies if the administering agency determined that an import was either directly or indirectly subsidized, and the International

Trade Commission determined that a domestic industry had been injured or threatened with injury.

Customs Valuation. It established five methods of determining the value of imports to simplify the process of assessing duties:

1. *Transaction value,* the price actually paid or payable for the merchandise when sold for exportation to the United States, with additions for extra costs such as packing costs and selling commission,
2. *Transaction value* of identical merchandise. If the transaction value cannot be determined, then the customs value of the imported merchandise is appraised as the transaction value of identical merchandise.
3. *Transaction value* of similar merchandise is the customs value based on the value of similar merchandise
4. *Deductive value,* is the customs value based on the resale price of similar merchandise in the United States with subtraction of additional costs for insurance, transportation, taxes, and commissions,
5. *Computer value,* is the customs value based on the sum of production and materials costs, profit, general expenses, packing costs, and assists not included as part of production materials and other listed costs of production.

Government Procurement. The act gave the president the authority to waive the application of discriminatory government procurement laws such as the Buy American Act; to designate major industrial countries as eligible for non-discriminatory bidding under the agreement; and to bar purchases from ineligible countries.

Product Standards. The Trade Agreements Act of 1979 indicated that the Act does not prohibit any private person, federal agency, or state agency from setting standard-related activities; however, this cannot create unnecessary obstacles to foreign trade and such standard-related activities must be deemed necessary to achieve legitimate domestic objectives such as: the protection of health or safety, essential security, and environmental and consumer interests. Imported products should be tested with comparable methods to those employed on domestic products, unless international standards need to be applied.

Tariffs. It allocates authority to the president to give least developed countries full tariff reductions on products that are not import-sensitive.

Civil Aircraft Agreement. It eliminated all duties on civil aircraft, engines, and parts intended for use in civil aircraft.

Agricultural Agreements. It implemented bilateral agreements on cheese, other dairy products, and meat. The approved bilateral agreements resulted in an increase of the annual cheese quota to 110,000 metric tons in a quota coverage of about 85 percent of cheese imports. The agreements also set a floor of 1.25 billion pounds of meat import limitations and a countercyclical formula to increase or lower imports in accordance with domestic supply.

Liquor Duties. Liquor is taxed solely on the basis of alcohol content, with tax based on the finished product after it has been diluted and bottled.

The Caribbean Basin Initiative. This legislation provides authority to grant duty-free treatment for all eligible articles from any beneficiary country that meets the provisions specified. Countries eligible for designation as beneficiary countries are:

Anguilla	Haiti
Antigua and Barbuda	Honduras
The Bahamas	Jamaica
Barbados	Montserrat
Belize	Netherlands Antilles
Cayman Islands	Nicaragua
Costa Rica	Panama
Dominica	Saint Christopher-Nevis
Dominican Republic	Saint Lucia
El Salvador	Saint Vincent the Suriname
Grenada	Trinidad and and Tobago
Grenadines	Turks and Caicos Islands
Guatemala	Virgin Islands, British
Guyana	

The countries are designated as "beneficiary countries" and only these countries and territories or successor political entities will be eligible for duty-free treatment. Eligible articles that receive duty-free treatment under the CBI are any articles that are the growth, product, or manufacture of a beneficiary country and are imported directly from a beneficiary country into the customs territory of the United States. An additional proviso is that the sum of (1) the cost or value of the materials produced in a beneficiary country or two or more beneficiary countries plus (2) the direct costs of processing operations performed in a beneficiary country or countries is not less than 35 per centum of the appraised value of such article at the time it is entered.

Duty-free treatment does not apply to some articles:

Textile and apparel articles that are subject to textile agreements;

Footwear, handbags, luggage, flat goods, work gloves, and leather wearing apparel;

Tuna, prepared or preserved in any manner, in airtight containers;

Petroleum, or any product derived from petroleum;

Watches and watch parts (including cases, bracelets, and straps) of whatever type including, but not limited to, mechanical, quartz digital, and quartz analog;

Sugar and beef products.[16]

The Wine Equity and Export Expansion Act of 1984. There is a substantial imbalance in international wine trade resulting, in part, from foreign wines' relative accessibility to the U.S. market while the U.S. wine industry faces restrictive tariff and nontariff bariers in virtually every existing or potential foreign market. The purpose of the act is to provide wine consumers the greatest possible choice of wines from wine-producing countries. The potential U.S. demand for wine is significant. Through this act, expansion into these markets is being encouraged. To make the wine trade more equitable, the United States is trying to achieve greater access to foreign markets through the reduction or elimination of tariff barriers and nontariff barriers to trade in wine.[17]

The Sociocultural Environment

Markets have to be understood before a marketing strategy can be developed. The marketing manager needs to comprehend how and why consumers buy. Demographic breakdowns provide an initial important insight into the structure of the markets. However, we draw from the sociocultural environment to understand other dimensions of consumer behavior:

Who buys?

Where do consumers buy?

When do consumers buy?

What do consumers buy?

How do consumers buy?

If marketers can anticipate future actions, then it may be possible to influence such actions with proper marketing strategies. Consumer behavior is a function of various influences: personal (life-style, occupation, economic circumstance, personality, motivation, beliefs, and attitudes) and environmental (family, social class, reference groups, and culture), which stem from the sociocultural environment. Understanding these factors and how they influence consumer behavior provides a clue as to how to reach and serve the consumer more effectively. These factors are discussed in the following chapter.

Summary

The United States is the largest single importer of manufactured goods in the world. The affluence and life-style of the American consumer make it the largest consumer market in the world as well. Rapidly increasing imports indicate that there is demand for imports in the marketplace, whose size and affluence present opportunities to the importer yet make it a difficult market to serve. The importer must be able to understand demographic, economic, legal/political, and sociocultural environmental variables and trends to frame an adequate and competitive marketing strategy. The complex U.S. foreign-trade legislation provides importers with access to a vast market yet frames the strict conditions under which they can serve this market.

Notes

1. *United States Trade: Performance in 1985 and Outlook* (Washington, D.C.: U.S. Department of Commerce, 1984).

2. Ibid., p. 15.

3. The following section is summarized from *United States Trade: Performance in 1987,* pp. 25–28.

4. For a complete discussion of the U.S. trade position, see *United States Trade: Performance in 1987,* pp. 67–70.

5. Reprinted by permission of Warner Books/New York from John Naisbitt, *Megatrends* (New York: Wainer Books, 1982).

6. P. Kotler, *Marketing Management: Analysis Planning, and Control, 5/E,* C 1984, p. 89. Reprinted by permission of Prentice-Hall, Inc., Englewood Cliffs, New Jersey.

7. See "The Graying of America," *Newsweek* (February 28, 1977).

8. "Wholesale prices rise 4% in 1988," *The Miami Herald* (January 14, 1989), p. 3C.

9. For more on U.S. trade policies, see *Trade: U.S. Policy since 1945* (Washington, D.C.: Congressional Quarterly, 1984).

10. See 19 U.S.C. 1862, Sec. 232.

11. See 19 U.S.C. 1303–677h.

12. See 19 U.S.C. 1751–56.

13. See 19 U.S.C. 1801–2033.

14. See 19 U.S.C. 2101–487.

15. See 19 U.S.C. 2501–82.

16. See 19 U.S.C. 2701–6.

17. See 19 U.S.C. 2801–6.

3
An Analysis of Import Markets

A key factor in the success of import activities is providing consumers with products and services that meet their needs. Consumers are concerned with the need-satisfying qualities of products and services, such as style, price, and convenience. In most instances, consumers are not concerned with the country of origin.[1] If a product meets the needs of enjoyment and other important considerations, the product will be accepted in the marketplace.

The basic utilities of form, time, place, and possession are key to the makeup of a product. First, the appearance of the product (in terms of packaging, branding, warranties, and so on) is significant as the product must "fit" the target market. The product should be available where and when the consumer wants it. Similarly, the consumer should be able to take possession of the product and use it. Import-marketing activities can provide these utilities to the consumer by expanding product offering, choice, and information. Marketing activities must be planned, coordinated, and controlled through a carefully designed plan. In order to develop an adequate plan to meet market and organizational needs, it is first necessary to analyze the marketplace in order to identify opportunities the firm can exploit.

Finding Attractive Opportunities

Opportunities come from the environment. One key factor in the success of the firm's marketing activities is the firm's ability to assess the needs of particular groups of consumers or target markets. In order to do this, the importer needs to monitor the environment, relying on marketing intelligence to identify changes that can pose a threat or provide an opportunity in the marketplace. This allows the firm to implement a plan of action that can help the firm take advantage of opportunities and defend it from threats in the environment. The implementation of the marketing strategy calls for the formulation of specific strategies relating to product, distribution, promotion, and pricing. For the importer to identify the opportunities in the market, there must be an understanding of what target market to serve. The needs of the consumer market must be profiled and the size of the market measured to identify market potential.

Prior to product introduction, a thorough analysis of the market should be conducted. This will provide information about the market size and needs of the target market. The volatility of the environment will determine how responsive the marketing strategy must be to maintain a competitive position. If the environment is dynamic in nature, the marketing approach must monitor all changes and either respond immediately or lead with evolutionary trends. Without the reaction or adaptation to shifts in the environment, any competitive edge the importer possesses will evaporate.

The U.S. Market

The United States is a huge market with tremendous potential, the single largest importer in the world. Statistics indicate that:

Imports extend across more than ten thousand product classifications.

Manufactured goods represented over two-thirds of total imports.

Approximately one-fifth of all consumer goods and one-third of industrial goods and supplies are imported.

The lucrative U.S. market is a target for exporters all over the world. The environment is very competitive with so many sellers vying for market penetration. This requires the formulation of an adequate marketing strategy that will recognize opportunities. However, the U.S. market is difficult to penetrate and serve, putting a premium on the importer's ability to develop an adequate marketing strategy to maintain market share in the import market. This is particularly relevant in a market such as the United States where demographic changes and social and geographic mobility have pushed marketers to pursue product-differentiation and market-segmentation strategies to better identify potential consumers with a wide range of preferences, tastes, and needs. The importer, therefore, needs to formulate strategies that respond to the specific realities of the marketplace.

Vignette 1
The Marketing of Imported Beer

Years ago, the beer industry was simple. If you wanted a draft, you went to your local bar and had a beer on tap. Alternatively, you could pick up a case or six-pack at the neighborhood liquor store or supermarket. There was a view that beer was beer. However, this is not the case today as Americans are being saturated with a huge assortment of beers. Will it be a domestic, imported, light, regular, draft, bottled, canned, twist-top, lager, ale, and so on? The industry is becoming more complex and more competitive with imports penetrating the market.

Imported beers have been increasing their share of the beer market in the United States. Statistics show that in 1984, while consumption of domestic beer decreased less than 1 percent, consumption of imported beer rose approximately 10 percent. On the aggregate, imported-beer sales volume has been growing approximately 4.3 percent a year in a market that appears to have stagnated with very little growth being observed.

Between 1980 and 1985, beer imports grew by 72 percent. One explanation for the strength of imported beer was the strong dollar, which gave imported beer a competitive price edge over domestic beer. However, consumer preferences play a significant role as high-quality advertising efforts appear to have had an impact on the sudden success of imported beer. A case in point is Corona Beer, one of Mexico's leading brands. Corona beer entered the U.S. market in a rather unorthodox manner. California surfers tasted the beer when they visited Mexico and brought the beer back to the trend-setting beach communities. In a short period of time, Corona—with its clear, gracefully curved bottle and painted-like label—was the "in" beer in Southern California. The Mexican producer quickly took advantage of the rising preference for Corona beer and began aggressively marketing the product in California and the rest of the United States.

Corona beer appeals to the baby-boomer market. The typical Corona drinker is the stereotyped yuppie: young (between 21 and 35 years old), professional, and in the middle to upper income groups. According to *Advertising Age*, the young consumer has a larger likelihood of beer consumption than older age groups—61 percent among the 19–24 age group as compared to 25 percent among those 50 years and older. The yuppie market is expanding at a 9 percent yearly rate and Corona has performed quite well among this group, outselling other major beers.

Sources: *Industry Surveys: Food, Beverages and Tobacco* (June 26, 1986).
Michael O'Neal, "A Mexican Beer Whose Cup Runneth Over," *Business Week* (Sept. 1, 1986).
Patricia Winters, "Mexican Brews the Hot Category in Imports," *Advertising Age* (April 7, 1986).
Mary Williams Walsh, "A Mexican Beer Scores in the U.S.," *The Wall Street Journal* (Dec. 17, 1986).

The Consumer Market

The consumer market, being as large as it is in the United States, provides for an infinite number of products as long as the design is commercially viable and meets the needs referred to earlier. Population is approximately 237 million and annual expenditures on goods and services total approximately $2 trillion or the equivalent of $9,000 per capita. The market grows by about 1.5 million people each year, which adds $100 billion to purchasing power. However the profile of the market has evolved over the years, resulting in significant variations in buying behavior. These distinctions exist across age groups, income ranges, regions, social classes, and numerous other criteria that can be used to segment the population. The importer is almost required to distinguish between groups of consumers and think in terms of viable segments. If the segment is significant in size and is reachable, a customized strategy should be implemented to meet its needs. Although a segment may be substantial in size, a key factor is being able to reach this group and communicate the product/ service that is being offered to them. A major objective in formulating a marketing strategy is to better understand the consumer in the target market and stimulate demand in the segment. Instead of selling the steak as meat, you sell the "sizzle" of the steak. Success will be determined by how well you are able to market the sizzle to the target market. The segment need not be large, as is the case for some luxury items, as long as there is a need or want. The group can be reached if proper communication channels are utilized. For example, the Hispanic market is regionally located; thus, selective communication modes must be chosen. The assumption when the market is segmented is that consumers will respond in a similar manner to communication stimuli. Thus, when the segment is being analyzed, it is important to determine the motivational forces that affect consumer behavior. Understanding consumers allows the marketer to serve their needs, raising the probability of a good "fit" between the product and the specific target market.

Market Segmentation. In segmenting a market, one identifies submarkets of a segment that has potential for the imported product sales. Segmentation starts with the disaggregation of the market into segmentation bases. For example, segmentation bases could be defined according to customer-related dimensions, such as purchasers' geographic location and demographic characteristics (gender, age, and income, for example). Segmentation bases can also be created from situation-related dimensions such as rate of use (heavy, light, or none), time of purchase, and buying situation (kind of store, type of product). For example, the method used in purchasing is significant because it tells much concerning the convenience and packaging that is expected. The purchase may have been on impulse or after major internal and external search. Was a specific brand requested or was a generic product purchased? The unit sizes, number of units purchased, and purchase frequency tell the importer the expectations of a product in a specific target market.

Segmentation strategies must consider the following:

A segment should be homogeneous within itself in terms of purchasing behavior, desires, and so on, so that consumers within the market segment can respond in a similar way to marketing-mix stimuli.

All components of a segment should be accessible by the same communication media, channels of distribution, promotions, and so on.

A segment should be measurable and large enough to be profitable.

Micromarkets. In the previous chapter, demographic environmental factors were analyzed to ascertain what forces can create opportunities or present threats to the import activity. These forces were identified as:

The slowdown of U.S. birthrate

The aging of the U.S. population

The changing American family

The growing number of single-member and nontraditional households

Geographic shifts in population, such as Sun-Belt migration

An increased percentage of women in the work force

Rising average household income

A better-educated population

Changing ethnic and racial breakdowns in the population

These changing environmental factors point to a significant shift from mass markets to micromarkets. This has significant implications in the marketing of imported consumer goods. As life-styles and purchasing behavior change, the firm must respond in its strategy formulation. A case in point: during the 1950s, there existed a strong cultural value of conformity. With strong uniform values, it was possible to think of this rather homogeneous group as a huge mass market. As socioeconomic and cultural changes settled in, by the 1980s, marketers face a market where conformity no longer exists in the magnitude of the '50s. Lack of uniformity in societal values has fragmented the market and increased segmentation.

The ability to mass-market products aided the growth of corporations such as General Foods, Procter & Gamble, and Sears, Roebuck. Beer companies such as Anheuser-Busch and Miller were able to flourish with mass-marketing. However, today, the middle-class mass market is disappearing and segmented markets are being targeted according to life-style, psychographic, and demographic profiles.[2] These changes were caused by numerous factors. Increased affluence among the U.S. population, a decrease in the birthrate, more women in the workplace, and higher levels of education among white-collar workers have expanded demand for products and life-styles available that have traditionally been only for the upper classes, such as designer clothes, customized items, vacations abroad, eating out, and exotic foods. They are part of what the affluent consumer expects and wants.

Affluence has caused people to pursue the life-styles of their choice, resulting in a variety of life-styles. The consumer is looking for uniqueness and individualism. Importers must adapt their strategies to these changes in society. For example, the soft-drink industry has responded with tremendous variety to satisfy a diverse market. Coca-Cola has Original Formula Coke, New Coke, Diet Coke, Cherry Coke, and so on. The days of bottled Coke in one size and taste for all are long gone in the United States. It is now difficult to market a uniform product because of the lack of uniformity and/or homogeneity in the market. "It's become much more difficult to think of the middle class as some big monolithic group of people," says Susan Guianinno, director of research services at the advertising agency Young & Rubican.[3] The middle class years ago was populated with groups of belongers and conformists. Today, the middle class is dominated by numerous groups including "achievers," "experimentals," and the "society-conscious." The demographic changes are being fueled by divorce, which is permeating the middle class. The statistics indicate that a child born today has a 60 percent chance of being brought up through at least one separation and a 20 percent chance of experiencing two. The values that were established in the family of years ago are shifting away. With parents taking a lesser role in rearing their children, middle-class teens are looking outside of the family to define their social values. The family has lost much of the structure that teens need. Middle-class values have been muddled up and today's teens are more materialistic, less realistic, and more difficult to motivate than in previous generations. The malls with their specialty shops satisfy teenagers' wants and are a place to hang out.[4]

Importers need to understand the market and the segments they serve in order to focus the marketing effort to reach them effectively. Market segmentation, therefore, has become a necessary strategy to enter the U.S. market. It should be clear that the level of marketing expertise needed to establish a successful segmentation strategy is relatively high. The import marketer must be able to identify opportunities by scanning environmental factors and understanding the impact of changes occurring in the marketplace. Similarly, the marketer must be able to define, measure, and reach the appropriate market segments. Moreover, the firm needs to command significant resources to be able to pursue strategies that can elicit response from a consumer market that is saturated with product offerings from domestic as well as foreign sellers. Thus, marketing expertise is especially significant in the formulation of marketing strategies for consumer markets.

Vignette 2
The Marketing of Imported Rum

Imported products are making an impact on the markets for distilled liquors. One of the most significant trends seen in recent years has been the increased consumption of rum, spearheaded by a shift from hard to soft liquors, which in turn was influenced by an aging population becoming increasingly health-conscious and rising popularity of rum among the youth on what has been termed a boom in entertainment.

The increase in rum consumption observed from 1974 to 1979 (when sales jumped from 4 to 11.3 million cases) continued into the 1980s. Given the forecast of sales and consumption increases, it can be expected that there is the potential to absorb additional brands in the marketplace. However, one important aspect of the imported-rum market is its competitive structure. One major company (Bacardi) dominates, commanding a significant 60 percent of the market. Moreover, Puerto Rican rum has the largest market share of imported rum into the United States. However, other countries have been competing in the rum market with significant success. To compete in a market where one company dominates so strongly, competitors have significantly increased promotional efforts. New entrants must be prepared to spend heavily on promotion up front to establish brand awareness and to distinguish its brand from the others. The liquor industry with its overall growth attracts new entrants and thus the market remains highly competitive.

The boom in rum sales was caused in part by the success of the Puerto Rican rum. The statistics show that in 1979, Puerto Rican rum accounted for 90 percent of total rum sales. During the 1969–79 ten-year span, Puerto Rican rum experienced a 227 percent growth in sales, while total rum sales grew by 189 percent. Still, vodka remains the market leader in the overall distilled liquor market, outselling rum three to one. However, rum sales are increasing at a faster rate due to imported rums' inroads into the vodka market as aggressive marketing converts vodka and whiskey drinkers to rum.

Globally, dark rums appear to be the favorite. However, in the United States, light rums are more popular. Consumers like the way light rum mixes with other ingredients to make drinks such as daiguiris, cocktails, rum and collins, and the traditional rum and coke. Rum appears to have a unique feature of blending well with mixes and has its own distinctive flavor. With this advantage, rum drinkers increase quantity and frequency of usage.

The demographic profile of rum drinkers is somewhat unique when compared to the general liquor drinker. The significant characteristics are persons in age group 25–49, university students and graduates, and persons with incomes in excess of $20,000 per year. Rum is rapidly becoming a favorite drink of ex–vodka drinkers and is a preferred drink among women. Similarly, rum is a favorite among lower-income groups and single swingers who are familiar with many types of drinks.

Similarly, blacks are accounting for an increasing proportion of the rum consumed in the United States. They consume 14 percent more than the average population. Another growing segment that prefers rum is the Hispanic population. Since Hispanics consume mainly rum, strong sales regions are New York, California, Florida, Illinois, and Texas. The areas that lead in consumption are the District of Columbia, Hawaii, Florida, Nevada, and New Hampshire.

Source: Summarized from *Perfiles de Mercado de los Estados Unidos* Serie VI. Washington, D.C.: Secretaria General de la Organizacion de Estados Americanos-OAS, 1980.

Industrial or Producer Markets

Producer markets or industrial markets constitute all the organizations or individuals who buy goods and services to produce other goods and services that are rented, leased, and/or sold to other intermediate buyers or producers. Industrial or producer markets can be broadly grouped according to the type of product purchased:

Materials and parts: Products purchased in this category include raw materials and component parts used in the production process and included in the final product.

Capital goods: These are products needed to develop the production process and include machinery and equipment.

Supplies: These are products needed to maintain a smooth production operation. The products purchased in this category include maintenance and repair supplies, office materials, and other related supplies.

Since industrial buyers make their purchasing decisions in a different way than consumers, it is important to understand their buying process. This will enable the importer to segment the possible markets to serve and develop an appropriate marketing strategy. The industrial market is a lucrative market if served well, since it includes a wide range of products used in or to maintain the production process. These markets include farming, mining, communication, construction, manufacturing, public services, transportation, banking, and insurance. It is estimated that there are approximately fourteen million industrial buyers in this buyer group.

Detailed information for analysis can be readily found in government publications. For example, data can be obtained by Standard Industrial Classification (SIC), a system that classifies manufacturing activities under twenty major industrial groups each having a two-digit number, with further product-group breakdowns at the three- and four-digit levels. For example, food manufacturing is classified under SIC code 20, tobacco manufacturing under code 21, and so forth.[5] The *Census of Manufactures* provides detailed data on number of establishments, location, number of employees, annual sales, and so on under this four-digit classification system.

The most salient characteristics of the industrial-buying process are:

Demand faced by the industrial sector is derived demand, i.e., demand is derived from the demand in consumer markets. It is for this reason that industrial buyers are greatly concerned with cost, productivity, uniform quality, and defined specifications. Since demand is therefore specific for each product group, industrial buyers are usually experts in their field. Dependability is a key selling factor as buyers rely on their suppliers for timely and adequate delivery. Thus, the importer seeking to serve these markets needs to incorporate these features in the marketing strategy and to assure consistent quality, product-specification adherence, and dependable supply. A close relationship between buyer and seller should be one important objective in the marketing strategy.

Industrial or producer markets are concentrated in geographic areas, not dispersed throughout the United States, as is the case of many consumer markets. The location is usually close to sources of supply or where transportation links the firm with major market areas. Many corporations also keep purchasing offices in cities such as Boston, New York, and Miami and on the West Coast. This characteristic facilitates the entry strategy and coverage of the market. The importer should look for specific geographic areas to reach potential markets and analyze location patterns to integrate the marketing strategy accordingly.

Industrial-market purchases are usually large in volume. However, since the buyers do wish to avoid dependency on one or two suppliers, they seek different suppliers and split their orders. Thus, the importer can expect to have competitive bidding in industrial markets and must react accordingly.

Industrial buyers prefer to deal directly with suppliers, especially where large-ticket items are concerned. Consequently, channels of distribution tend to be more direct. In certain product categories, such as supplies, a more indirect channel can be followed. Thus, the importer should be prepared to deal directly with industrial customers. This can have significant implications in terms of the importing channel structure, as the importer will have to bypass importer wholesalers except where an adequate product category is involved.

Industrial buyers set precise product requirements and specifications. This involves careful negotiations and knowledgeable buying behavior. Consequently, the importer needs to develop a well-trained sales force as personal selling becomes a salient promotional tool. Similarly, the importer needs to carefully research buying procedures, contract negotiations, and contractual obligations required in the sector served.

The industrial-buying process is usually carried on by one person. In some cases, however, the buying process may be conducted by more than one person or a purchasing center. In the first case, the selling strategy for the importer is relatively simple, as it is easier to deal with one contact. However, when a buying decision requires more than one decisionmaker, the selling effort becomes more complex. In such situations, the importer needs to identify the buying process as well as the ultimate decisionmaker in order to best serve the market.

It can be seen, then, that an importer's reaching industrial or producer markets requires a significantly different marketing strategy and effort than for reaching consumer markets. Understanding the basic differences between these markets and their behavioral characteristics serves as the basis for developing a comprehensive and adequate marketing strategy.

Vignette 3
The Cut-Flower Industry

The cut-flower industry in the United States is a $4.3 billion industry. Imports account for 70 percent of domestic supply in both producer and consumer markets. Principal flower-exporting countries are Colombia, Chile, Mexico, Costa Rica, Ecuador, Peru, Canada, and Kenya. The flowers that are imported are carnations, roses, alstromeria, pompoms, statice, and gypsophilia.

The cut-flower industry has been growing steadily as consumer behavior changes. Americans traditionally purchase flowers for special occasions. Flowers are now being purchased when sending messages, as a token of friendship, as a get-well wish, or just to convey to someone "have a nice day."

Since this product is sold by the reputation of the establishment rather than the image of the product, a crucial aspect of the marketing strategy is to serve intermediate markets in an efficient way. The product must pass through distributors or brokerage houses quickly. Moreover, cut flowers must meet the requirements of the selective U.S. consumer who seeks quality, variety, long life, and color in the product. In addition, the product must comply with the U.S. Plant Protection Quarantine Inspection Program (in terms of product quality), U.S. antidumping regulations (concerning pricing). Since the product is highly perishable, it is necessary to use air transportation to reach the market and process it rapidly through customs. Consequently, for the marketing strategy to be successful, key factors such as harvesting, special packaging, and timely delivery are required to meet the needs of the marketplace.

Source: Industry sources.

Reseller Markets

Individuals and firms that purchase products and services with the intent of reselling or leasing them for a profit are classified as *resellers*. Wholesalers and retailers are examples of reseller markets. There are approximately 380,000 wholesalers and 2,000,000 retailers in the United States. Resellers are not as dispersed geographically as consumers, nor are they concentrated geographically. However, since the basic role of these organizations is to distribute products and serve as links between producers and consumers, they seek locations to link them to major market areas. Thus, wholesalers will be strategically placed, linking major market areas, while retailers will similarly serve major local market areas.

Reseller organizations handle a large variety of products that they buy from domestic as well as foreign suppliers. As is the case with industrial buyers, reseller buyers are usually experts and their buying decisions take into consideration product demand, variety, inventory-carrying costs, and merchandising. Retailers, for example, typically carry a large number of individual items. Groceries carry about 10,000 items, drug stores on the average carry approximately 12,000 items, and hardware stores about 25,000 items. Even with such diversity, buyers attempt to make purchasing a routine for efficiency purposes. Buyers, on the most part, must adhere to strict purchasing budgets and will consider products until their funds are depleted.

For the importer, reseller markets provide a viable alternative to sell consumer products without the substantial commitment required to go directly to the market. Since location and size of the organizations vary significantly, the importer can concentrate on specific locations and market areas. Careful planning, timing with budgetary allocations, and product/market fit should direct the marketing strategy. The importer should strive to identify reseller market groups that offer potential for volume and market coverage.

The main advantages to the importer in selling to the reseller market are:

1. Wholesalers/retailers are accessible regionally and can open the doors to large consuming markets in the United States.

2. The market is established and heavy start-up capital is not required.

There is however a loss of control on the part of the importer because the wholesaler and retailer select high-turnover items, which dictates the type and quantity of the order. For importers whose marketing expertise is limited and whose products are unknown in the marketplace, the reseller market can open doors to the U.S. market.

Summary

In order to succeed in the marketplace, the importer must be able to provide form, time, place, and possession utilities. While form utility is traditionally considered a production utility, import-marketing activities can supplement and enhance form utility by identifying a product that fits the market segment's needs. An important aspect of providing utilities in the marketplace is to understand behavioral dimensions in the different markets that the importer wishes to serve. While searching for attractive opportunities, the importer can concentrate marketing efforts in serving consumer, industrial, or reseller markets. Each type of market provides for different opportunities and the importer must be able to recognize important behavioral characteristics of the market to be served.

Notes

1. "Clothing Shoppers Talk Domestic But Look First for Style, Savings," *Wall Street Journal* (October 15, 1987), p. 32.

2. Jack Z. Sissors, "What Is a Market," *Journal of Marketing* (July 1966), p. 21.

3. John Koten, "Upheaval in Middle Class Markets Forces Changes in Selling Strategies," *Wall Street Journal* (March 13, 1987), p. 29.

4. Jeffrey Zaslow, "Children Search for Values Leading to Shopping Malls," *Wall Street Journal* (March 9, 1987), p. 25.

5. For more detailed information on how to find SIC codes, see *Standard Industrial Classification Manual* (Washington, D.C.: U.S. Government Printing Office).

Part II
The Import-marketing
Strategy

4
Import-product Strategy

S trategic product decisions are an important component of the import-marketing strategy. This chapter attempts to familiarize the importer with the factors influencing a product strategy, the major elements of the product strategy, (which include defining the product and product-strategy decisions), and the sources of import products. It also addresses specific import regulations that dictate the makeup of the product and allow for successful importation.

One of the most important decisions in the import-marketing strategy is the selection of the proper product to serve the identified target market. The highly complex nature of the U.S. markets requires that the importer carefully chooses the product and product strategy to match product with market needs. The U.S. market is characterized by its dynamism—demographic and life-style changes, a highly competitive climate, and aggressive marketing by the sellers of products have resulted in target marketing. This strategy identifies segments with different needs, interests, and ways of satisfying them. Technological changes and rapid obsolescence constantly change and improve the product offerings in the marketplace. Thus, the product-choosing and -marketing activities that enhance need-satisfying capabilities are crucial to the success of an imported product.

The challenge to the importer is to identify world-class products for specific market segments. This match between product and target market is not only the concern of marketers of consumer goods; this challenge is prevalent in all product areas, consumer or industrial, whenever a seller has to turn to foreign markets to supply the U.S. market. Importers that serve the U.S. markets have an important advantage: they sell established products having marketing potential in the United States. However, the importer must match the product with a target market and develop an adequate product strategy to reach the target market and convince consumers to buy the product.

What Composes the Product

The importer must be cognizant that the product is more than its physical attributes. It is a complete concept of tangible and intangible dimensions that make up a firm's product offering. The tangible aspects of the product are the physical aspects, including product features. The intangible aspects are those aspects that enhance the product in the eyes of the consumer, and they include such things as quality perceptions, brand name, aesthetic characteristics, prestigious image, presale and postsale services, and warranties that complete the "product image" in the eyes of the consumer. Thus, a complete product includes the tangible and intangible characteristics that represent the product offering of the firm in the marketplace, that is, the product strategy to meet the needs of the target market.

Marketing is important in that it enhances the intangible aspects of the product offering. The marketing strategy, then, calls for decisions not only concerning the tangible aspects of the product, but also the intangibles that complement the physical aspects of the product and make it more marketable and consumable.

Factors Influencing Import-Product Decisions

Several factors influence the import-product decisions:

customs regulations,

product liability,

quality,

transportation costs.

Customs Regulations

The U.S. import requirements can greatly affect the type and quantity of products that can be imported into the United States. Generally, most peaceful goods can enter the United States without significant problems or barriers. However, importation of certain classes of merchandise may be prohibited or restricted to protect U.S. markets, the economy, the security of the United States, or the health and well-being of the American consumer as well as to preserve plant and animal life.

It is impractical to list all products specifically. However, numerous classes of products will be discussed next. The U.S. importer should contact the agency mentioned for detailed information.[1]

Product Restrictions. Certain consumer products must meet with efficiency and labeling standards to indicate energy-consumption estimates. Products included in this category are:

refrigerators and refrigerator freezers,

freezers,

dishwashers,

clothes dryers,

water heaters,

room air conditioners,

home heating equipment, not including furnaces,

television sets,

kitchen ranges and ovens,

clothes washers,

humidifiers and dehumidifiers,

central air conditioners,

furnaces,

certain other types of household consumer appliances, as appropriate.

Importation of these products must meet the requirements of the Department of Energy and/or Federal Trade Commission. Consumer products offered for importation will be refused admission if they fail to comply with the applicable consumer-product–safety rule or specific labeling or certification requirements, or are determined to contain a defect that constitutes a substantial product hazard.

Electronic products that emit radiation (such as television receivers, microwave ovens, X-ray equipment, and laser products) are subject to the Radiation Control for Health and Safety Act of 1968. As such, entry notices must be filed with the Food and Drug Administration's Bureau of Radiological Health. Electronic products classified as radio-frequency devices (such as radios, tape recorders, stereos, televisions, and citizens-band radios) must meet radio-emission standards of the Federal Communications Commission.

The importation into the United States of *foods, drugs, cosmetics, and medical devices* is regulated by the Food and Drug Administration of the Department of Health and Human Services. Imported products that do not meet regulations must be altered to comply; if not, they will be destroyed or reexported. Any alteration costs will be incurred by the importer. Biological drugs for human consumption require licensing. Additional labeling is needed for animal drugs. Biological materials and vectors that include therapeutic serum, toxin, antitoxin, or analogous products must be accompanied by samples of the licensed product. The importation of controlled substances (including marijuana, narcotics, and other dangerous drugs) is prohibited except when regulations of the Drug Enforcement Administration are adhered to.

Agricultural commodities include dairy products, fruits, vegetables, insects, livestock, meat products, plant products, poultry products, and seeds. Inquiries concerning requirements and restrictions for this product class should be addressed to the Food and Drug Administration and the Department of Agriculture. Commodities are inspected and an inspection certificate or permit will be issued to indicate import compliance.

Individuals or firms who wish to import *alcoholic beverages* such as distilled spirits, wines, or malt beverages must initially acquire an importer's permit from the Bureau of Alcohol, Tobacco and Firearms, which enforces the Federal Alcohol Administration Act. The U.S. Customs Service will not release alcoholic beverages destined to any state for use in violations of its laws, and the importation of alcoholic beverages in the mails is prohibited. Imported wines in bottles and other containers are required to be packaged, marked, branded, and labeled according to regulations. Malt beverages must also be labeled. The labels of distilled spirits and wine must have approval labels issued by the Bureau of Alcohol, Tobacco and Firearms. This agency provides foreign documentation guidance that is required for the import of wines and distilled spirits. In addition to the Bureau of Alcohol, Tobacco and Firearms, the Food and Drug Administration has specific requirements that must be met.

Textile, wool, and fur products are regulated by the Federal Trade Commission. Textile products are subject to the requirements of the Textile Fiber Products Identification Act. Information such as fabric content and manufacturer's name and country are required. A commercial invoice must accompany the shipment if its value exceeds $500.00. Wool products require comparable disclosure. Documentation specifics can be found in the Wool Products Labeling Act. Fur products must meet similar requirements, which are found in the Fur Products Labeling Act.

Wildlife and pets fall under the jurisdiction of several government agencies. Entry is limited to certain designated ports of entry unless an exception is granted by the U.S. Fish and Wildlife Service.

Motor vehicles and boats are subject to rigid safety standards when imported into the United States. If an automobile or automobile equipment does not conform to the specifications of the National Highway Traffic Safety Administration, a period of grace is available to conform to regulations. Emission standards prescribed by the Environmental Protection Agency must be met also. Here is a word of caution to importers if modifications are necessary. Nonconformity with safety standards and/or emission standards may be extremely expensive due to additional engineering, labor, and material costs. Imported boats and associated equipment must meet the safety regulations of the U.S. Coast Guard or standards under the Federal Boat Safety Act.

Importation of *pesticides and toxic and hazardous substances* is regulated by the Environmental Protection Agency (EPA). Pesticides are classified as economic poisons and devices. They include insecticides, fungicides, herbicides, and rodenticides. All imported pesticides must be registered by the EPA and meet their approval prior to being released through customs. Toxic substances that may present an unreasonable risk of injury to health and environment must be approved by the EPA. Hazardous substances of a caustic or corrosive nature that are suitable for household consumption must meet labeling, packaging, and transportation guidelines administered by the Materials Transportation Bureau of the Department of Transportation.

Gold, silver, currency, and stamps is another product classification having import restrictions. Gold and silver must meet specified levels of fineness to obtain permission to be imported. The guidelines are specified by the National Stamping Act and enforced by the Department of Justice. Monetary instruments, which are outlined in the Currency and Foreign Transactions Reporting Act, include U.S. or foreign coin, currency, travelers checks, money orders, and negotiable instruments or investment securities in bearer form; they do not include bank checks, travelers checks, or money orders made payable to the order of a named person that have not been endorsed or that bear restrictive endorsement. If the monetary instrument is in excess of $5,000 and is transported (by mail or other means) on any occasion in or out of the United States, of if a person receives more than this amount, a report must be filed with the Customs Service. Postage stamps are prohibited except for educational, historical, or comparable purposes. Further information is available from the Secret Service within the Treasury Department.

The importation of *arms and ammunition* is prohibited unless a license is issued by the Bureau of Alcohol, Tobacco and Firearms. *Radioactive materials and nuclear reactors* (which includes all forms of uranium, thorium, and plutonium) must meet the regulations of the Nuclear Regulatory Commission and those of any other agency of the U.S. government.

Importers should consult the appropriate administrating U.S. agency for further information. The vast majority of agencies just discussed are located in Washington, D.C. Many have offices in other locations too. Sufficient lead time should be allotted to allow for processing of documents. This will smooth the importation process.

Import Quotas. An import quota is a limit on the quantity of imported merchandise for a given time period. Quotas are established by specific legislation. The U.S. Customs Service is empowered to administer the majority of import quotas. In the United States, import quotas are divided into two types: *absolute* and *tariff-rate*. Absolute quotas are quantitative; a limited amount can enter during a quota period. If imports have exceeded the quota, two alternatives available are to export the excess or warehouse the product for entry in a future quota period. Tariff-rate quotas allow for entry of a specific quantity of product at a reduced rate of duty. There are no limits on quantity that may be entered. However, when a quantity quota is met, the duty rate increases.

An example of quotas being enforced and the changes taking place that affect importers can be seen in the U.S. footwear industry. U.S. manufacturers in 1985 were being seriously injured by importers. The International Trade Commission recommended that a quota system be imposed on footwear imports. Some U.S. lawmakers have proposed that a surcharge be directed at countries harvesting significant trade benefits from their liberal access to the U.S. market.[2]

For specific information on import controls, the Commissioner of Customs should be consulted. Trade restrictions and quotas are undergoing constant change, and knowledge of current legislation is vital for importers.

Trademarks, Trade Names, and Copyrights. It is unlawful to import into the United States any merchandise manufactured abroad if this merchandise or its label, sign, packaging, or general makeup bears a trademark owned by a citizen or corporation of the United States. The U.S. citizen or corporation is required to register this trademark in the Patent Office or Trademark Office. However, with the permission of the U.S. trademark owner, the importer can obtain authorization to distribute the trademarked articles abroad. A counterfeit trademark is a trademark that is virtually indistinguishable from a registered trademark. If these articles are seized by customs, the government may then

distribute the articles to any federal, state, or local government agency,

donate them to a charitable institution, or

sell them at a public auction after one year if no eligible organization has requested the articles.

Infringement of copyright occurs when there is importation of copies of an article obtained outside the United States without authorization of the copyright owner. Articles that meet these criteria will be seized and destroyed or, if the Customs Service is satisfied that there was no intent to violate copyright laws, could be returned to the country of origin. The similarity test is performed to determine if the article is a copy.

The importer would be well advised to become aware of a country's intellectual-property laws and practices prior to deciding to do business in that country. *Intellectual property* refers to a broad collection of rights that include trademark and copyright protection. The rights granted in the United States extend only through the United States and its possessions.

The patent law is unique in the United States because it grants a patent to the first inventor regardless of whether another individual who independently makes the invention files an application first. Many countries require that an invention be developed within their country in order to retain the benefit of the patent.

A trademark can be a word, symbol, or device that identifies the source of an article or service. The device/service mark can represent quality. In the

United States, these trademarks and service marks are protected by regulatory agencies. Protection abroad will vary from country to country.

The owners of a copyright have the work that they originated protected by regulation. In the United States, the owner has the exclusive right to reproduce the work, distribute copies, and perform or display the work to the public, as protected by copyright regulations.

These protective rights are available to importers, but it is up to the owner to pursue them and derive the benefits provided in the United States. In general, the United States views intellectual property as a private right that should be enforced by the owner. The importer must take the necessary steps to assure that importation will not result in violation of U.S. rights held by U.S. citizens, corporations, or others. In the United States, intellectual-property rights can be enforced by a civil suit for infringement. The intellectual-property owner may be awarded damages or an injunction against infringement. If the circumstances are serious, criminal penalties such as fines and/or imprisonment are common.

A firm should protect its intellectual property at the outset, which will provide a competitive advantage in the United States in the future.

Product Liability

Importers selling in U.S. markets must be cognizant of the fact that consumer safety is a major aspect of marketing in the United States. Practically every consumer product must be designed and packaged to protect consumers who use them.

The concept of product liability illustrates that manufacturers and marketers are responsible for injuries and damages caused by their products. Product-liability suits have increased significantly over recent years as consumers' awareness of their rights to damages have increased.[3] The result is greater emphasis on product safety in the production and engineering stages (as well as safety warnings on labels.) The Consumer Product Safety Commission has established standards for virtually all consumer products. Manufacturers are required to conduct a "reasonable testing program" to insure that their products conform to establish safety standards.

The laws of product liability have been changing to keep up with the shifts in the political environment. Previously, manufacturers and sellers were held liable only when negligence or lack of due care on their part was ascertained. Currently, the courts are taking a tougher stand referred to as "strict liability." The concept of strict liability says that if a defect in a product is legally established, the manufacturer is liable, regardless of what precautions were taken.[4] To protect themselves, importers must incorporate product-liability insurance as an essential ingredient in their product strategy. Premiums for this insurance have risen by leaps and bounds. In some cases, coverage is almost impossible

in. In many industries, producers have established their own insurance
ᴗcause of the costliness of product-liability insurance. However, the pic-
ɩure is not totally bleak as efforts are underway in several states to exempt companies from liability for injuries or property loss resulting from misuse of the
products or from consumer negligence.

Quality

Most American consumers base their purchasing decisions, in part, on the quality or perception of quality of the product. This consideration is very important in consumer evaluation of the value of the product and its need-satisfying
capabilities. No area of the product strategy is of more importance and concern to the importer than product quality. American consumers are accustomed
to consistent quality levels. Consequently, searching for imported products
means assuring that the foreign producer can consistently provide the level of
quality that is required.

It is important that the importer view quality control as an integral component of the product strategy. This should include a process to oversee quality control either during the production process or before shipment. Success
of importing activities can, in many instances, be contingent upon the foreign
producer's ability to manufacture products to agreed-on or acceptable industry
standards of quality. The importer should, in all instances, exercise control
over quality. The lack of a uniform or consistent product quality can quickly
undermine the marketing efforts and the opportunities in the U.S. markets,
as the importer will need to turn away from the foreign producers that cannot
meet industry quality standards.

Transportation Costs

How transportation costs affect the landed cost of the product will vary according to the type of product, the transportation mode used, and the distance
traveled from importing country to U.S. port of entry. As a general rule, the
higher the value of the product relative to its weight and volume, the higher
the transportation costs that the product can absorb.

Transportation costs include not only the explicit costs but implicit cost
as well. Implicit transportation costs represent the cost/benefit that is forgone
by selecting one alternative of transportation versus another. These costs/
benefits may be tangible or intangible in nature. Implicit costs arise because
of events such as delays, loss, damage, pilferage, and theft that result in additional charges, customer dissatisfaction, and possibly lost sales.[5] It is difficult
to forecast implicit costs. Consequently, few importers estimate insurance
coverage needed to recover losses from all possible events. Transportation insurance may provide some protection in the event of a loss, but may not cover
all explicit and implicit costs if a shipment is delayed, rerouted, or lost.

Sources of Imported Products

The importer searching for imported products needs to have an understanding of manufacturing locational arrangements of the world's productive capabilities. Each country's industrial capabilities are different. The structure of the manufacturing sector, the size of the firms, and the financial capabilities of the different firms vary from country to country, resulting in a myriad of ways in which a country uses and organizes its resources in the industrial sector.

While manufacturing exists in one form or another in practically every country in the world, not all producers can make products adequate for the U.S. markets. Even though there has been a very rapid diffusion of manufacturing technology throughout the world, not all process innovations and technology transfers have been the same. Consequently, the industrial sectors of the different countries in the world give rise to different supplying capabilities. Table 4–1 gives us an overview of selected countries' manufacturing capabilities. The lower- and middle-income countries tend to predominate in food and agriculture as well as in textile and cloth. The high-income countries predominate in machinery and transportation equipment. Technological advancement may be one variable that accounts for this difference.

Production in Foreign Countries

As importers research the potential supply sources, they should be aware that manufacturing occurs even among the most impoverished nations in the world. However, the type of industries, technology used, and ability to adapt to the rigorous requirements of the U.S. markets may not be present in all instances. Even as industrial development is growing throughout the world, the composition of the manufacturing sector in a country reflects its level of economic development and resource availability.

Traditional Industries. These sectors manufacture basic goods such as food, clothing, textiles, leather, and furniture. They generally use domestic raw materials and some intermediate imported semifinished goods and supplies.

Assembly-Type Industries. These are manufacturers that assemble parts or final products often with imported component parts. These industries include radios, televisions, metal furniture, certain forms of wearing apparel, cosmetics, pharmaceuticals, and consumer durables such as refrigerators, cars, and washing machines.

Intermediate Industries. These are manufacturers of semifinished goods and component parts sold for replacement or used by other industries. These groups of manufacturers include building and packaging materials.

Table 4–1
Manufacturing Value Added by Sector as a Percentage of Total Manufacturing Value Added, Selected Countries

	Agriculture and Food Processing	Textiles and Clothing	Machinery and Transportation Equipment	Chemicals	Other Manufactures	Manufactures as % of GDP
Lower-income countries						
India	15%	16%	20%	14%	35%	15%
Kenya	26	10	30	8	26	12
Middle-income countries						
Brazil	15	10	23	13	39	27
Colombia	26	15	11	7	41	17
Dominican Republic	69	4	1	6	20	18
Indonesia	29	7	7	12	45	13
Peru	26	13	11	12	38	26
Philippines	39	13	9	9	30	25
Saudi Arabia	4	—	—	—	96	6
Venezuela	27	6	8	8	51	17
High-income countries						
Japan	7	5	39	8	41	30
Sweden	10	3	35	7	45	22
United Kingdom	13	7	35	10	35	18
United States	12	6	32	12	38	21
West Germany	10	5	38	10	37	36

Source: Excerpted from The World Development Report 1985. Copyright 1985 by the International Bank for Reconstruction and Development/The World Bank. Reprinted by permission of Oxford University Press, Inc., New York.

Metal/Machinery Industries. This last group of manufacturers represents the most developed and capital-intensive aspect of manufacturing. It includes the basic type (iron foundries) as well as more sophisticated production of automobiles, aerospace products, electronic and electric machinery, transportation equipment, and specialized metallurgic goods.

An analysis of the countries throughout the world indicates that the poorest, least developed countries are least likely to produce metal/machinery products except at the most basic level, while developed countries have advanced metal/machinery sectors offering a full range of products. As the industrial sector evolves (producing electromachinery and computer-based technology), the intermediate sector also expands to offer component parts and semifinished goods for all types of manufacturers.

In countries such as the United States, where technological innovation and application at the industrial level is high, the traditional types of industries and some basic intermediate industries (such as packaging materials) lose out to foreign competition, where foreign manufacturing enterprises have been able to move into sectors not yet affected by large-scale innovation, namely light industries of nondurable consumer goods and industrial supplies and where opportunities lie for the enterprising importer.

Other Sources of Imported Products

Importers need not import directly from the foreign country in all instances. U.S. customs regulations permit the temporary importation of raw materials, semifinished, and finished products to be stored, repackaged, assembled, processed, or manufactured within U.S. territories prior to payment of duties.

Foreign Trade Zones and Bonded Warehouses. Foreign trade zones (FTZs) and bonded warehouses are enclosed areas within or close to a port of entry. For U.S. customs purposes, they are considered to be outside the United States Customs Area. The merchandise that is held and that remains in transit within the enclosed areas is considered outside of the country and duty-free.

Foreign Trade Zones. Foreign trade zones have two main functions: export/import processing and warehouse rentals. Such areas can be used to promote international trade and commerce into the United States. While in the foreign trade zone, goods can be altered or combined into merchandise not subject to quota. Repackaging can change the duty classification and goods can be assembled, processed, or manufactured either for reexport without paying customs duties or for the U.S. market upon payment of U.S. import duties. Warehouse may function as bonded warehouses, where goods remain duty-free until imported into the United States (paying duties at the port of entry).

Other operations that are also included in the foreign trade zone are container frieght stations, where less-than-one-container loads are opened and separated. They then either are cleared for customs clearance, remain in the FTZ, or are reexported to other countries.

There are numerous advantages available to the importer. Products entering the U.S. market may be brought to the threshold of the market to reduce delivery delays. The importer is permitted to exhibit its product to potential consumers. The merchandise can also be remarked or relabeled to meet the requirements of the governing agency. There is no time limit as to how long the foreign merchandise can be stored in a zone. General information on U.S. foreign-trade zones may be obtained from the Office of Foreign Trade Zones, U.S. Department of Commerce, Washington, D.C., 20230.[6]

Bonded Warehouses. Foreign merchandise can be stored in customs bonded warehouses, but there are time limitations. Goods can be transferred to the foreign-trade zone for the purpose of eventual export, destruction, or permanent storage. With the transfer to the FTZ, the bond is canceled as are all obligations to duty payment, or as to the time the merchandise is to be exported, are terminated.[7]

Elements of the Import-Product Decision

The Product Life Cycle

One of the most important aspects to consider when serving U.S. markets is that products, consumers, and markets change over time. This not only means that the importer must carefully choose the product to sell in the market, but that markets must be developed and products managed in changing market conditions. Products, like consumers, have a life cycle. That is, products are first new to a market; some then grow and mature; and some eventually decline and are removed from the market. Product categories too have life cycles, and within these, improved and innovated products may also have a life cycle independent of the product category. However, it is important to understand the product category's life cycle as well as the particular product's life cycle in order to manage and prepare an adequate strategy to respond to competition and market conditions over time.

Introductory Stage. The importer's objective when a product is introduced to the market is to develop widespread awareness of the product benefits and obtain trial by early adopters. At this stage of the product life cycle, competitors are not viewed as important. With regards to product design, quality and quality control are extremely important.

Growth Stage. The objective in the growth stage is to establish a strong market and distribution niche. Within this niche, consumer loyalty must be maintained and strengthened. At this point, the marginal firms that entered the market emulating the importer's product begin to drop out of the market because of the shakeout. The product design has added modifications for new segments that market research has identified. Product improvement and trimming of unnecessary specialties are in order at this stage.

Maturity Stage. At maturity, the importer must defend its position against competing brands and the product category against other products. Efforts must go into tightening dealer relationships. The competitive outlook is relatively stable, with market shares not likely to fluctuate significantly among the players. Should a firm introduce a substantial product improvement, it could result in shifts in market share. Product design policies concentrate on production-cost cutting and elimination of weak products and services. New uses for the product are sought to increase the frequency of use by the current segment served.

Decline Stage. The strategic objective in this final stage is to milk the offering of all possible profits. Only necessary costs should be incurred. The number of competitive players in the market begins to decline, which could result in increased market share for the firms that can hold on in the marketplace. The product line should be pruned to those items that return a direct profit.

Product Positioning

Most products consist of tangible and intangible aspects that exert influence on consumer decision making. The marketing strategy defines the kinds of attributes that the selling effort would bring in front of the would-be purchaser to influence his or her decision to buy the product. Since the consumer's buying behavior is complex and variable, it is important for the seller to understand which are the most attractive attributes to the consumer. Thus, if the marketer can understand how consumers perceive their product in relation to a preferred product, then the marketer can adjust the marketing strategy to position its product in such a way that it can improve its performance in the marketplace.

Planning should be an ongoing process for all marketers. Successful planners have the ability to add the appropriate products at the correct time. Besides the addition of new products, it is important to know what products to delete and the right time to do so. As planners, importers must ask themselves:

Are there customer needs that no existing products are satisfying well?

Could a modified product better satisfy customer needs?

The solutions to these types of questions are not simple, but can be resolved by product positioning. Product positioning employs market research techniques that measure consumer perceptions of products or brands according to several product attributes (for example, is product A high-priced or low-priced?). In addition, consumers can be asked the salience of numerous attributes (for example, what price would you prefer to pay?). The purpose of positioning research is to show how products are positioned relative to each other and to the consumer's perception of an ideal product. This technique allows the marketer to discover opportunities to resposition existing products through product and/or promotion changes. Market opportunities that have not been satisfied may necessitate the introduction of a new product into the market, thus filling a void.

Product Adaptation

Products imported into the United States will be greatly influenced by

> import requirements
> consumer preferences
> cost
> quality

Import Requirements. Import requirements in the United States are regulated by government agencies that enforce the legislation enacted. Prior to importation, the firm should consult the appropriate agency to obtain specific requirements for the product.

Consumer Preferences. Consumer preferences are unique in the U.S. market, where buyers are very demanding of a product's performance. In the products strategy, focus should be placed on marketing the product attributes to the lifestyle segment targeted.

Cost. Cost/benefit analysis must be made to ascertain the viability of the U.S. market, taking into account shipping, insurance, packaging, duty, taxes, and successful marketing of the product.

Quality. Quality is a vital component of any product. The level of quality is perceived in the U.S. market by variables such as price, packaging, and promotion. Rival firms' quality levels should be evaluated to determine if the imported product will be competitive.

Branding

By definition, a brand is a name, term, sign, symbol, design, or some combination of the preceding used to identify the products of one firm and to differentiate them from competitive offerings. A brand name is that part of the brand consisting of words or letters that comprise a name used to identify and distinguish the firm's offering from those of competitors.[8]

A firm's name is often the only thing that competitors cannot copy. If an importer wishes to further penetrate an import market and protect its position, the brand can have legal protection by registration as a trademark. This brand name can then be the takeoff on a major marketing program to convince consumers that this brand best meets their needs and desires. From the consumer's perspective, the brand name simplifies shopping, usually guarantees the same level of quality, and allows self-expression. The brand name develops product-like qualities of its own. In sum, branding is valuable to both the firm and consumers.

Labeling

The design of product package and label is important in presenting and promoting the product to the consumer. The creative aspects of labeling need to accommodate the words and symbols of the brand itself. Moreover, the importer needs to carefully research the legal requirements surrounding labels. Sellers must make sure that the required information is on a package and label before importing a new product. In the United States, labeling is strictly regulated under the Fair Packaging and Labeling Act of 1966 to provide consumers with product information that is helpful for their decision making in the marketplace. Products must also meet the safety standards of the Consumer Product Safety Act of 1972. Information pertinent to product usage that is deemed harmful has to be printed on the package and/or label (cigarettes being an example).

Packaging

Packaging is a vital component in the import-product strategy. Fundamentally, the package must prevent damage while the product is in transit. Upon importation, it will tell the consumer what this product is all about.

Protection. When a product moves in international trade over long distances and timeframes, it must be well packaged for no damage to result. The purpose of bulk protective packaging is to avoid loss damage, pilferage, spoilage, and vandalism.

Import Cost and Transportation. A second important consideration is the cost associated with transportation and importation of the product. Gross weight is usually used to determine total transportation costs and import duties. These costs can be significant, so attention must be placed on the protective aspects of packaging.

Promotional Considerations. How does the importer present the product to the consumer? Packaging plays a major role in formulating perceptions of quality in the mind of the consumer. An analysis should be conducted of the packaging used by the importer's competitors. The package must be in line with the market/life-style the product was designed for. Whatever market segment an importer is attempting to reach, the product attributes must be conveyed through its packaging (for example, through package shape, makeup, graphic design, and color). The packaging communicates what the product is and who may need it. If an importer is uncertain of appropriate packaging for the U.S. market, the guidance of a package-design consultant could pay large dividends. The package must convey the message desired to the market segment targeted. The importer must not promise too much because if the product does not perform according to expectations, repurchases of the product will be low.

Customer Services and Warranties

The service component of the product strategy is a vital factor in obtaining consumer satisfaction. Many products require customer service for presale and back-up warranties for postsale. For the product to be successful it must be used adequately and for the purpose intended. Similarly, the consumer needs to be reassured that he or she made the correct purchase decision.

Customer Services. Many products require installation, repair, financing, delivery, and instructions for proper use. These responsibilities should not in all cases be left to the distribution network. Inadequate attention to customer services may result in product failure and market demand evaporating. Customer service is a competitive tool that requires a cost/benefit analysis to fine-tune the level of service required in a particular market.

Warranties. Another component of product strategy is a warranty, which is a promise by the importer that the product will perform as intended with an offer to replace or repair a defective product. The warranty may raise product satisfaction and ratain and enhance demand of the product. The importer must compare the cost of a warranty with the advantages that accrue and make a decision on offering it based on economic return.

Product Line and Mix

Most firms today sell more than one product, hence the term *product line*. A product line is a group of related or similar products that represent a firm's offering in the market. The number of product lines represents the width of the company's product mix. Importers can realize a competitive advantage in two ways. First, the firm can stimulate demand by offering customers a line of allied products. Second, by combining these products, marketing and production economies will lower costs. This approach will strengthen the importer's position in the market with a diversified product portfolio rather than a single product.

Summary

An importer must define an adequate product strategy to tap the target market the company proposes to serve. Important considerations in developing the product strategy are customs requirements, import quotas, product restrictions, consumer safety, quality, and transportation costs. The objective of an import-product strategy is to import a good that meets the legal requirements for its importation but also best meets the needs of the target market. Foreign trade zones and bonded warehouses can be a boon to the importer. As firms scan world markets for supply sources, they need to understand the nature of the productive capabilities of the countries from which products are sought and the stages of the product life cycle. The importer must then decide on critical strategy elements (branding, packaging labeling, level of customer services and warranties, and so forth) in order to develop a comprehensive strategy to serve the market.

Notes

1. The following section is summarized from *Importing into the United States* (Washington, D.C.: U.S. Customs Service, 1986), pp. 46–51.

2. Sandler and Travis, *Update* (June 1985), p. 2.

3. "Product Safety: A New Hot Potato for Congress?" *U.S. News & World Report* (June 14, 1982), p. 62.

4. Thomas C. Kinnear and Kenneth L. Bernhardt, *Principles of Marketing* (Glenview, Ill.: Scott, Foresman, 1983), p. 304.

5. Marta Ortiz-Buonafina, *Profitable Export Marketing: A Strategy for U.S. Business,* p. 197.

6. See Foreign Trade Zone Act of June 18, 1934. 19 U.S.C. 81a–u.

7. See Tariff Act of 1930. 19 U.S.C. 1311.

8. Reprinted from *Marketing Definitions: A Glossary of Marketing Terms,* compiled by Ralph S. Alexander (1960), published by the American Marketing Association.

5
Import-channel Strategy

The purpose of this chapter is to provide the importer with an understanding of the very complex distribution system that has developed in the United States. This includes both the organizational system (retailers, wholesalers, and so forth) and the extensive physical distribution system (including rights of way, facilities, and organizations) in commercial use today. The importer needs to understand these intricate channels of distribution for they are an essential component of successful marketing and can be of help in efficiently reaching the targeted segments in the vast U.S. market.

As shown on figure 5–1, a product should follow a path from producers to consumers to insure that such a path leads to the desired target market. Example 5–1 shows the path followed by processed foods: an importer-distributor can go to wholesalers and retailers or, alternatively, to institutional markets. Each market has different product requirements. For instance, products destined for consumer markets usually require smaller packages, while those destined for institutional markets are sold in industrial-size containers.

Example 5–2 shows a typical channel flow for mass-produced wooden doors with flush panels. As depicted in the diagram, these doors can be routed to wholesaler-distributors and then to retailers for the do-it-yourself market, or to building contractors and independent contractors who do not buy enough volume to justify going to the wholesaler-distributor directly.

Example 5–3 depicts a typical channel of distribution for nontraditional agricultural products, namely fruits and vegetables. As shown, the importer deals with either the producer or foreign export agents such as cooperatives, independent distributors, and export brokers. These products are then routed to consumer and institutional markets.

As revealed in these examples, the import-distributor is a very important link in the import channels of distribution. Foreign producers need to rely on these channel members to provide important marketing services:

- Importers know the local markets well. They are, therefore, best qualified to identify potential markets, determine product/market match, and develop an adequate channel of distribution strategy.

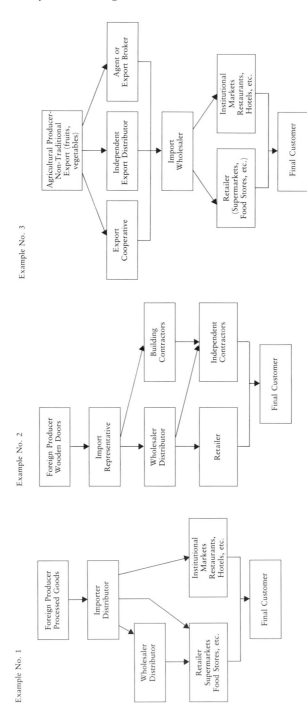

Source: Adapted from *Perfiles de Mercado* (Washington, D.C. Secretaria General de la Organization de Estados Americanos, 1980).

Figure 5–1. Import Channels of Distribution

- Importers can assemble the required inventories to meet local demand and make major commitments to inventory holding and promotional activities.

- Importers can provide presale and postsale services as required by the product as well as financial services to other channel members to promote continuity, cooperation, and productivity from the channel system.

Importer-distributors are, therefore, the link between the foreign producer and the domestic channel of distribution. Consequently, the importer needs a thorough understanding of the marketing system that connects the import product with the final consumer: the functions performed by channel members, the factors affecting import channels of distribution, and the type of channel members that form a product's marketing system.

Import-marketing Channels of Distribution

Placing goods and services where and when they are needed and facilitating change of ownership and transfer of title occur within the channels of distribution. In some instances, the path goods and services take during these functions is relatively short and simple. Other paths are more complex and lengthy. However, the importer must have a working understanding of the complex route that a foreign product must take to reach stores in any U.S. city or town.

Defining Channels of Distribution

Channels of distribution can be formally defined;

> The structure of intracompany organization units are extracompany agents and dealers, wholesale and retail, through which a commodity, product, or service is marketed.[1]

The various marketing institutions and organizations that are responsible for the title flow and the physical movement of the goods and services from producer to consumer form the path that the products or services move through as they go from point of production to point of final consumption. These units perform the following important functions:

- Channels of distribution facilitate the flow of goods and services, reducing the number of transactions required to reach the final consumer. Channels provide time and possession utilities, that is, channels of distribution put products where consumers are and facilitate the transfer of title by taking possession of goods and transferring them to final consumers at the time that the consumers buy them.

- Channels of distribution adjust discrepancies between supply and demand. Producers generally want to produce and sell in large quantities of one or a few products. Consumers, on the other hand, want to buy by the piece, one product at a time. Channels of distribution adjust these discrepancies by accumulating products from different producers and breaking bulk orders into smaller quantities to sell to the middlemen closer to the market.

In order to serve these functions, channels of distribution perform the following activities:

Transfer of title: Facilitating exchange of ownership from producer to consumer.

Promotion: Development of promotional mix to inform and persuade potential consumers.

Negotiating: Searching out and negotiating the terms of sale with potential and current customers so that the transfer of title can be effected.

Physical distribution: Transporting and storing the goods.

Financing: Acquiring and dispersing funds to cover the cost of channel work.

Risk taking: Assuming risks in connection with channel work performed.

Ordering: Anticipating consumer needs and fitting the company's offer to the marketplace. This involves activities such as assembling from a large number of suppliers, breaking bulk, inspecting, testing, and judging products for quality.

Payment: Backward financing from buyers to producrs.[2]

The Import-Channel Structure: Transfer of Title

An import marketing strategy entails an explicit set of objectives and policies that define the type of marketing system desired, the level of services needed to deliver the product to the consumers, and the level of control desired, given competitive conditions and company resources. These factors, discussed later in this chapter, affect channel decisions and strategic choices. In the process, the import-marketing channel must be integrated with other elements of the marketing mix to enable the importing firm to effectively and efficiently reach its target market.

Channel strategies and objectives are critical to the success of the firm and have some important characteristics. First, marketing-channel decisions are infrequently made. Most marketing-channel systems, once implemented, become a semipermanent feature of the marketing strategy. Other marketing factors (such as new-product introduction, promotional activities, and pricing decisions, to name a few) become more relevant to recurrent marketing decisions. The management of the marketing channel reverts to day-to-day repetitive activities aimed at maintaining cooperation and productivity at desired levels of the different organizational units that comprise the marketing-channel system.

Second, there is an inherent perception of risk involved in changing established patterns of distribution. Once the channel system is implemented, there is tendency for maintenance and stability. Change occurs only under very stressful circumstances (for example, nonperformance or lack of productivity). In many product categories (such as clothing, processed foods, shoes, and automobiles), there is a well-defined marketing-channel structure that functions effectively to reach significant market segments in the United States.[3]

The just-mentioned characteristics clearly indicate that the channel decision, when first implemented or revised, needs very careful and conscientious consideration by the import manager. Marketing-channel decisions are critical inasmuch as these decisions affect the ability of the firm to reach its target market. Similarly, these decisions involve financial risks as the firm must implement, develop, and maintain the existing channel system.

Factors Affecting Import-Channel Decisions

The decisions involved in developing an effective and efficient import channel of distribution are usually made by the manufacturer. In import activities, however, an importer middleman usually has a major say in the decision-making process. This evolves out of the nature of the import process itself. The producer of the goods is located in a foreign country. Very often, the foreign producer has little or no expertise in the U.S. market and must rely on the business acumen and expertise of the import middleman. Since none of the channel decisions can be made independently of other elements of the marketing mix, the foreign producer and its principal channel member(s) must develop very close cooperation. Consequently, one of the major factors affecting channel decisions in import activities is the degree of expertise of the foreign producer. Other factors are the type of marketing system desired, the degree of control desired, the competitive situation, and cost.

Degree of Marketing Expertise

Most foreign producers, particularly smaller firms, have little marketing expertise to set up a comprehensive import-channel system to adequately cover the complex and vast U.S. market. Instead, they work through an importer middleman who acts as distributor or channel leader. There are degrees of directness in importing that are highly related to the perceived need of marketing expertise and familiarity with the U.S. market.

The foreign manufacturer must be able to penetrate the U.S. market effectively. The foreign producer has two basic options when first entering an import market:

> direct import channels of distribution,
>
> indirect import channels of distribution.

In developing a *direct import channel of distribution*, the foreign manufacturer decides to sell directly to agents, distributors, and other middlemen who comprise the import channel of distribution. This direct method demands significant marketing expertise and financial involvement. An example of this channel of distribution is the one used by the Japanese automobile industry in the United States.

When a foreign manufacturer decides that the most attractive import channel of distribution is direct, then a *wholly owned or jointly owned subsidiary* should be considered as an alternative channel to serve as importer, distributor, and/or wholesaler. Similarly, an importer may decide to form a joint venture with a foreign producer to import and distribute the exporter's products. Such an arrangement allows the importer's wholly owned or joint venture a means to control the firm's marketing strategy, developing its own product strategy, managing its own sales force and sales effort, and using all the means available in the United States to promote its products, without having to depend on an independent importer or distributor to do these marketing tasks.

Importing through a subsidiary can assure the importing venture the continuing presence of a product in the marketplace and allow the foreign producer to provide a full range of buyer-support services. Similarly, it allows the importing venture to obtain the market-related expertise and be in a position to respond to threats and opportunities posed by environmental changes. Similarly, this type of channel arrangement can facilitate further expansion in the marketplace, allowing the importing venture to exploit fully its competitive advantages in the target market and to control production and marketing activities.

Indirect import channels of distribution entail the relationship with one import middleman, usually an import distributor, who serves as channel leader on behalf of the foreign manufacturer (as in the case of an agent or commission house) or on its own behalf (as in the case of an import merchant who buys the goods outright from the foreign producer). The role of the middleman becomes pivotal in the success of the import-marketing strategy as the importer becomes a vital and critical link between the producer and consumers, providing the expertise to gain access to the market and designing the channel system needed to tap a particular market segment.

Type of Marketing System Desired

The decisions affecting import-marketing channels are influenced by the type of marketing system desired. This entails decisions regarding channel length, coverage, middlemen types, and quantity and quality of each middleman type.

Channel Length. Channel length involves the number of channel levels to be used. Length refers to the number of middlemen performing specific functions within the channel to bring the title to the consumer. Figure 5–2 illustrates the channel level options.

A *zero-level* channel consists of an importer selling directly to consumers. Such a channel requires extensive use of direct contact with consumers through personal selling. This type of channel is most frequently used with industrial products.

A *one-level* channel involves selling through one intermediary, usually an importer-retailer. Many large retail-chain stores (such as Allied Stores, Federated Stores, and Sears, Roebuck) buy directly from foreign manufacturers. Thus, foreign manufacturers can in effect establish control over most aspects of their marketing strategy.

A *two-level* channel system involves selling to an importer-wholesaler, who in turn will move the goods through the channel, selling to retailers. This is the most common type of channel system. Many products, such as processed foods and consumer goods, typically move through this type of channel.

A *three-level* channel involves three middlemen. The additional intermediary is usually a jobber that buys from wholesalers and serves retailers. The type of goods moving through such a channel are specialty, impulse,

---

Zero-level	Importer --- Consumer	
One-level	Importer --- Retailer -- Consumer	
Two-level	Importer -- Wholesaler ------------------------------ Retailer -- Consumer	
Three-level	Importer -- Wholesaler -- Jobber ------------------- Retailer -- Consumer	

Source: Adapted from Philip Kotler, *PRINCIPLES OF MARKETING* 2/E C 1983, p. 357. Reprinted by Permission of Prentice-Hall, Inc., Englewood Cliffs, New Jersey.

Figure 5–2. Channel Level Options

and unsought goods that are usually bought in small lots. Inventories at the retailing point usually consist of a very few items kept at a time. Examples of these goods are kitchen utensils, candy, and personal-care items.

The type of channel length chosen generally reflects established practices in many marketing areas. Figure 5–3 presents the different middlemen types and possible length in a conventional import-channel of distribution for consumer goods.

Coverage. The importer must decide the degree of coverage of the market. The choices range from *exclusive* distribution (selling to one intermediary or import distributor), to *selective* distribution (selling to a selected number of importers) to *extensive* distribution (selling to a large number of importers of the different middleman types). The benefits of each market coverage vary, but generally speaking, the greater the degree of exclusivity, the greater the influence

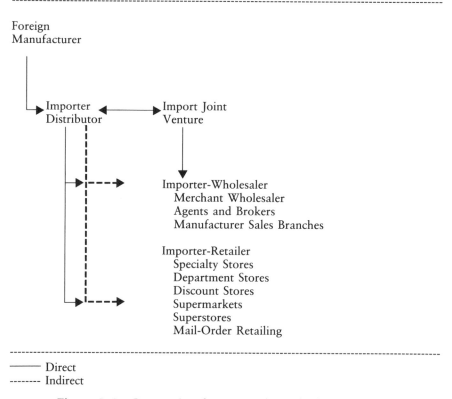

Foreign
Manufacturer

Importer
Distributor

Import Joint
Venture

Importer-Wholesaler
    Merchant Wholesaler
    Agents and Brokers
    Manufacturer Sales Branches

Importer-Retailer
    Specialty Stores
    Department Stores
    Discount Stores
    Supermarkets
    Superstores
    Mail-Order Retailing

———— Direct
-------- Indirect

Figure 5–3. Conventional Import-Channel of Distribution

and control that the foreign manufacturer and/or importer can exert on the channel-system marketing practices. On the other hand, extensive distribution dilutes the control the importer has over the marketing system. However, one important consideration (namely, consumer shopping patterns) will have a primary influence on the coverage that is necessary to reach market segments effectively. For example, convenience products are those products for which consumers are not willing to spend time and effort to buy. The channel strategy for this type of products must recognize this fact and provide outlets in as many locations as possible to accommodate this type of shopping behavior.[4]

Degree of Control Desired

A strong determinant of the marketing strategy and policies is the degree of control the importer wishes to exert on the channel system to achieve stated objectives and implement formulated strategies. One form of channel control is the formation of vertical channel systems. In this situation, the foreign manufacturer and/or importer may decide to bypass existing channels of distribution and perform channel functions by forward integration, that is, by entering into import-distributing and -wholesaling activities to increase control over marketing strategies. Channel integration requires the coordination of effort through the channel system, and the importer eliminates the need of intermediaries if the channel objective is to improve channel efficiency and performance. In the United States, more and more firms are trying to bypass existing independent channel systems by curbing or eliminating the independence of channel members. The result has been an increase in the number and types of vertical marketing systems (VMS).[5]

The Competitive Situation

In U.S. markets, where product availability and marketing practices are highly sophisticated, a channel strategy cannot be adequately developed without an evaluation of the competitive environment. A foreign manufacturer or importer cannot ignore competitive strategies, which entail evaluation of the competitive strategies, of domestic manufacturers as well as other foreign importers in the United States.

Cost

All the factors previously described have an impact on the firm's resource allocation and marketing costs. Developing, maintaining, and motivating channel members also becomes an integral part of the channel strategy. Consequently, cost—cost of developing and maintaining a channel of distribution—is the balancing factor in channel decisions. A careful balance must exist between marketing objectives, company resources, and costs associated with channel development and maintenance. In many instances, there are no clear-cut, prearranged import channels of distribution. The importer must be able to assess its own marketing expertise, the type of marketing system desired, the degree of control desired, and the competitive situation in terms of target markets in order to develop a comprehensive channel strategy to achieve goals and objectives.

Import Channels of Distribution

Importers can choose from a variety of channel arrangements to enter and cover the U.S. market. The previous section discussed the major factors affecting channel decisions. In addition to these factors, other influences (such as the characteristics of the product, the market area, and the company itself) will have an impact on whether a channel is direct or indirect, long or short. For example, a foreign manufacturer producing a few simple products (such as screws, paper clips, or working gloves, for which there is a need for a long channel) can enter a particular region through an importer-distributor that can provide the adequate channel system to tap the U.S. market effectively. On the other hand, industrial suppliers, knowing the needs and location of their markets, may decide to go directly to their customers using a manufacturer's representative or agent.

In order to set the framework to enable the importer to evaluate the alternative channels available to form a channel system, this section focuses on retailing and wholesaling and the prototype institutions that make up these sectors.

Retailing

Retailing is defined as all the activities involved in selling goods and services directly to final consumers. The U.S. Bureau of the Census indicates that there are approximately 1.5 million single unit and over 330,000 multiunit retail stores and about 150,000 direct-selling operations in the United States. In 1984, retail sales reached $1.573 billion. Retail institutions deliver a huge assortment of domestic and imported goods to the American consumer in an attempt to satisfy the affluent and highly discriminating needs of U.S. markets. As the consumer demand an extensive assortment of items, wide-ranging prices, quality, and innovative product lines, retailing activities are continually evolving to meet these demands. Supermarkets, convenience stores, and mass merchandisers meet consumer demand with convenience, competitive prices, and a wide variety of products. Planned shopping centers, designed to satisfy the needs of specific target markets, provide consumers with a variety of products and services in urban and suburban areas.

Retailers must determine the product offering, which includes convenience, shopping, and specialty goods. The nation's retailers come in all sizes and organizational types. New retailing types keep emerging in response to changing consumer preferences and shopping patterns. According to product line sold, retailers can be classified as specialty stores, department stores, supermarkets, convenience stores, discount stores, superstores, and mail-order retailers.

Specialty Stores. A specialty store offers a wide variety of services and specialty merchandise. Examples of such stores include fashion apparel and shoe shops, furniture stores, and florists. Most specialty stores carry a single or limited product line. Specialty stores having product-specialization strategies are called superspecialty stores. Some examples of these include Tall Men (tall men's clothing) and 5–7 (small women's sizes). Specialty stores are typically found in shopping centers, where they occupy 60–70 percent of the total shopping area. Specialty stores allow retailers to specialize in product offerings and tap well-defined target markets. Most specialty stores are independently owned. However, chain specialty stores are rapidly gaining market share in the retailing sectors.[6]

Given their product strategies, specialty stores offer significant opportunities to the importer. Importers, however, must conform to the product/market strategy of the different stores and provide products that meet the needs of the store. Since this type of retail outlet places strong emphasis on market segmentation, the importer must emphasize standardization of product and quality in order to adequately serve this market.

Department Stores. Department stores handle a large variety of merchandise organized in departments that are actually limited-line specialty stores within one organizational unit. Department stores are located in central shopping areas and/or major shopping centers. Their product line is varied, mostly concentrating on clothing, furniture, and household goods. Examples of department stores are Bloomingdale's (New York, Miami, etc.), Burdines (Miami), and Filene's (Boston). Department stores today are facing strong competition from mass merchandisers (discount stores), and their relative share of the retail market has been declining. However, these large retailers do a large volume of business. Many are part of chain stores such as Allied Stores and Federated Stores.[7] These retail outlets show a significant blend of imported as well as domestic product offerings. Consequently, they provide a significant opportunity for the importer as they can obtain a large volume of business and good market coverage in their regions.

Supermarkets. The supermarket is a large grocery retailer specializing in processed foods, produce, laundry, and household items. Supermarkets are typically high-volume, low-margin operations that capitalize on fast turnover of a large variety of products. Currently, the product lines of most supermarkets are being expanded to respond to changing trends in the marketplace, adding such lines as nonprescription drugs, beauty aids, housewares, magazines, toys, and books. Consequently, these retail outlets are opening opportunities to importers. However, the product must be adaptable to the high-volume, low-margin mass-merchandising approach. Importers must be willing to support the supermarket's sales efforts with other elements of the marketing mix, including extensive advertising, branding, packaging, and so forth.

Convenience Stores. Convenience stores are relatively smaller stores offering a limited line of convenience products. Examples include 7-Elevens and Farm Stores. While individual retail units are low-volume, high-margin operations, their total volume of sales is significant, and they are a potentially lucrative market for the importer, especially in specialty-food items. 7-Eleven, for example, is the world's largest convenience-store chain, with over 7,000 stores in the United States, Canada, and five other countries. Yearly sales are nearly $5 billion from customers that spend an average of $2.08 a trip.[8] Importers offering convenience products with mass-consumption potential can find a significant opportunity in these retail outlets.

Discount Stores. Discount stores are high-volume, low-priced operations that specialize in appliances, televisions, radios, soft goods, and some processed foods. The typical discount store is a large outlet concentrating inventories on national brands of best-selling sizes, models, and so forth in a given product category. As sales volume of discount stores has grown, so have their product offerings. Importers can tap this growing and important segment of the retail market by offering product lines that conform to the firm's product line and pricing strategy. It is important to bear in mind that selling to discount stores could jeopardize alternative coverage of the market through department stores and specialty stores.

Superstores. Some of the larger or more successful discount stores have grown into huge superstores. These retail organizations are giant mass merchandisers that operate on a high-volume, low-price basis. A typical superstore sells "food, hardware, soft goods, building material, auto supplies, appliances, and prescription drugs; and it has a restaurant, a beauty salon, a barber shop, a branch banker, and a bakery."[9] Importers catering to this type of retailer must conform to the product offering and operating basis, as is the case of the discount stores. Today, a few thousand such retail outlets operate in the United States and represent an opportunity to generate a high volume of orders if the product is adaptable to this particular mass-merchandising approach.

Mail-Order Retailers. Mail-order retailing is a direct-to-consumer method. Retailers offer merchandise for sale by mail, by telephone, or by visiting a mail-order desk at a retail store. Its popularity is growing rapidly due to the rising cost of gasoline and the movement of women into the labor force. These retail outfits reach a highly selective market segment with a variety of novelty items, specialty gift items, and crafts. More recently, mail-order retailers have expanded their product lines, offering such products as televisions, luggage and other leather goods, and sporting goods. The importer must bear in mind that the product offered to the mail-order retailer must meet the special requirements of the medium, that is, the product must be describable and not need complicated presale or postsale services or installation.

The retailers just described continually make decisions on product-assortment width (a few or many product lines) and depth (a few or many product lines) as well as the quality of the product. Retailers look for items that meet the quality standards of their product line. Consequently, importers should continually search for opportunities to meet the needs and requirements of the different retail types in order to tap these markets effectively.

Wholesaling

Wholesaling is defined as the activities of persons and establishments that sell goods and services to other merchants and/or institutional or commercial users for resale or business use.[10] Wholesalers are a vital link in channels of distribution as they provide services that create efficiencies in the flow of goods from producers to consumers. First, wholesalers transport and store products at locations convenient to retailers and consumers. Due to wholesalers' buying in large quantities in bulk and carrying large inventories, manufacturers and retailers benefit as their inventory needs are reduced. Second, wholesalers buy in bulk and assemble assortments from different manufacturers and then break bulk, that is, sell in smaller quantities to a large number of jobbers, small wholesalers, and retailers according to the needs of the market. Third, wholesalers serve as a source of marketing information, a function especially useful to foreign manufacturers. The type of information provided includes market acceptance, market trends, and competitive strategies. Last, wholesalers perform a financing function that improves the efficiency of distribution channels. They buy from manufacturers and in turn sell to retailers and other middlemen on credit, allowing manufacturers and middlemen to minimize inventory costs. In these ways, wholesalers absorb a significant amount of risk in the marketing transaction, which results in a higher degree of efficiency in the exchange process.

In 1984, there were approximately 415,000 wholesalers in the United States. Sales volume in this sector amounted to $1.360 billion. According to product line handled, wholesalers fall into three general categories:

merchant wholesalers,

brokers and agents,

manufacturer's representatives and/or sales branches.

Merchant Wholesalers. Merchant wholesalers are independent businesses that buy on their own account from suppliers. This group represents the largest element in the wholesale sector and accounts for approximately 50 percent of the total wholesale trade. Merchant wholesalers can be classified as:

full-function wholesalers offering a full assortment of services or

limited-line wholesalers, which offer a limited number of wholesaling functions.

Examples of the latter are cash-and-carry, truck wholesalers, drop-shippers, and mail-order wholesalers. These limited-line wholesalers usually operate with narrow product lines and do not hold large inventories. However, they monitor the retailer's inventories and replenish these when necessary.

Merchant wholesalers prevail in industries where the product is small, relatively inexpensive, and not perishable and does not require control over retailing operations. Drugs, groceries, and hardware are examples of products carried by merchant wholesalers.

Brokers and Agents. Agents and brokers are independent wholesalers who do not take title of the goods, that is, they do not buy the goods outright from the manufacturer but rather act on behalf of a supplier to obtain market coverage on a commission basis. *Brokers* are specialized agents who bring buyers and sellers together in industries where large numbers of buyers and sellers are geographically dispersed, as is the case with the commodity market, frozen foods, and used machinery. *Agents* are commission-based individuals who may act on behalf of one or many suppliers and sell a wide assortment of goods. Agents may represent manufacturers on an exclusive or nonexclusive basis, depending upon the needs and size of the market.

Manufacturer's Representatives or Sales Branches. In many instances, the foreign manufacturer may decide to use one specific representative or establish company-owned facilities to handle wholesaling functions rather than use established independent wholesalers or agents. An increasing volume of sales may make this a viable alternative. The establishment of these types of wholesale arrangements requires a significant investment in market development and maintenance.

Wholesalers keep continual tabs on manufacturers worldwide for new and potentially profitable products. Since they buy large quantities, maintain inventories to service channel members, and scan new markets and opportunities, they can provide the foreign producer with the critical expertise needed to enter the U.S. market. The key to being able to serve these channel types is to provide the product mix that offers the wholesaler an opportunity to enhance productivity and market position.

Physical Distribution

The delivery of goods to U.S. markets is an integral part of the channel decision and a very important component of the import activity. The logistics function, like any other business function, requires efficient management. Efficiency, or lack of it, can be found at different levels of physical distribution. However, it is the responsibility of the foreign producer and/or importer to assure adequate transportation modes and prompt, efficient delivery of the goods at the importing point.[11]

The Logistics Concept

The logistics concept in physical distribution entails a recognition that physical distribution is central to the importing activity and should be managed in a coherent, cost-effective manner. It is the process of organizing supply and overcome time and space.[12]

The logistics concept involves two central ideas: product flow and systems trade-offs. A total-cost concept, it entails a careful balancing of all system factors (such as transportation modes, time, cost, transportation requirements, product considerations, and customer needs) that affect costs and delivery of the goods. The task of the importer is to develop and coordinate an adequate system to achieve the essential goal of minimizing costs and maximizing service performance.

The logistics function, then, is very closely associated with the channel strategy as it is precisely to each channel member that the goods must be delivered in all instances whether the channel is direct or indirect, long or short. Consequently, the decisions related to channel strategy must incorporate efficient physical distribution in order to reach the target market efficiently and effectively.

Modes of Transportation

U.S. ports can be reached by airways, waterways, railways, and roadways. Shipping companies serving the U.S. ports offer the importer services from every corner of the world. Each transportation mode has distinguishing characteristics that affect the time involved in transporting the goods, the capacity or space available to transport goods, and the cost of transportation services.

Airways. Air transportation is becoming one of the most important modes of transportation, particularly in international trade. Airlines serving U.S. markets have expanded air-cargo capacity over the past decades by introducing wide-bodied airplanes and containerization. However, airplanes are still low-capacity vehicles in terms of horsepower–to–ton-mile ratio. This results in the highest per–ton-mile cost of all transportation modes. Air transportation is well suited for certain types of goods such as high-priced, fragile, or perishable goods and emergency shipments. Manufactured goods are especially suited for air transport due to their high cost relative to their mass or bulk. Most air carriers are combination carriers, that is, they carry both passengers and cargo shipments. The major type of carriers are domestic trunk carriers, international carriers, and foreign-flag carriers.

Domestic Trunk Carriers. Domestic trunk carriers are airlines' common carriers, that is, carriers that deliver transportation services to the public for a fee. These carriers have regularly scheduled arrival and departure services and cannot refuse such service except for good cause. Since airline deregulation in 1978, many domestic trunk airlines fly international routes and have expanded the available cargo capacity in international trade.

International Air Carriers. These are called U.S.-flag carriers and operate between the U.S. and most foreign countries. These carriers, prior to deregulation, had exclusive rights to fly international passengers and cargo between the United States and foreign countries. These carriers still enjoy access to more foreign ports than many domestic trunk airlines and fly across international waters between foreign countries. They account for a significant amount of international air cargo.

Foreign-Flag Carriers. Foreign airlines operate between their home country and the United States. As such, they are the counterpart of the domestic trunk airlines. These airlines offer regularly scheduled services and all-cargo services. For the most part, foreign airlines are heavily subsidized by their government and consequently offer highly competitive air-freight rates.

Waterways. This transportation mode involves using deep-sea or shallow-draft vessels. Deep-sea transportation is the backbone of international trade and accounts for the largest tonnage transported in international trade. Ocean shipment, also referred to as marine transportation, is characterized by its low cost relative to its large cargo capacity, permitting bulky and heavy cargo to be transported comparatively economically. The main disadvantage lies in the time required to move the goods. (Speeds seldom exceed 30 miles per hour.) With improved container technology and higher fuel costs, the shipping industry continues to emphasize large capacity at a lower cost. Goods moving by marine transportation include raw materials, foodstuffs that are bulky, and heavy manufactured goods.

Ocean shipping is mostly conducted by common carriers, liner ships that offer cargo services to all shippers who required their services except for good cause. Services can be also obtained on a chartered, time, or per-voyage basis. Ships offering these services are called tramp ships, which are general traders that rely on market supply and demand.

Inland waterway carriers are slow-moving vehicles specially suited to move heavy, bulky, low-value–per–unit cargo at very low cost. Internal waterways (such as lakes, canals, and rivers) provide geographic specialization only where such a mode is available. Many internal points of entry in the United States are accessible through inland waterways, and use of the flat-bottomed boat or barge has increased as improved technology allows some specially designed barges to be lifted into barge ships to be moved across larger bodies of water and then unloaded for continued use of inland waterways.

Roadways. The U.S. highway system is the major means of intracountry transport. It also accounts for a significant proportion of all goods shipments from importing point to final destination and from the United States to contiguous nations (Canada and Mexico).

Land carriers are similar to air carriers in that they are relatively low-capacity. The horsepower–to–ton-mile ratio, however, is much lower than for air-transportation carriers, so land transportation costs about a fourth less. Roadway transportation is especially flexible for short-haul cargo shipments of goods from importing point (by air or sea) to internal points of destination. It also provides a certain degree of flexibility in longer-haul destinations by providing a significant lower-cost alternative for a portion of the trip.

Railroads. This mode of transportation is also an important mode for inland transportation. Railroads are principally internal modes of transportation and are particularly important in hauling cargo between entry ports and major urban areas. Most railroads offer cargo-handling facilities close to or in ocean-port berths so that the cargo can be unloaded from the carrier into the railroad car. Railroads are common carriers particularly suited for heavy and bulky goods. Destination points are determined by established routes (tracks), giving this transportation mode less flexibility than others.

Intermodal Transportation. While sea transportation is the backbone of international trade, moving goods from exporting to importing port and then to their final destination may require the use of two or more modes of transportation. This approach is in conjunction with the logistics concept of coordination and careful balancing of all factors affecting transportation costs and objectives. Intermodal transportation involves the combination of two or more types of transportation to increase efficiency and reduce the total cost of shipment. The particular geographic link of export and import market is an important determinant of the type of intermodal combination that can be used.

Summary

The wise importer pays close attention to channels of distribution—the intracompany network that facilitates the flow of goods and services while bringing supply and demand into harmony. These channels are needed for transfer of title, promotion, negotiating, physical distribution, financing, risk taking, ordering, and payment. Based on an importer's market knowledge and degree of marketing expertise, it may choose either a direct or indirect distribution channel.

Other variables include channel length (number of levels), coverage, and types and number of middlemen. Importers must also consider the competitive situation and the amount of control they wish to maintain over the channel system.

Distribution options for wholesaling span merchant wholesalers; brokers and agents; and manufacturer's agents and sales branches. Specialty stores, department stores, supermarkets, convenience stores, discount stores, superstores, and mail-order houses are the retail alternatives. Choice of transportation mode (air, water, road, rail, or intermodal) will be affected by time, cost, and capacity restraints, the nature of the good, and customer needs.

Notes

1. Reprinted from *Marketing Definitions: A Glossary of Marketing Terms*, compiled by Ralph S. Alexander (American Marketing Association, 1960).

2. L. Stern and A.I. El Ansary, *Marketing Channels* © 1982. (Englewood Cliffs, New Jersey: Prentice-Hall, 1982), pp. 13–14. Reprinted by permission of the publisher.

3. Kenneth R. Davis, *Marketing Management*, 5th ed. (New York: John Wiley & Sons, 1984), pp. 407–08.

4. D.J. Rachman, *Marketing Today* (Chicago: Dryden, 1984), p. 358.

5. Philip Kotler, *Principles of Marketing* 2/E (Englewood Cliffs, New Jersey: Prentice-Hall, 1983), p. 390. Reprinted by permission of the publisher.

6. The Bureau of the Census considers a chain store system to be eleven or more stores handling the same kind of merchandise and under common ownership and management.

7. For example, Federated Stores based in Cincinnati is the parent company of Burdines and Bloomingdale's in Florida, Abraham & Straus in New York, Sanger & Harris in Dallas, Bullock's in Los Angeles, and I. Magnin in San Francisco, among others.

8. R.T. Hise and S.W. McDaniels, *Cases in Marketing Strategy* 1984), p. 269. Reprinted by permission of Charles E. Merrill Publishing Co., Columbus, Ohio.

9. T.L. Kurts and L.E. Boone, *Marketing*, 2/E © 1984), p. 503. Reprinted by permission of Dryden Press, Chicago, Illinois.

10. This is the definition used by the U.S. Bureau of the Census.

11. For a complete discussion on transportation modes, see Marta Ortiz-Buonafina, *Profitable Export Marketing*, pp. 198–207.

12. See P.B. Schary, *Logistic Decisions* (Chicago: Dryden, 1984), p. 3.

6

Import-promotion Strategy

S trategic promotion decisions are a key variable of an import-marketing strategy. This chapter will discuss the basic elements of an import-promotion strategy, highlighting the importance of cross-cultural factors in creating a marketing strategy that will reach the target market.

THE PROCESS OF COMMUNICATION
IN MARKETING

Communicating the elements of the firm's offering in the marketplace is one of the key components of the marketing strategy. In a market such as the United States, promotion becomes a critical tool in the marketing mix, inasmuch as it is necessary to be able to reach the appropriate target market.

Promotion refers to the forms of communication used by the company to inform and persuade consumers about a product offering.[1] Promotion can be defined as seller-oriented, market-oriented, profit-centered communication. All components of the promotion mix have the mission to communicate the seller's offering to the buyers and to inform them of the product's uses, value, availability, and price. Promotion is aimed at persuading the potential buyer concerning a desired course of action. It can be said that persuasion is the heart of the promotion effort.

The Promotion Mix

The promotion mix consists of four major tools:

Advertising: Any paid form of nonpersonal presentation and promotion of ideas, goods, or services by an identified sponsor.[2]

Personal selling: Oral presentation in a conversation with one or more prospective purchasers for the purpose of making sales.[3]

Sales promotion: Relates to marketing activities other than personal selling, advertising, and publicity that stimulate consumer purchasing and dealer effectiveness, such as displays, shows and exhibitions, demonstrations, and various selling efforts aimed at elevating consumer interest, attention, and action.[4]

Publicity and public relations: Nonpersonal stimulation of demand for a product, service, or business unit by planting commercially significant news about it in a published medium or obtaining favorable presentation of it on radio, television, or stage that is not paid for by the sponsor.[5]

The promotion strategy entails the planning, implementation, and coordination of communication with customers. The strategy involves the allocation of the promotion effort among the different elements of the promotion mix. These elements are not mutually exclusive, but each one adds an important dimension to the promotion strategy. The importer needs to blend these elements in such a way as to maximize the promotion objectives. Defining promotion objectives and a target market is a necessary prerequisite to developing an adequate import-promotion strategy. Such a strategy may involve some minimum effort of hiring a few salespersons, or it may even involve undertaking a comprehensive advertising campaign. In order to insure a proper focus for the promotion strategy, each element is analyzed in terms of the overall import-promotion strategy.

Importers are faced with the task of distributing the total promotion budget over the four promotion tools of personal selling, advertising, sales promotion, and publicity. The key is to determine the optimal mix to achieve sales objectives.

Changing the mix of promotion tools, often by selecting one to replace another, is a common strategy of firms in their quest for greater sales. A number of firms have opted for print and electronic advertising, direct mail, and telephone solicitation in lieu of sales activity in the field. Still others have boosted their sales-promotion budgets relative to advertising outlays in order to increase sales more quickly. The need to efficiently and flexibly alter the promotion mix is ample reason to centralize the marketing functions.

The features and costs of the different promotion tools vary. Importers must clearly comprehend the differences between advertising, personal selling, sales promotion, and publicity in order to choose the proper mix.[6]

Advertising

There are many kinds and applications of advertising. The principal features include:

Public nature: Advertising is a communicative vehicle that is clearly public in nature. This gives it a certain amount of acceptability and a relatively standard variety of communication choices. Purchasing motives for a particular product will be publicly known, given the same advertising message to a large section of the population.

Omnipresence: The pervasiveness of advertising enables the seller of imported goods to communicate his or her message again and again. The prospective purchaser, therefore, can evaluate the messages from different advertisers and make his or her buying decision accordingly. The size, acceptability, prominence, and success of an importer are often indicated by the scope and budget assigned to advertising.

Dramatization: Advertising employs an array of audio and visual media to vividly convey an importing firm's image and products.

One-way communication: As effective as advertising often is, it cannot substitute for a salesperson making a pitch to consumers and soliciting a response from them. A monologue—an ad communicated to the consumer—does not require the consumer to pay as careful attention.

Two distinct ways that advertising is used are to establish a long-term image for an advertised import (for example, Perrier water) or to achieve quick sales in the short term (as with drastically reduced airfares during off-peak time). The various types of advertising have differing cost structures, with electronic media requiring a much larger budget in terms of cost per consumer reached than print media.

Personal Selling

Few methods are as effective as personal selling in shaping a buyer's choices, beliefs, and decisions. As compared with advertising, personal selling has the following features:

Person-to-person interaction: Personal selling provides the face-to-face contact between two or more persons, enabling each party to assess the other's wants, desires, and buying motivation and allowing the seller to adjust the selling pitch immediately.

Relationship building: Personal selling provides various types of relationships, from a simple sale to a long-term account. The latter necessitates greater marketing (and human-relations) skills on the part of the sales representative.

Feedback: Personal selling places a greater obligation on the consumer to become involved in the sales representative's presentation. The buyer often feels a need to listen and respond, even if "Thanks for your time. I'll think about it" is the answer.

Personal selling is by no means an inexpensive activity. In fact, it is an importer's most expensive device for contacting buyers. Sales calls cost companies on the average $153 per call in 1982, and the expenses associated with personal selling are expected to steadily increase in the future.

Sales Promotion

Sales promotions (coupons and premiums, for example) are specific tools to complement advertising and personal-selling efforts. These promotion tools have some unique features:

Communication: It heightens the consumer's awareness of the importer's product and can help trigger a decision that may result in consumption of the product.

Value: Sales promotion provides some incentive, such as an entitlement or bonus that is deemed valuable by the consumer.

Importers may use sales-promotion devices to have a faster impact, to highlight and enhance product offers, and to generate additional sales. Nevertheless, this tool is not effective in building long-run brand preference.

Publicity and Public Relations

This tool is a double-edged sword for it can be positive or negative depending on public opinions. The attractiveness of publicity is based upon:

Credibility: Independent news stories appear to be more real and believable to readers than ads.

The element of surprise: Publicity will reach individuals that avoid salespeople and advertisements. The information reaches the consumer as news rather than as a sales pitch.

Marketers usually do not emphasize product publicity. When they do use it, it tends to be after the fact. Hence, a well-organized publicity effort that manages to consort with the other promotion-mix tools can be especially effective in implementing the import-promotion strategy.

Cross-Cultural Factors

International companies that wish to enter a market such as the United States can pursue several strategies for market penetration.[7] To seek market penetration effectively, a framework for considering alternatives is required. Given any product/market base, five strategic alternatives are available to the company seeking to introduce a product into a specific target market.

Import-Product–Communications Extension. In introducing a product into the U.S. market, importers can employ product extension which is the easiest and in many cases the most profitable marketing strategy. In every market in which a comparable product is sold, the importer attempts to offer its own product and use advertising and promotion themes and appeals similar to those of domestic competitors.

The importer must ascertain through market research whether consumer preferences are satisfied by the attributes of the product. CPC International was faced with this dilemma in its attempts to popularize Knorr dry soups in the United States. Dry soups are by far the most popular in Europe, and the firm attempted to replicate this in the United States. Unfortunately, due to poor market research, CPC woefully misread the potential for this product in the U.S. market. Taste-panel comparisons of Knorr dry soups with popular wet soups led it to go forward with Knorr. The problem was that while test-panel results strongly favored the Knorr product, the panel tests did not account for the real-life market conditions for soup, which include preparation as well as eating. Wet soups are ready to serve when heated. Dry soups, on the other hand, take 15 to 20 minutes of cooking time. This factor is crucial in soup-purchasing decisions, and it illustrated a misapplication of the extension strategy.

The product-communication–extension strategy is popular with multinational companies because of the cost savings involved. The two saving features are manufacturing economies of scale and elimination of product research and development costs. Considerable savings can also be made with the efficiencies stemming from the standardization of marketing communications.

Cost savings can be significant but should not distract importers from a more important objective: profit maximization. This may necessitate strategy adjustment or creation. In sum, product extension may well provide immediate cost savings, but it can often be extremely costly and financially calamitous.

Import-Product Extension–Communications Adaptation. For products that satisfy a different need or serve a different purpose under similar conditions in the domestic market, the only changes necessary pertain to marketing communications. For example, bicycles and scooters are considered recreation vehicles in the United States, given their usage patterns, whereas they are a basic mode of transportation in many other countries. The same is true for outboard motors, which are considered recreation-related sales in the United States but fishing- and transportation-fleet supplies overseas.

An import-product transformation results when a product designed to meet one particular need winds up serving multiple needs or one for which it was not initially intended. Surveying and monitoring consumers are excellent means by which to discover different and new uses for an imported product.

Food products provide some of the best illustrations of product transformation. For example, in Europe, dry soup powders are marketed as soups only, whereas in the United States, they are sold as appetizer dips and sauces. The difference is in marketing communications: the identical product—dry soup powder—is illustrated and described on the label to reflect the distinct uses in the European and U.S. markets.

One great advantage of this strategy is that the cost of implementation is relatively low. The necessary changes will be cosmetic since research and development, technology, production process, and inventory control do not require adjustment. Where costs do enter in, they center on the identification of different import-product functions and recasting marketing communications (such as advertising, promotion, and point-of-sale material) around the newly identified use.

Import-Product Adaptation–Communications Extension. This strategy assumes that the imported product will have the same function but under different use conditions in import markets. The approach used in international-product planning extends, unchanged, the communications strategy developed for the domestic market (source of the imported good) but adapts the product to conform to local use conditions.

Many products have been modified to function the same globally under varying environmental situations. Soap and detergent manufacturers who are involved in international business must alter their formulas to account for local water conditions, environmental regulations, and washing equipment. Agricultural chemicals (including fertilizers, herbicides, and insecticides) must be adjusted for different soil conditions, climate variations, and the kind and intensity of insect resistance. Household appliances and clothing are additional categories of imported goods that must be adapted to local-use conditions and preferences. Almost always the basic communication approach remains the same.

Dual Adaptation. Both the import product and communications content have to be adapted when there are the differences just cited. For example, certain Asian beers are bottled in dark, half-liter bottles with somber labels. U.S. import consultants would be prone to suggest, instead, a six-pack in cans or light-colored bottles with cheerful and imaginative labeling.

Import-Product Invention. Strategies based on adaptations and adjustments can certainly prove effective in international marketing; however, they fall short in responding to global market opportunities. U.S. importers of small appliances and personal-care goods who also distribute to South America would do well to source from a manufacturer whose product can be used with either 110- or

220-volt current. This would also indicate that the manufacturer has experience in international markets, can achieve greater economies of scale, and can provide the importer with a competitively priced, quality product.

In sum, certain products—and markets as well—must be adapted. Some are good candidates for adaptations, and others require no change at all. Just as companies' manufacturing costs differ, so too do their abilities to select and turn out profitable product adaptations.

THE IMPORT-PROMOTION MIX

In designing a promotion mix for an imported product, the firm must consider the effectiveness of each promotion tool in relation to the type of product market it has defined as its target market. The promotion mix varies significantly if the product is targeted for consumer or industrial markets. Consumer products require greater emphasis on mass-selling media, with other promotion tools as supportive of the mass-selling effort.

Sales promotion can be very helpful in increasing brand switching, attracting new uses for the product, strengthening the company's brand image, increasing awareness, and initiating trial and evaluation by new users. Personal-selling efforts should complement sales promotion activities by timely visits to wholesale and retail outlets to replenish orders, set up point-of-purchase displays, organize sample distribution, and so on.

On the other hand, industrial products require greater emphasis on personal selling and sales promotions. The more expensive and complex the industrial good is, the more it relies on personal selling. Advertising supports the personal-selling efforts by creating awareness, reminding the industrial buyers of the product, providing lead generation for sales representatives, and telling customers how to use the product and reassuring them of their purchase.

Mass Selling

The importer is in a better position to make mass-selling decisions than the foreign manufacturer of imported goods. The importer has knowledge of the market, familiarity with the sociocultural enviroment, and understanding of the role of mass selling for the success of the marketing strategy.

The development and design of a campaign requires the importer to weigh the changing conditions in the international environment such as government regulation, media availability, and marketing costs. From country to country, these conditions will differ markedly from those existing in the U.S. environment.

Media Mix

The importer's next task is to select advertising media to get the message across. Decisions must center on desired reach, frequency, and impact; merits and availability of the major types of media and specific media vehicles; and the timing of media.[8]

It is vital that the media planner know the capabilities of the principal media types to deliver reach, frequency, and impact. Naturally, there are certain advantages and disadvantages to each medium. In choosing among media categories, media planners place greatest emphasis on the target audience's media habits, the product, message content, and cost. Key media types include:

> newspapers
>
> television
>
> direct mail
>
> radio
>
> magazines
>
> outdoor

Newspapers. This media type represents about 29 percent of total volume in major-media expenditures. For example, one page in the *Miami Herald* costs $11,800 during the week and $15,530 on Sunday. The newspaper provides flexibility, timeliness, and good local-market coverage. Moreover, this form of media is widely accepted and has high believability. Its drawbacks are that it has a short life and its reproduction quality is poor. It is also limited to the individual reading the newspaper, with little pass-along readership.

Television. The use of television as a media source accounts for approximately 22 percent of total promotional disbursements. A 30-second slot in prime time costs $4,500 in the fourth quarter (the Christmas season) with the other three quarters ranging from $500 to $1,500. Its cost fluctuates depending on the urban market being served and the time of day, based on when there are more or fewer viewers. Television allows for tremendous creativity through the combination of sight, sound, and motion. Effective artistic talents will enhance the spot's appeal to viewers' senses. However, it is important not to lose the message amid the artistic embellishments of the advertising. The cost is significant. Also, television is cluttered with numerous ads prior to and after the ad has been aired. With this type of media, there is little audience selectivity.

Direct Mail. Direct mail accounts for approximately 14 percent of promotion expenditures. This media type has strong advantages for the importer attuned to market segmentation. While there is not the large volume of competition that the other media have, this is becoming less the case as more media planners use this approach. A significant aspect of direct mail is its personalization. However, in comparison to other media types, this strategy has a relatively high cost.

Radio. Radio advertising represents approximately 7 percent of total promotion expenditures. For example, one minute of prime time in Miami costs on average from $80 to $120. There is fluctuation in rates here, as is the case with television, depending on the time of day and the coverage area of the radio station. With fairly low cost, radio allows high segmentation due to its geographic and demographic selectivity. However, the presentation is only audio and the attention span is lower than with television.

Magazines. This media type accounts for approximately 6 percent of total promotion expenditures. Due to its selective contents, magazines allow for high geographic, demographic, and life-style segmentation. Magazine advertising is perceived as prestigious and enhances the product's credibility. The quality of the reproduction is high and there is good pass-along readership. The media planner normally does not have a say about the location of the ad, and long ad-purchase lead times are required.

Outdoor. The lowest amount of promotion expenditures is allocated to outdoor advertising. A prime billboard costs $8,000 per month in Chicago, with location the major factor. Its low cost relative to high repeat exposure and low competition are its strong points. However, there is limited selection of audience and creativity.

Creative Decisions

Differences in creative strategies are vital to advertising success. Advertisers seek the different and the unique in individual campaigns. They have to realize, as well, that large advertising expenditures alone do not assure success. One study has concluded that the creativity factor is more important to a campaign's quality than the number of advertising dollars spent.[9]

A product has numerous attributes from which the most distinctive must be chosen. An ad should present just a few of these attributes and emphasize the most significant ones. Once alternative messages are developed, they are tested and the best one chosen. Creative designers employ various methods to obtain their advertising objectives. One method is to approach consumers and experts and extract good ideas. Their views concerning a product's strengths and limitations provide a wealth of data to develop a creative strategy. Importers should focus on consumer research that can help monitor consumer satisfaction in order to fine-tune the product to meet consumer needs and provide satisfaction.

Some creative people employ a deductive framework for producing advertising messages. One framework viewed purchasers as expecting one of four types of reward from a product:

rational

sensory

social

ego-satisfaction

Buyers visualize these rewards from result-of-use experience, product-in-use experience, or incidental-to-use experience. Using a four (reward type) by three (experience type) matrix produces twelve types of advertising messages. Themes can be produced for each of twelve advertising-message types depending upon the product. For example, the appeal "gets teeth brighter" is a rational-reward promise following results-of-use experience; and the catch phrase "be all that you can be" is a sensory-award promise tied to product-in-use experience.[10]

Basic promotion objectives can be aimed at getting the consumer to go through the Attention-Interest-Desire-Action (AIDA) model as illustrated in table 6–1. In essence, promotional efforts start with informing the consumer to build awareness and attention and develop his or her interest. The second phase involves persuading via communication efforts to stimulate evaluation and trial (desire) that will lead to repeat purchase decisions. As the product moves through its life cycle in penetrating the market, promotion efforts turn to reminder types of advertising to reinforce the decisions made by consumers and confirm and reassure consumers of their purchase.

Personal Selling

Of all the promotion tools available to the importer, personal selling is the most important, since it provides various options via person-to-person communication,

Table 6–1
AIDA Model and Promotion Objectives

Promotion Objectives	AIDA Model
Informing	Attention
	Interest
Persuading	Desire
	Action
Reminding	Action

oral presentations, and direct-selling activities. Effective communication is critical in dealing with foreign sellers. Interaction with potential customers is the key dynamic of personal selling, and it variously involves contact with other importers, foreign agents, import wholesalers, retailers, brokers, distributors, and, ultimately, the consumer. The greater the complexity of the product, product line, or system (such as flexible machine tool manufacturing), the greater the emphasis on personal contact and, therefore, on personal selling.

Personal-selling Strategies for Imports

Personal-selling strategies for imports include:

The importer: The importer has the option of acting as his or her own salesperson. This is often the practice with a small importing firm or a firm new to the import activity. The selling strategy will emphasize personal contact and developing better knowledge of the consumer and the market.

Sales representatives: The importer can use sales representatives to penetrate the market by establishing trade leads and contacting new customers. This strategy is effective in developing and expanding market opportunities.

Foreign sales force: The use of a foreign sales force can be a relatively inexpensive way of way of covering the market. However, a foreign sales force may not be as effective in the U.S. market context as the two previous strategies.

The critical factor in a successful import-selling strategy is establishing the right local distributorship. A careful and deliberate search for intermediaries who can offer highly effective sales support, combining traveling sales representatives and local sales operations, can surely strengthen the selling strategy. Additional promotion efforts that emphasize personal selling include:

Trade fairs. Specialized marketing events are one of the best ways to contact potential sellers from overseas markets. The foreign exporter of goods or services exhibits his or her wares, import orders are taken, and business leads can result. Whether the importer is new to the business or well established, trade fairs serve as a forum for contacts and commercial relationships between exporters, distributors, and intermediaries. There are many of these events in the United States throughout the year that can enable the importer to exhibit products to potential buyers.

Trade missions. Foreign governments—usually national, but also provincial/state and municipal—assist their private sectors in developing and expanding export activities. Foreign business executives and government representatives travel to the United States to stimulate trade, investment, joint ventures, licensing, franchising, and contract manufacturing. The importer can use these missions to acquaint potential buyers with products and suppliers.

The Sales Force

A company's link to its customers is its sales personnel. The customer may never have any direct dealings with the company as all transactions may be handled through the salesperson. The salesperson can also provide valuable information about the consumer to fine-tune marketing strategies. Therefore, the importer must analyze the issues of sales-force design, such as setting sales-force objectives, strategy, organization, size, and compensation.

The objectives of the sales force must center on the feature of the importer's target markets and the position it hopes to achieve in these markets. A company must recognize personal selling's role in the marketing mix for effective customer service. Personal selling is costly but indispensable at certain stages of the buying process, such as the buyer-education, negotiation, and sales-closing stages.

As companies become more market-oriented, the sales force too must also become more market-oriented. Generally, salespeople are perceived as being concerned solely with sales volume, with the marketing department responsible for marketing strategy and profitability. Increasingly, however, salespeople are expected to know how to achieve customer satisfaction and generate company profit. They should be skilled in analyzing sales data, assessing market potential, collecting market intelligence, and developing marketing strategies and plans. Analytical marketing skills are becoming much more important for sales representatives, particularly at the higher echelons of sales management. Marketers view a market-oriented, rather than a sales-oriented, sales force as the more effective in the long term.

By organizing contacts between people in the buying and selling organizations, the importer serves as the account manager. Selling requires support from various functions in the organization. Teamwork is required from top management, particularly when major accounts are concerned: technical people furnish technical information to the customer prior to, during, and after the purchase; customer service representatives offer installation, maintenance, and miscellaneous services to the customer; and office staff back all in-house phases of the sale.

Sales-Force Structure. The structure of the sales force is relatively simple if the import firm offers one product line to one end-using industry whose customer base is scattered. In such a case, the firm employs a territorial-structured sales force. A product-structured or customer-structured sales force is common if the company sells a variety of products to many different kinds of customers. The various structures are described next.

Territorial-structured Sales Force. The sales representative is assigned a specific territory and handles the company's total product line in this region. This structure avoids all ambiguity as to the responsibilities of each salesperson. All positive/negative results, within the scope of activities the salesperson can control, can be attributed to the salesperson's efforts. Given this autonomy, the salesperson is motivated to cultivate local business and develop personal ties. There are cost savings, as well, because of the limited area that needs to be covered. Decisions about the shape and size of the territories are fundamental in designing sales regions. In carving out these territories, specific criteria are applied:

ease of access and administration,

facility in estimating sales potential,

travel time,

sufficiency and fairness of workload distribution among the sales force.

Product-structured Sales Force. In some industries, sales representatives' knowledge of the technical aspects of the product is vital. In this case, companies structure their sales force along product lines. Where the products are extremely complex, not related to one another, or very numerous, product specialization is required.

Customer-structured Sales Force. Import firms often structure their sales force along customer lines. Different sales forces can be assigned to serve different industries, large versus small accounts, and current versus potential customers. This structure may help the sales force accumulate wealth of information concerning the needs of the customer. This information is valuable for strengthening the development of marketing strategies. Additionally, a customer-specialized sales force can be cost-effective, since the sales force can be staffed by technically knowledgeable persons where needed, but less skilled persons elsewhere as appropriate.

Complex-Structure Sales-Force. For import firms that sell a broad range of products to many kinds of customers all over the country, a combination of arrangements shapes the sales-force structure. The team may be organized by region-product, region-customer, or even region-product-customer. It is not uncommon for a sales-force representative to report to one or more line and staff managers.

Compensation. An attractive compensation package is essential in attracting talented sales representatives. Sales representatives are interested in a regular income, performance bonuses, and remuneration based on experience and longevity. Management, however, is concerned with cost-effectiveness, control, and simplicity. These differences in outlook explain the wide variety in compensation packages among the employers in the import business.

Management is responsible for establishing the features and extent of its compensation package. One of the first decisions it must make is how to position its import firm in comparison with the going market price. In some cases, the market conditions will dictate what rate it will pay its salespersons; however, given the tremendous variation in remuneration packages, making comparisons is extremely complex.

An import company must decide on the components of compensation for its sales force. These comprise a fixed amount, a variable amount, expenses, and fringe benefits. The fixed amount generally means a salary and meets the need for a regular income. The variable amount (which includes commissions, bonuses, and profit sharing) is to enhance motivation, effort, and performance. Expense accounts allow the salesperson to incur costs deemed necessary for selling (such as Broadway theater tickets for important foreign exporters visiting the United States to seek a distributor for their products). Fringe benefits include paid vacations, health care, annuities, life insurance, and stock options. Their purpose, collectively, is to provide job security and promote satisfaction in the workplace.

Management must determine the breakdown of each type of remuneration for its particular operation. For example, one formula may allocate 70 percent to a fixed income and the remaining 30 percent to other components in the package. There is no set formula to use as a guide. However, in jobs where most of the tasks are nonselling and in jobs where the selling function is technically complex, fixed compensation should have greater weight.

Structuring remuneration policies and plans should be based on the impact each feature has on sales-force motivation, specific product emphasis, and overall administration, including nonsales duties. Utilizing both fixed and variable components in the compensation mix, management controls the sales incentives and assures that administrative duties will be maintained. Adding to the complexity is employers' growing tendency to provide employees with a choice of fringe benefits. In this way, the employer attempts to satisfy the employee's personal needs in the hope that this will lead to increased effort and performance. The result is a sales force where each salesperson has his or her own customized compensation package.

SALES PROMOTIONS

Aimed at stimulating consumer buying and awareness of the imported product or product lines, sales promotions can be effectively used by importers. These activities include point-of-purchase displays, specialty advertising (such as T-shirts, pens, matches, and ashtrays), samples, coupons, and contests among the dealers and consumers.

Importers who use these devices find them to be quite an effective sales tool and complementary to their overall promotion efforts. This type of activity keeps the consumer's awareness of the product and the company high. Importers will find that consumers are appreciative of these devices as most consumers enjoy receiving something free. However, the cost of these items, including import duties and shipping costs, must be incorporated into the promotion budget of the import firm.

The arsenal of sales-promotion tools consists of a wide variety of promotion devices aimed at stimulating earlier and/or stronger market response. These are tools for consumer promotion, trade promotion, and sales-force promotion. Most organizations (including manufacturers, distributors, retailers, trade associations, and nonprofit institutions) use sales-promotion tools.

The tremendous increase in sales promotion in consumer markets may be attributed to several factors. Internal factors include promotion's ready acceptance as an effective sales tool by senior management; product managers' increased ability to use sales-promotion tools; and pressure on these same managers to boost sales performance. External factors that have spurred the growth of sales promotion are:

the sheer number of brands available (a continuing trend),

the industry itself becoming more promotion-oriented,

economic hardships (such as inflation and recession) making the consumer a "deal-seeker,"

importers demanding more deals from foreign vendors.

Sales promotion and advertising are often used to erode competitor brand loyalty. The promotion mix must blend the right combination and dosage of the two. Sales-promotion–to–advertising ratios can range from 20:80 to 80:20 with current trends being toward higher ratios due to consumers' greater price-sensitivity. Management's concern is that the ratio not rise too high lest it cheapen the perception of the product.

Sales-Promotion Tools

Sales-promotion tools serve many purposes. The intent is to find new customers and reward loyal customers. Brand switchers and consumers looking for bargain prices or premiums are also attracted. This means that the increase in sales will be, for the most part, short-term. Long-term sales increase is not attained in this manner, unless consumers are very satisfied by the product and discontinue switching. In planning an effective sales-promotion campaign, the importer must consider the type of market, promotion objectives, competitive factors, and cost and efficacy of each promotion tool. Some key tools are samples, coupons, price packs, premiums, and point-of-purchase displays and demonstrations, which will be discussed next. Other types include dealer promotions (push money, buying allowances, free goods, contests, and so on) and sales-force promotions (such as bonuses and contests). These sales-promotion tools are used to gain the cooperation of wholesalers, retailers, and salespersons.

Samples. These offers to try the product free of charge are the most effective (yet most costly) means for introducing a new product.

Coupons. These vouchers provide the bearer with a discount on the purchase of a particular product. This method is effective in boosting sales when a product has "peaked" (reached the mature stage of the product life cycle) and in promoting early testing of a new brand. To be effective, the appropriate range of savings should be 15–20 percent of the purchase price.

Price Packs. This promotion entails savings off the regular price of a product. These include the "reduced-price pack" (for example, two for the price of one) and "banded pack" (such as two related products together, such as hair shampoo and conditioner). Price packs are even more effective than coupons in achieving short-term sales.

Premiums. Goods are offered cheaply or free to entice the buyer to purchase a specific product. The premium can be the package itself, if reusable (such as a tote bag). The importer can offer the consumer a variety of premiums (T-shirts, decals, or buttons) carrying the importer's name.

Point-of-Purchase Displays and Demonstrations. These promotional devices are employed at the point of purchase or sale. This approach is often seen in food retailing, where a large display is shelved with the product and a sales representative is distributing the product, demonstrating its capabilities and educating the consumer about its use.

Timing and Implementation

Each sales-promotion program must be carefully planned, implemented, and controlled, with special attention up front to cover lead time and sell-off time. Early on, the marketing and sales-promotion group needs to plan, develop, and change, wherever necessary, the packages or materials to be distributed. At the same time, the team needs to design the advertising campaign and point-of-sale materials; alert and organize the sales representatives in the field; and allocate, produce, position, and release inventories for the various distribution locations.

Although the assessment of sales-promotion effectiveness is vital to sound import marketing, it is often neglected by import companies. When sales-promotion effectiveness is measured, however, it is usually done by evaluating sales performance prior to, during, and folllowing the promotion program. It is important for import managers to allow a sufficient period of time before a final assessment of the impact of sales promotion on sales.

Essential to the total promotion mix, sales promotion must be well conceived, goal-oriented, equipped with the proper tools and techniques, and effectively implemented.

Publicity

Publicity, another key promotion device, entails obtaining editorial space (as opposed to paid advertisements) in any mass medium that might reach the target audience or customers. Among the most versatile of promotion tools, publicity can be utilized to promote an imported product or product line, a brand name, a location, a concept, an activity, an organization, or a country. To illustrate, a number of Caribbean Basin nations engaged Washington-based government or public relations firms to develop or improve their image, to lobby for economic and/or military-support funds and improved trade terms, and to promote tourism and foreign direct investment.

At the firm level, publicity aids in the company's overall public-relations efforts. These efforts are aimed at creating or strengthening a positive image of the firm (including that of a socially responsible enterprise) and successfully dealing with negative, damaging, and unfounded rumors and stories. Among the tools used are media relations, product publicity, corporate public affairs and communications, lobbying, and public-issues management.

Publicity can definitely yield great benefits to the firm vis-à-vis its public image at a much smaller cost than advertising. But the media must judge the story angle newsworthy. If they do, media space and time are free, and benefits could be equal to six or seven figures in advertising expenditures—not to mention greater credibility.

Promotion Strategies

A sound import-promotion strategy requires management to design, implement, and manage communication with customers. The strategy entails the assignment of each important promotion activity to the various facets of the promotion mix. Each one adds an important dimension to the promotion strategy, and they are by no means mutually exclusive. The importer needs to combine these elements in a manner that will optimize the promotion objectives. The first task in developing a sound import-promotion strategy is to set promotion objectives and identify a target market. The import-promotion strategy may require a modest effort employing only a few sales representatives, or it may entail the launching of an advertising program. To properly focus the promotion strategy and assure the effectiveness of each component for the import strategy, every component is evaluated within the context of the overall import-promotion strategy.

Push versus Pull

The company's choice of a push or pull strategy as a promotion objective strongly influences the promotion mix. With a push strategy, the sales force and trade promotion are used to push the product through the channels. The manufacturer heavily promotes the product through wholesalers; the wholesalers, in turn, do the same vis-à-vis the retailers; and retailers aggressively promote the product to consumers. With a pull strategy, large advertising expenditures and heavy consumer promotion are used to develop consumer demand. An effective strategy results in consumers asking for the product from their retailers, the retailers passing on the request to wholesalers, and the wholesalers turning to the producers to supply goods, which effectively results in the product being "pulled" through the channels of distribution. An import firm's preference for push or pull will depend on the product and its strategy.

The optimal or proper mix depends upon the type of product and its relative value. For example, the pull strategy would be appropriate for a consumer product that is frequently purchased, that has a relatively low unit value, and whose target market is relatively large, geographically dispersed, but highly accessible through mass media. Conversely, a product that has a complex technical nature, is infrequently purchased, and enjoys a relatively high unit value might require a strong emphasis on personal selling and would use a push strategy.

Pull or push promotion techniques also use different sales-promotion strategies. For example, a pull strategy requires sampling, premiums such as free-in-pack or free-in-mail premiums, as well as point-of-purchase promotions. Push strategies require cooperative advertisement, promotion allowances, and sales-force contests. Additionally, merchandise-incentive programs (such as merchandise allowances, "push"-money bonuses for middlemen, management assistance to channel members through sales-force training, and inventory control) as well as financial assistance in the form of credit and discounts are also very important techniques.

There is, really, no absolute or optimal mix that can be mentioned as the strategy to follow for a given product. The market is dynamic and consumer preferences are in a constant flux. Competition can also influence the strategy to follow. Consequently, an understanding of the marketplace and the competition's marketing strategy should help the importer in focusing on the right strategy to follow.

Promotion in the Product Life Cycle

The product–life-cycle theory of international trade is one of the major concepts in explaining trends in importing. It argues that products, like human buyers, develop in stages: birth, growth, maturity and decline. As the theory applies to promotion, one can observe the following pattern:

Introductory (Birth) Stage. The objective of communications at this stage is to build a general awareness of the imported product or service and its advantages over the competition. The optimal media mix at this stage emphasizes personal sales, testing, and publicity, along with a large dose of introductory advertising. The extent of the effort during this stage depends on the compatibility of the imported product with the U.S. market.

Growth Stage. The development of brand preference among wholesalers, distributors, and consumers is the principal objective of communications at this stage. The media mix emphasizes mass media and the design of sales promotions aimed at attracting dealers. The thrust of the promotion effort in this stage is to penetrate the market and secure a market niche as competitors are likely to imitate the product moving into the later growth stages of the Product Life Cycle (PLC).

Maturity Stage. This stage calls for maintaining the loyalty of consumers and the trade. Dealer promotions and sales-force promotions are the principal tools used in this stage. Creative methods are needed to boost the frequency of product/service usage, and the most effective use of mass media and dealer-oriented sales promotions are again emphasized.

Decline Stage. Costs are kept to a minimum, with expenses incurred only to maintain a profitable distribution. All media efforts are withdrawn. Consequently the product will float (or sink) on its own.[11]

Evaluating the Promotion Strategy

The importer—and the import-management company, as well—are the pivotal points for an effective promotion strategy. Since the manufacturer is a foreign supplier, sound communication with the market begins with the importer as the nexus between the foreign exporter and the import market. This link is critically important, as the importer very often must serve as the "eyes and ears" of the foreign manufacturer, gathering business intelligence, monitoring the competitive environment, and suggesting necessary marketing (and, at times, manufacturing) changes.

At the heart of a successful import operation, then, is an effective importing organization. The performance level of the import strategy lies in the effectiveness of the importer.

A successful responsive importing organization will:

Know and identify with the foreign manufacturer. Importing organizations should understand the company's history, objectives in the U.S. market, organizational structure, financial structure, and sales volume.

Know the company's products. Importers need to understand how a product is produced (the production methods and technology) as well as the target market(s) that the product might satisfy.

Know the characteristics of both customers and competitors. Understanding the target market and competitors' product offerings in the marketplace is the starting point for an effective marketing/promotion strategy.

A comprehensive marketing strategy requires the design and development of a promotion strategy and the implementation and coordination of the strategy to convey the company's product(s) to the target market. The import company must formulate a promotion-mix budget, allocating funds for advertising, personal selling, sales promotion, and publicity. Funds allocation and, of course, budget levels are decided upon by the importer, although it is not unusual for the exporter to contribute financial resources to this activity and to work closely with the import firm. In any case, the budget funds will be allocated taking into account the objectives of the promotion strategy. Effective and efficient implementation of these decisions are crucial along with the monitoring of results. The strategy at this point is fine-tuned to increase the likelihood that the promotion program will produce the desired results.

Summary

Promotion—the company's communication with the consumer about a product—is a vital component of the import-marketing mix. Importers wishing to enter a product into a market have the options of import-product–communications extension, import-product extension–communications adaptation, import-product adaptation–communications extension, dual adaptation, and import-product invention.

Advertising (newspaper, magazine, television, radio, direct-mail, or outdoor), personal selling, sales promotion, and publicity comprise the marketing mix. Personal-selling strategies require attention to sales-force design (territorial, product, customer, or complex structure) and compensation package. Sales-promotion programs include specific tools (samples, coupons, price perks, premiums, and point-of-purchase displays), publicity, timing, and implementation. A "push" technique or "pull" technique can be used to move a product through the distribution channel. Consideration must be given to competition as well as to the product's life-cycle stage.

Notes

1. J.M. Rathmell, *Managing the Marketing Function* (New York: John Wiley & Sons, 1969), p. 41.

2. Reprinted from *Marketing Definitions: A Glossary of Marketing Terms*, compiled by Ralph S. Alexander (American Marketing Association, 1960), p. 18.

3. Reprinted from *Marketing Definitions: A Glossary of Marketing Terms*, compiled by Ralph S. Alexander, published by the American Marketing Association (1960), p. 9.

4. Reprinted from ibid., p. 20.

5. Reprinted from ibid., p. 19.

6. The following section is summarized from Philip Kotler, *Marketing Management: Analysis, Planning and Control*, 5/E C 1984, pp. 623–625. Reprinted by Permission of Prentice-Hall, Inc., Englewood Cliffs, New Jersey.

7. This section is adapted from Warren J. Keegan, "Multinational Product Planning: Strategic Alternatives," *Journal of Marketing*, vol. 33 (January 1969), pp. 58–62.

8. Philip Kotler, *Marketing Management*, p. 645.

9. John C. Maloney, "Marketing Decisions and Attitude Research," in *Effective Marketing Coordination*, George L. Baker, editor, published by the American Marketing Association (1961), p. 595.

10. John C. Maloney "Marketing Decisions and Attitude Research," in *Effective Marketing Coordination*, George L. Baker, editor, published by the American Marketing Association (1961), p. 618.

11. The following section is excerpted from Kotler, *Marketing Management*, pp. 680–684, 661–662.

7
Import-pricing Strategy

Importing is a profit-oriented activity and, as such, is a key aspect of company operations. Similarly, pricing strategies relate the organization to its environment. The competition, the target market, and the importer's marketing effort all converge in these strategies. What the optimum price may be is governed by a series of factors that may or may not be under the importer's control. Hence, importers must develop an appropriate pricing strategy. This strategy includes setting pricing objectives, pricing methods, and implementation to address the issues that come under consideration in developing a pricing strategy: the cost of obtaining or supplying the product, the demand for the product in the marketplace, the environmental factors affecting the pricing strategy, and the company's profit objectives. This chapter examines the unique import-pricing constraints in the U.S. market as well as the fundamental aspects of the import-pricing strategy.

The Import Price

Pricing Strategy. The pricing strategy is a key element of the overall marketing strategy because of its impact on revenue to the company. As such, it is a very important aspect of the import-marketing mix. It is important to recognize that a company's dollar sales, sales volume, and profit are a function of how well the price is related to demand and environmental conditions in the marketplace. Similarly, pricing strategy can be a source of problems for the importer when the pricing strategy is first implemented as the firm has to consider a large number of factors that, in addition to product costs, affect the price of an imported product.

Price Escalation. An important consideration in formulating a pricing strategy is the additional costs of importing the product, which can affect the selection of foreign products. The increase in a foreign products's cost and price when transportation costs, importer costs (such as custom-house brokerage fees and freight forwarding charges) are added to a foreign factory price is referred to as price escalation. In addition, as the product moves through the channels of distribution, the landed cost of the product (that is, the cost of the product ex-customs in the United States) will reflect a price escalation that frequently increases the price significantly. Let us examine this price escalation via the example in the following table.

FOB value	U.S. $ 500
Freight and insurance	200
CIF value	$ 700
Markup (40%)	280
Quoted CIF price	$ 980
Import duties (10% of CIF price)	98
Landed cost to importer	$1,078

FOB: free on board, named point of destination

CIF: cost, insurance, freight, named point of destination

These costs incurred in the import activity are allocated to the importer. However, the landed cost to the importer will greatly vary depending on the terms of delivery to the final destination. The cost will also vary based on the risk and costs absorbed by the exporter in moving the goods. Also, the longer the channel of distribution, the more frequent the markups as goods travel through to their final destination.

The importer should be aware that in the United States, the typical markups range from 25 to 40 percent at wholesale level and as high as 150 percent at the retail level.[1] Consequently, the length of the channel of distribution and the type of distribution structure used will greatly affect the price-escalation factor as each channel member adds its markup to the landed-product cost.

Factors Affecting Import-price Decisions

Since pricing is the mechanism through which the firm attempts to meet its profitability objectives in the marketplace and insure the success of the firm, the importer (like the wholesaler and retailer that sell domestic products) must assess demand in the marketplace and other environmental factors that may affect the import-pricing strategy. Some of these factors are similar to those impacting domestic products. Others are unique to the import-pricing decision, including U.S. trade legislation and the economic and cultural situations.

Government Regulation

The import-pricing decision in the United States is affected by the legal/political environment, which includes the body of laws, government agencies, and lobbying groups that influence the legal and political processes. Government legislation on imports has increased steadily over the years, a trend that will probably continue, one of the major reasons being mounting pressure from lobbyists as the U.S. trade deficit rises. The U.S. government is being placed in the "hot seat" to protect consumers and the environment from a flood of imports.

Since 1986, there have been increases in imports from the EEC. This provides a favorable situation for consumers who may experience a higher quality of living with consumption of higher-quality and/or less expensive products. However, for the domestic producer, this is an unfavorable situation as the competitiveness of the market is intensified. The significant point for the importer is that current, reliable information is needed to understand the legal/political environment. As changes in the legislation are ongoing, any legislation that affects the importer's pricing strategies must be considered.

New Tax Reform Act of 1986. The New Tax Reform Act of 1986 is a prime example of changes in the legal/political environment. It contains changes that may significantly affect the pricing of imports from related companies. The act provides that an import-transfer price, for income-tax purposes, should not be higher than the value claimed for customs purposes. An import-transfer price is the price that a foreign company or subsidiary charges for its products to an importing unit that is a related company. For an international corporation, the transfer price has major impact on net income, since such pricing could, in theory, help achieve such objectives as tax minimization and avoidance of duties. The law purposely seeks to equate transfer pricing and custom valuation to determine the correct value of imported merchandise and accurately calculate duties.

This aspect of tax reform will doubtlessly be refined by future regulations. As a result, integration is needed for tax and customs planning. Competent counsel should be sought to review the importer's procedures for transfer pricing and customs valuation. Proper procedures are of value to the importer as the occasion may arise when the Internal Revenue Service and the Customs Service request verification that procedures are in accordance with the law. The 1986 law specifies that importers may claim a transfer price for customs purposes that is too low to be consistent with the transfer price they claim for income-tax purposes. The price cannot be higher than would be consistent with the value they claim for customs purposes. The term *customs value* means the value taken into account for purposes of determining the amount of any customs duties that may be imposed on the importation of any property.[2]

Price Discrimination. This is another aspect of the U.S. legal/political environment that has a bearing on the import-pricing strategy. In the United States, price discrimination occurs when sellers charge different prices to the same category of buyers for the same product sold in the marketplace. This can become a source of legal problems for the firm, if such price discrimination is found to be in violation of the Robinson-Patman Act. The Robinson-Patman Act of 1936 is most important to importers developing a price strategy. The Clayton Act outlawed price discrimination, but the Department of Justice was not very effective in prosecuting cases under the Clayton Act due to its vague references to price discrimination.

The 1930s saw the rise of large chain stores in the United States. This resulted in a feeling of discomfort by manufacturers because these large stores demanded large quantity discounts, advertising allowances, and brokerage fees when no brokerage services were performed. The discounts the larger stores could provide were taking away the market share of the small independent "mom-and-pop" stores, and brought about the anti–chain-store sentiment leading to the Robinson-Patman Act (which has been called the Anti-A&P Act). The courts have always felt that any form of price discrimination or price fixing "results in elimination of some form of competition."[3]

The objectives of the Robinson-Patman Act can be generally stated as follows: The primary aim is to amend the Clayton Act, which became outdated with the numerous changes in the marketplace. Second, the act outlaws price discrimination (not based on cost differential) between different purchasers of commodities of like grade and quality, where the effect is to lessen competition or tend to create a monopoly. Finally, the act regulates discrimination by not permitting advertising allowances, brokerage fees, and special services, unless these services are actually provided and available in equal terms to all buyers of the same category. For example, the services and allowances provided to consumers in the northeastern United States must be available in the southeastern United States for comparable products at comparable prices.

The implications to the importer are that for price discrimination to be permissible, the cost must be justified as a result of a marketing effort, manufacturing, selling, and/or delivery. Also, a level of good faith is expected to meet the competition. Finally, physically similar products must have a cost justification and package differentiation in order to have price differential.

Antidumping and Countervailing Duties. Another important consideration in import-pricing strategy is antidumping legislation. When the price of a product moving from one country to another is lower than the manufactured price, governments may intervene, alleging dumping by the importer. Before antidumping laws can be applied, the government in the importing nation must show that the price in the importing country is lower than the price in the exporting country and that, as a result, producers in the importing country are harmed. Most countries are signatories to the General Agreement on Tariffs and Trade (GATT) convention covering antidumping subsidies and countervailing duties and/or they have antidumping legislation aimed at protecting local producers from unfair foreign competition.[4] The GATT code defines dumping as a product priced at less than the normal value of the product in the exporting country. Theoretically, dumping benefits the consumer through lower prices. However, concern with unbridled business practices has led the U.S. government to carefully consider the impact of dumping in the U.S. market where such practices unfairly discriminate against the domestic producers. While dumping is difficult to prove, the courts have recognized it in such cases as steel from Japan, golf carts from Poland, and tomatoes from Mexico.[5]

The development of the International Antidumping Code dates back to the 1960s during the Kennedy Round. It entails a set of rules whose objectives insure that antidumping practices do not constitute an unjustifiable impediment to international trade. The code provides relief from injurious dumped imports (that is, those whose export prices are lower than home-market prices) and insures fair and equitable treatment of all parties concerned with antidumping proceedings.[6]

The countervailing-duty statute works to offset the unfair advantage arising from foreign-government subsidization of goods sold in the United States. In general terms, a subsidy is a bounty grant (usually provided by a government) that confers a financial benefit on the production, manufacture, or distribution of goods or services. This is not a unique concept, for all governments—including the United States—maintain a subsidy program of one type or another.

The impact of subsidies is significant, which caused the United States and other trading countries to formulate policies for the use of subsidies in the General Agreement on Tariffs and Trade. The GATT also contains provisions regulating the use of countervailing duties (special customs duties imposed at the border by importing countries) in an effort to offset the economic effect of a subsidy. This will prevent injury to domestic industries that might otherwise result from subsidized imports.

U.S. acceptance of the Subsidies Code was approved by the Congress on July 26, 1979, with the enactment of the Trade Agreements Act of 1979. Under the new Trade Agreements Act, countervailing duties are to be imposed on all subsidized imports originating in countries that apply the Subsidies Code to the United States, only where the subsidized imports are found to cause or threaten to cause material injury to a domestic firm in the United States. Imports of subsidized dutiable products originating in countries that have not signed the Subsidies Code generally will not benefit from this test of material injury. Duty-free imports will benefit from a material-injury test consistent with international obligations of the United States. The Trade Agreements Act of 1979 provides for numerous changes in U.S. trade laws as it applies to subsidies, countervailing duties, and other countermeasures. We will not provide great detail of this act. Suffice to say that if an importer is included under the act's classification, further details should be obtained.[7]

These laws and codes are complicated and sometimes it is difficult to understand how they operate. Some ambiguous areas may become more comprehensible if we analyze common areas of misunderstanding.[8]

Antidumping and countervailing-duty laws correct inequities to U.S. firms. The United States levies duties on merchandise sold in the United States at "less than fair value" if such sales cause or threaten material injury to or materially retard the establishment of a U.S. industry. By imposing penalties, countervailing-duty legislation checks the unfair competitive advantage foreign manufacturers and exporters receive from foreign-government subsidies such as grants, loans, preferential rates, or special tax exemptions. Merchandise is considered to have been sold at a price below fair value when the producer's charge for the product in the United States is less than the producer's home-market price for the same or similar products, after adjustments have been made for differences in the merchandise, quantities purchased, and circumstances of sale.

It is all fine and good to have policies and laws to protect U.S. producers, but the laws must be enforced. An investigation is usually started when a petition is filed with the U.S. Department of Commerce and U.S. International Trade Commission. The petition should allege unfair competition from either dumped or subsidized products and must support these allegations with information that is reasonably available to the petitioners. Persons or groups who are eligible to file antidumping or countervailing-duty petitions include:

A U.S. manufacturer, producer, or wholesaler of a product similar to the imports in question,

A certified or recognized union or group of workers that represents an industry engaged in manufacturing, producing, or wholesaling a product in the United States similar to the imports in question,

A trade or business association, the majority of whose members manufacture, produce, or wholesale a product in the United States similar to the import in question.

In the absence of a petition, the Department of Commerce is allowed to initiate investigations itself. The department exercised this authority in December 1985 when it began an antidumping investigation of certain semiconductors from Japan.

U.S. Trade Legislation. Pricing is affected by U.S. laws regulating pricing decisions in many instances, as indicated in the previous section. In the United States, generally there are fewer restricitons governing pricing than in most countries other than those coming under antitrust legislation. While the firm must comply with these regulations, recent U.S. trade laws may, in many instances, ease import restrictions, which may allow importers to offer products at lower prices.

Under U.S. trade laws, products eligible for entering U.S. customs under the Generalized System of Preference (GSP) and the Caribbean Basin Initiative (CBI) receive duty-free treatment. This can significantly affect pricing and competitive situations in the U.S. markets.

The GSP provides duty-free arrangement for imports of less developed countries (LDCs) and is in effect until July 4, 1993. The GSP continues the mandatory exclusions listed in the 1974 Trade Act:

textile and apparel articles subject to the Multi-Fiber Arrangements,

watches,

import-sensitive electronic, steel, and glass products,

certain footwear articles

In addition, the 1984 extension of the GSP adds the exclusion of:

leather handbags,

luggage,

flat goods,

leather and other leather wearing apparel.[9]

Other products must meet the legislation requirements listed in chapter 2.

The CBI was developed to help a specific group of LDCs, namely countries in the Caribbean and Central America.[10] Designated beneficiary countries can export products to U.S. markets and receive duty-free treatment if legislation requirements are met. Products that are not included in the duty-free treatment are:

textile and textile products,

watches and watch parts,

petroleum and its derivatives,

canned tuna,

leather and leather goods.[11]

In summary, the importer who is eligible for GSP and CBI treatment has the trade advantages of duty-free access to U.S. markets, which comes down to a favorable pricing position. More details on the GSP and CBI appear in chapter 10.

Foreign-Exchange Fluctuations

One important consideration in importing is the fact that a minimum of two currencies are involved in every transaction. While the problem of obtaining foreign exchange or payment is not within the immediate concerns of importers, who pay for their purchases with dollars, foreign-exchange fluctuations are an important consideration inasmuch as they can make the dollar "buy more" when the dollar is strong against another country's currency. For example, a supplying country that suffers currency devaluation will find its exports become cheaper, thus providing the exporter with more value for its dollar expenditures. Since adjustments begin to develop as a devaluation occurs, importers should be aware of currency developments in supplying countries to be able to reap advantages from such devaluations.

Similarly, the importer can seek to minimize loss of purchasing power of the dollar when the dollar devaluates or loses value vis-à-vis other currencies in world markets. The foreign-exchange market technique known as "hedging" can help reduce the company's exposure when faced with loss of profits resulting from an unfavorable exchange fluctuation. Hedging may be described as the actions that may be taken in foreign markets to minimize the cost of devaluations and revaluations of currency fluctuations.[12]

To illustrate the hedging process, assume that an importer needs to pay $100,000 for foreign goods quoted in Swiss francs at a prevailing exchange rate of SwF 1.7010 per U.S. dollar or SwF 170,100. The importer, knowing that a given amount of Swiss francs will have to be delivered at a future date and expecting the dollar to devalue, may purchase spot exchange at the time of delivery and take the loss. For example, if the dollar devalues so that the foreign-exchange rate now is SwF 1.65 per dollar, the amount due would be $103,090.91. This represents a loss of $3,090.91 from the foreign-exchange fluctuation. Consequently, the importer may choose to buy Swiss francs in the 30-, 90-, or 120-day forward market. A forward purchase of foreign exchange is a contract to obtain a specified amount of foreign currency on a specific date at a specific rate of exchange. In this case, the importer would buy a futures-exchange contract in the amount of SwF 1.688 for a dollar equivalent of $100,770.14. Thus, the importer is assured of paying the stipulated dollar amount and having the necessary foreign currency available at the price determined by agreement with the Swiss exporter. It should be noted that forward contracts of this kind should not be considered speculative as they are simply a way to offset or insure against a potential economic loss during periods when the U.S. dollar shows tendencies toward devaluation.[13]

Competition

The U.S. market is a highly competitive one in which products from all over the world are sold. Import-pricing strategies need to consider the competitive environment that a product encounters in the marketplace. It should be noted that in the U.S. market, country of origin may not be an advantage, because shoppers are so accustomed to foreign products that their purchasing behavior does not necessarily include country of origin as a determinant of purchasing decision. Therefore, pricing strategies must respond to the competitive environment. An example: A couple of New Yorkers go through the stack of men's dress shirts at Alexander's department store. They closely compare fabric contents, the shirts' cuts, and prices, but not their countries of origin. The shirts are made in Korea, but that is not an issue to the two shoppers. As the couple indicates, the family budget comes before nationalism.[14]

Channel Relationships

A given channel structure will affect the pricing strategy inasmuch as importers need to consider the different markups and incentives needed in order to maintain middleman interest in stocking and selling the imported product. The type of product, the type of presale and postsale services needed, and the incentives required to develop and maintain a channel structure influence the pricing decision.

Buyers' Reactions to Price and Product Strategies

In implementing the pricing strategy, the importer must recognize that consumers choose among products that might satisfy a given need. The guiding concept is value. In the consumer mind, the price of the product must be such that it provides him or her with the most value per dollar, assuming that the consumer is a rational, utility-maximizing person.

Buyers' reactions to product prices vary depending on the product cost in relation to their total income, their degree of need, and the availability of substitutes. Moreover, buyers' reactions to product prices are not universal, but rather change over time and may vary from consumer type to consumer type. Consumers do not always have a straightforward interpretation of prices or price changes. Understanding demand and the marketplace can help reduce error that may arise from an inadequate pricing strategy.

Cost and Profit Expectations

Price is a major factor in generating revenue. This can be expressed in a formula:

$$\text{total sales} = \text{summation of (price} \times \text{quantity)}$$

That is, the total sales of the company is the sum of the products of all items sold times their prices. This revenue should be high enough to cover all costs and profit expectations of the firm, including all the costs associated with importing the product.

Stage in the Product Life Cycle

After introducing a product in the U.S. market, the importer hopes the product will have a long life in the marketplace. However, the importer will need to reformulate pricing strategies to reflect the changing market conditions as the product moves through its life cycle. Strategies generally will be adapted as follows.

Introductory Stage. During the introductory stage, the importer's appropriate strategy depends both upon how distinctive its new product is and how long it expects this distinctiveness to last. The more distinctive and unique the new product is, the greater the range the importer has in pricing. If the product is highly distinctive, a revolutionary new product with no comparable product in the market, the importer has greater freedom to choose from a wide range of prices. However, if the product's distinctiveness is low, with comparatively minor changes from existing and substitute products, the importer has much less freedom in pricing and may select a level just above the competitive substitutes. Similarly, the longer the period during which an importer expects its new product's distinctiveness to last, the wider the range of possible profitable prices. During this stage, high trade discounts may be necessary to cover the market.

The importer must keep in mind that regardless of the product's distinctiveness, it will not be free from competition. The pricing strategy should take into consideration that the product distinctiveness will deteriorate in a relatively short time as competitors enter the market.[15]

Growth Stage. In the growth stage, the importer's pricing strategy must increasingly take direct account of the pricing strategies of its competitors, one by one, as they enter the market. If price skimming (high price) was implemented during the introductory stages, a switch may be made to penetration pricing (low price) in stages as the competitive factors become significant.

During the market-growth stage, while the pricing strategy becomes increasingly dependent upon those of its competitors, nonprice competition also increases. Greater emphasis should be placed on broadening the market by increasing promotion-pricing opportunities and product improvement.

Maturity Stage. At this stage in the product life cycle, competition stabilizes. The strategy is directed at defensive pricing to maintain market share. The leading brands generally cannot command as high a price as previously, unless the seller has been able to secure consumer and trade loyalty. The importer should keep a watchful eye out for innovative pricing strategies (rebates, dealer-oriented discounts, and so on) in order to stabilize market share. At this stage, the importer must also keep a careful watch for product improvements, new imports, and new brands making inroads into market share.

Decline Stage. Once the product has reached this stage of the product life cycle, the number of players in the game has decreased. Maintenance of profit levels is the name of the game. Promotion efforts are trimmed to maximize profits. This strategy is commonly referred to as run-out strategy, harvesting the product, or milking the product. Promotion costs are cut back and what is normally left are the hard-core consumers who habitually purchase the product.

Elements of the Import-pricing Strategy

The pricing decisions in U.S. markets are very complex and important. Price is a vital component in a successful import-marketing strategy that generates sales and revenue. Inadequate pricing strategies can quickly doom a product in the marketplace and hinder the company's efforts to enter the market with a salable product. Today, environmental factors force the firm to interpret the needs of its consumers and provide them with a product that is adequately priced to obtain their favorable response. The success of the firm may well depend on how well it interprets its target-market's needs and values and adjusts all elements of the marketing strategy to respond to these needs. Pricing is the key variable in the marketing strategy that brings the strategy elements into focus and provides the firm with the means (revenue) to carry out its marketing objectives in the marketplace.

Pricing Objectives

The initial step in developing an import-pricing strategy is to examine the pricing options available to a firm and to establish clear-cut guidelines that relate to the pricing variable in the import-marketing strategy. Pricing objectives do not stand in a vacuum, but should be consistent and be derived from the company's overall and marketing objectives. Pricing objectives are the broad guidelines that relate the company's product to its environment and its target market. Objectives provide well-defined guidelines that relate the role of price in the import-marketing strategy and the firm's purpose in developing and exploiting an identified export-market opportunity. There are three general types of pricing objectives:

> sales-oriented objectives,
>
> profit-oriented objectives,
>
> status-quo objectives.

Sales-oriented Objectives. These are stated in terms of entry and growth in a target-market through high volume of sales. The objectives may be stated in dollar sales, volume, or market share. The major efforts are directed toward securing market position by entering and growing in the market in a specific time frame. Profits are attained subsequent to gaining market share and increased volume of sales. Sales-oriented objectives are consistent with desire to obtain control in the targeted import market.

Profit-oriented Objectives. These are stated in terms of a dollar amount, a percentage markup over expenses, or return on investment. A major goal of profit-oriented objectives is to develop an adequate level of profits in the long term. Import sales, market development, and investment costs must meet profitability objectives. A secondary goal is to carve out a niche in the market, serving specific market segments as a means to attain and maintain profitability levels.

Status-quo Objectives. These are stated in terms of "meeting the competition," "maintaining market stability," or "sustaining competitive edge." Such objectives are suitable for the importer who wants to penetrate the smaller market segments without attracting the attention of the other players in the market. The objectives are not always emphasized, but meeting the competition or stable pricing policies are still significant goals.[16]

Pricing objectives are the fundamental guidelines of the import-pricing strategy. The importer should take into consideration the needs of the market, environmental influences and constraints, and the firm's commitment to its import transactions when expressing its objectives. Objectives underlie the pricing policies that the firm develops to enable it to implement its pricing decisions.

Pricing Policies

Import-pricing policies represent the strategic course of actions the importer selects after careful consideration of all the factors that affect the pricing decision. In developing strategic import-pricing policies, the importer must answer to the firm's international commitment, its financial capabilities, and the environment in which it competes. The strategic policies stated by the import firm will guide present and future decisions in the target market and will enhance the importer's chances for success. Pricing objectives enable the firm to insure growth, market share, profit, or noncompetitive position in the market. Import-pricing policies provide the guidelines for ascertaining these pricing objectives. Three types of policies merit consideration:

Penetration or low-margin pricing policy,

Skimming or high-margin pricing policy,

Competitive or market-oriented pricing policy.

Penetration or Low-Margin Pricing Policy. This is consistent with a sales-oriented objective. To enter and grow rapidly in a target market, the import firm needs to establish competitive prices. In order to capture a large segment of the target market, prices should be set below competitors'. The logic behind this approach is that sales volume will be high and acceptable profits will be made over the long haul. What is sacrificed in this case are short-term profits for long-term market share and market growth. Underlying this pricing option is the concept of elasticity of demand. When price changes by a small percentage and the quantity demanded changes by a larger percentage, then we can conclude that demand is elastic. The importer is making the assumption that the consumer is sensitive to price fluctuations (or, in other words, that demand is elastic). As a result, by coming into the market with a comparatively low price, larger volume sales are realized as consumers respond to this price by demanding larger quantities. Clearly, setting a price to generate desired volume of sales entails a thorough understanding of the important factors that affect demand in the marketplace. The overriding consideration is that gross margin or markup is low enough to penetrate a market, given the product's quality, costs, competition, and elasticity of demand.

Skimming or High-Margin Pricing Policy. This is consistent with a profit-based objective. To enter a market and obtain targeted profit levels, the import firm needs to establish a price that will generate the revenues required to reach profitability objectives. With this policy, the highest possible price is charged, taking into account the product's costs, quality, and competition. This option sacrifices long-term market growth for short-term profits. Demand is assumed to be inelastic when higher prices evoke only small percent changes in quantity demanded. In such a case, the high price will have no major impact on the sales volume needed to attain profitability. An important consideration in this pricing option is the relative distinctiveness, uniqueness, or need for the product in the import market so that a high margin can be applied without losing sales due to competitive pricing pressures.

Competitive or Market-oriented Pricing Policy. This is consistent with the status-quo objectives. The firm seeks to go along with established prices and minimize competitive pressures. Any price changes the importer undertakes should be in response to changes in the market. With this approach, the importer minimizes the chance to have a head-on confrontation with another competitor in the market. The pricing strategy here can be used effectively as a barrier to entry for potential new entrants. An important consideration in this pricing option is size of the firm relative to the competition and import-market size.

The strategic import-pricing policies selected must focus on the company's marketing and pricing objectives. A key ingredient in this process is flexibility to adapt to the environment as it changes from time to time. These policies must be audited periodically to appraise the impact of pricing on the corporation's competitive position, sales, and profitability.[17]

Pricing Methods

Importers frequently play the role of middlemen who buy goods outright for resale in import markets. They set prices by employing a standard markup, usually a dollar amount added to the costs of goods available for sale. The markup, which can be expressed as a percentage of selling price or cost, should be sufficiently large to cover the middlemen's overhead costs (clerical, inventory, administrative, and so on), all other costs (including those of estimated average returns, defective goods, and unsold inventories), and an adequate profit.

Imported-product cost includes the cost of acquiring the product plus all the related costs of importing (transportation costs, freight-forwarding costs, customs duties, brokerage fees). Having established the imported-product cost, the markup rate can then be applied to arrive at the final price for the importer.

Pricing Implementation

All previous pricing decisions will eventually be broken down into a series of prices that represent the company's offers in the marketplace. These are the actual prices that are quoted to potential customers. The actual price must include discounts or reductions on final selling price. These discounts may include special discounts for customers or trade discounts for intermediaries that reflect the cost of their services. An exporter selling through an importer-distributor might establish a 25 percent discount for the intermediary. These discounts are not arbitrary, but rather reflect the channel-strategy type of intermediaries to be used, channel functions required, and so on. Quantity discounts eliciting larger orders from customers and intermediaries can be offered and included in the price. There are different types of quantity discounts, and the firm should carefully examine the legal issues involved in granting them. Other discounts included in the basic price are cash discounts (for early payment when credit is extended), promotional discounts (which represent allowances made to intermediaries to advertise and promote the firm's products), and push money (money given to the intermediaries to pass on to the sales force or retailers to seek their cooperation in promoting the product). All of these discounts represent the export marketer's recognition that intermediaries need stimulation and compensation for services provided according to marketing objectives.[18]

Demand-responsive Pricing Strategies. Since the importer must respond to demand, this section will provide a "menu" of relevant pricing strategies that respond to demand:

Value-in-Use Pricing. This involves setting prices that will capture some of what customers will save by substituting the firm's product for one currently being used. For example, the manufacturer of an electronic word processor knows that its machine does not just merely replace a standard office typewritter, but also reduces secretarial costs.

Leader Pricing. This stategy involves setting some very low prices—real bargains—to get customers into retail stores. The idea is not to sell large quantities of the leader items, but to get customers into the store to buy other products.

Psychological Pricing. This invovles setting prices having special appeal to target customers.

Odd-Even Pricing. This entails setting prices that end in certain numbers. For example, product prices below $50 often end in the numbers 5 or 9, as in $49 or $24.95. For higher-priced products, prices are often $1 below the next even dollar figure, such as $99 rather than $100.

Prestige Pricing. This involves setting a rather high price to suggest high quality or high status. Some target customers want the "best" so they will buy at a high price. But if the price seems "cheap," they worry about quality and do not buy.

Price-Line Pricing. This approach involves setting a few price levels for a product class and marking all items at these prices. It assumes that customers have a certain price in mind that they expect to pay for a product.

Full-Line Pricing. This entails setting prices for a whole line of products. How to do this depends on which of two basic strategies a firm is using. In one case, all products in the company's line are aimed at the same general target-market, which makes it important for all prices to be related to one another. In the other case, the various products in the line are aimed at entirely different target-markets, so there does not have to be any relation between the various prices.

Complementary-Product Pricing. This involves setting prices on several products as a group. It may lead to one product being priced very low so that the profits from another product will increase, thus raising the product group's total profits. For example, Atari might set a low price for its video-game consoles. Once customers buy the console, they will buy Atari's games to go with it—at a nice profit for Atari![19]

Terms of Sale. In import pricing, it is customary to include in the price the delivery terms, indicating where the liability and obligations of the seller terminate during the actual physical movement of the goods. Shipping goods from one country to another entails a higher degree of risk than shipping goods within a domestic market. If the goods are lost or damaged, if delivery is delayed, or if goods are redirected to another destination, the delivery terms provide the basic tool to define the respective responsibilities of buyer and seller. In the U.S. market, it is customary to use FOB (free on board) terms. The "shopping list" that follows explains the terminology common to charges incurred in the importation process. Under all terms listed, the seller must supply the goods according to the contract of sale for timely delivery. This includes providing packaging, checking operations (measuring, weighing, and counting), and assisting the buyer, at the latter's request, in obtaining the documentation needed for importation. The buyer must take delivery for the goods as soon as they are placed at his or her disposal and bear liability for loss or damage, as well as other charges that apply from point of delivery to final destination. The buyer is usually bound to designate point of delivery; otherwise, when no specific point is named and there are several points available, the seller can select a point at the place of delivery that is most suitable to the seller's purpose.[20]

Ex works (ex factory, ex mill, ex plantation, ex warehouse, and so forth): *Ex works* means that the seller agrees to make goods available at works or factory and is not responsible for loading the goods on the vehicle provided by the buyer. The cost and risk of moving merchandise to the final destination must be incurred by the buyer.

FOR/FOT (free on rail, free on truck, named point of departure): *FOR/FOT* relates to railway wagons and trucks, respectively. With the specific delivery terms, the seller must place the merchandise on a specific vehicle, in sufficient weight to take advantage of quantity rate, in an appropriate type of vehicle, with proper loading and covering as per the sales contract. Should the carload or weight be insufficient for quantity rates, then delivery of goods must be made to a transporting company when such facilities are included on the rate of freight. The seller bears all risk and losses until the wagon (or truck) is loaded. The buyer assumes full responsibility from named loaded vehicle at named point of departure.

FAS (free alongside ship, named point of shipment): With FAS, the seller delivers merchandise at the loading berth alongside the ship within a specific time frame. Delivery of merchandise by the seller at the loading berth takes place within a specific time frame. It is the responsibility of the buyer to incur the cost and time of loading and the clearance of merchandise for export. During the transfer of merchandise from seller to buyer at shipside, liability for loss or damage to the merchandise is also transferred.

Free carrier (named point): This classification was developed to meet the requirements of modern transportation, such as multimodal transport and containers. It implies that the seller will deliver the goods into the possession of the carrier, who assumes complete responsibility. It is at this point that all liability for loss or damage is transferred to the buyer. The seller is required to obtain an export license or other official authorization needed for the export of goods.

FOB (free on board, named point of shipment): Under FOB terms, the seller places the goods on board a ship at port of shipment, incurring the cost and time of loading the merchandise on the carrier. The seller must obtain any export license or other government authorization required to export the merchandise. Liability for loss or damage is transferred to the buyer when the merchandise passes the ship's rail.

FOB (free on board, named airport of departure): This classification is comparable to *FOB vessel*, however the carrier is air transport. *FOB* in this case means that the seller delivers the merchandise into the possession of an air carrier/agent. At this point, the seller's responsiblity ceases but the arrangements for transport are conducted by the seller at the buyer's expense.

Freight/carriage paid to (named point of destination): Under this classification, freight costs are incurred by the seller to deliver merchandise to named point of destination. At the time goods are transferred to the first carrier, liability for loss or damages on the part of the seller ceases. If requested by the buyer, the seller must provide assistance in obtaining export documents.

C&F (cost and freight, named port of destination): *C&F* means that the seller must pay the costs and freight required to have the merchandise arrive at a specific port of destination and on board a seagoing vessel. The risk of loss and damage is transferred from seller to buyer when the merchandise passes the ship's rail. This seller must furnish the documents requested by the buyer, including a clean bill of lading.

Freight/carriage and insurance paid to (named point of destination): This classification is comparable to *freight/carriage paid to*, but included here is insurance for loss or damage to merchandise while in transport. The seller incurs all costs such as insurance and assumes responsibility until merchandise is transferred to the first carrier. The seller may be required to provide necessary export documentation if requested by the buyer.

CIF (cost, insurance, freight, named point of destination): This classification is comparable to *C&F*, but the difference is that insurance is included under this classification for merchandise during transit. The risk of loss and damage is still transferred at ship's rail and must be delivered with a policy of marine insurance in transferable form against the risks of carriage. Also, documents must be provided by the seller if requested by the buyer, including a clean bill of lading.

Ex ship (named port of destination): In this case, the seller makes the merchandise available to the buyer on board the ship at point of destination. Hence, the liability of loss is also transferred to the buyer at this time. The seller must provide the buyer with export documents and other documents that may be necessary to enable the buyer to take delivery of the goods.

Ex quay (named port of destination): Under this classification, the seller has the merchandise available to the buyer in the quay or wharf in point of destination. All costs to have merchandise available at this wharf are incurred by the seller. *Ex quay* has two derivatives: *Ex quay, duty paid* and *Ex quay, duties on buyer's account.* To avoid confusion, the full description should be used so both parties will know who is responsible for import duties.

Delivered duty-free (named point of destination in the country of importation): This classification requires the seller to deliver the merchandise and to pay for import duties and transport costs from import point to buyer's destination. This classification is all-inclusive with almost all responsibilities falling upon the seller and minimal responsibilities upon the buyer. The seller will accommodate the buyer by clearing the goods for import and delivering merchandise to the buyer's premises.

Summary

In conclusion, it should be stressed that when importers are setting a price, consideration must be made as to what consumers will be willing to pay, for in that acceptable range of pricing lies the firm's profits. Even though sellers spend a lot of time on pricing procedures and many people think companies go about pricing scientifically, pricing often remains an art. An adequate pricing strategy can go a long way in helping the importer determine the most marketable price.

In developing a pricing strategy, an importer should understand such legislation as the Tax Reform Act of 1986, the Caribbean Basin Initiative, and the General System of Preferences as well as regulations covering price discrimination, dumping, and countervailing duties. Other factors to consider include price escalation, foreign-exchange fluctuations, competition, channel relationships, cost and profit expectations, buyers' responses to price and product strategies, and the good's stage in the product's life cycle.

Pricing objectives may be sales- or profit-oriented or may merely be status-quo–related. The optimum pricing policy (penetration, skimming, or competitive) will be based on the pricing objective. Among the demand-responsive pricing concepts are value-in-use, leader, psychological, odd-even, prestige, full-line, and complementary-product pricing and price lining. Finally, an importer must be familiar with the various terms of sale when figuring prices.

There are also numerous regulations and economic and market conditions that an importer should be aware of when developing a pricing strategy for the U.S. market. In addition, the pricing strategy should be incorporated into the company's overall objectives and marketing strategy to have the good fit between the importer and the environment.

Notes

1. See also Edward W. Cundiff, Richard R. Still, and Norman A.P. Govoni, *Fundamentals of Modern Marketing*, 4th ed., (Englewood Cliffs, New Jersey, Prentice-Hall), p. 422.

2. See 19 U.S.C. 402.

3. For a summary of this and other related antitrust laws, see Richard P. Bagozzi, *Principles of Marketing Management* (Chicago: Science Research Associates, 1986), p. 527.

4. Tariff Act of 1930, 19 U.S.C. 1671.

5. Steven Plant, "Why Dumping Is Good for Us," *Fortune* (May 5, 1980), pp. 211–22.

6. *A Preface to Trade*, p. 95.

7. 19 U.S.C. 2501–82.

8. Antidumping and countervailing duties laws are well summarized in Phillip Otterness, Francis McPaul, and Kenneth Cutshaw, "The ABC's of American Trade Laws on Foreign Dumping and Subsidies," *Business America* (December 8, 1986), pp. 4–6.

9. Trade Act of 1974, subchapter V, 19 U.S.C. 2463(c).

10. For a complete list of designated countries, see chapter 2. See also 19 U.S.C. 2702(b).

11. See 19 U.S.C. 2703(b).

12. *Foreign Exchange Handbook for the Corporate Executive* (New York: Brown Brothers Harriman, 1970), p. 31.

13. Ibid., p. 32.

14. "Clothing Shoppers Talk Domestic But Look First for Style, Savings," *Wall Street Journal* (October 15, 1987), p. 31.

15. A complete discussion on this subject can be found in Cundiff, Still, and Govoni, *Fundamentals of Modern Marketing*, p. 281.

16. Adapted from Marta Ortiz-Buonafina, *Profitable Export Marketing*, pp. 144–45.

17. See ibid., pp. 145–46.

18. See ibid., p. 151.

19. E.J. McCarthy and W.D. Perreault, *Basic Marketing*, 9th ed. (Homewood, Illinois: Richard D. Irwin, 1984), pp. 504–9.

20. The following terms are summarized from *INCOTERMS* 1980 Edition (Paris: International Chamber of Commerce, 1980).

Part III
The Import Function

8
Processing the Import Transaction

The purpose of part III is to present the detailed steps necessary to initiate and complete the import transaction. Each of these steps will be traced in the import flow chart (figure 8–1). Also highlighted will be the three flows in the import activity:

financial flow (financing to pay import purchases), physical flow (traffic insurance),

documentation (documents necessary to comply with regulations of exporting and importing countries).[1]

A key feature of these import functions is that each is a separate activity, operating independently from the others. Nevertheless, all must be completed before the merchandise can be released by customs authorities and enter the importing country. To illustrate, in the financial flow, the importer must present and negotiate payment terms with the seller/exporter. The importer must then pay for the purchase by paying the seller directly or indirectly through a third party or enterprise such as a bank or other financial institution. The only activities involved in the financial-flow process relate to the facilitation of funds transfers from one nation to another. The accompaniment of shipping documentation may or may not be included. In the actual physical, shipping companies move the merchandise from one country to another (from export point to import point). The physical movement of goods, from warehouse to warehouse, requires documentation. Since evidence must be given that the merchandise has actually been shipped, an array of regulatory documents must be completed and filed. It is the shipping document, issued by the transportation firm, that ties together the financial, physical, and documentary flows. This document is, therefore, the most important certificate in the import process.[2]

This chapter will focus on the initial processing of the import transaction and financial flow. The subsequent two chapters address the physical and documentary flows.

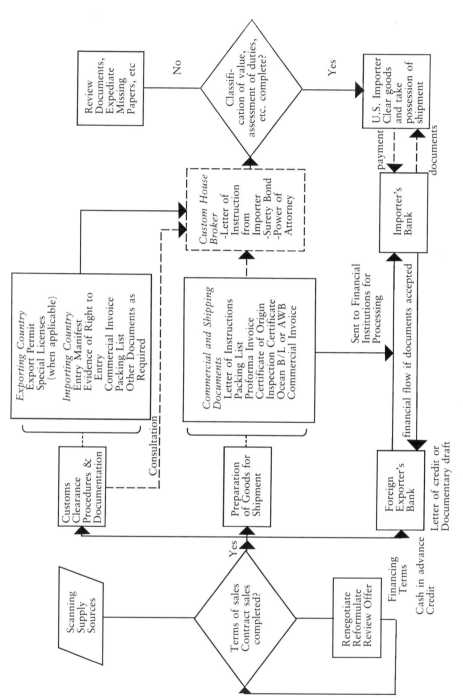

Figure 8–1. Import Process

The Import Process

Scanning Supply Sources

One of the most basic activities in import operations is scanning supply sources. In an import transaction, the two essential parties are the importer and the foreign supplier. The relationship with the supplier with regard to quality control is a major issue in successful business relationships. To successfully sell imported goods in the U.S. markets, it is extremely important that the supplier guarantee product quality for the initial as well as subsequent orders. Negotiations on quality and quality-control issues are among the key aspects of this initial phase of the import process. It is not enough to have an assurance of such quality. The importer should analyze and certify the quality-control procedures used by foreign suppliers. If minimum quality standards are not met, the importer may quickly lose customers and gain a poor reputation in import markets. Consequently, quality-control issues should be conducted in a spirit of mutual cooperation for the benefit of both importer and exporter.

A second consideration in scanning supply sources is spatial separation. In an import transaction, the foreign producer and the importer are separated by geographic distance, increasing the complexity of business transactions. Also, because of the special separation of buyers and sellers, it is necessary to enlist the services of many specialized institutions (such as transportation carriers, freight forwarders, customhouse brokers, and banking institutions) that play an important role in the completion of an efficient and successful import process.

A third consideration influencing the search for suppliers is the disparities in manufacturing development in the world today. While the rapid development of technology during the twentieth century has made possible the diffusion of manufacturing into previously underdeveloped industrial sectors and regions, this process has been uneven. As such, the sources of supply vary from one country to another, as do transportation services. For example, in many developing countries (such as Brazil, Taiwan, Hong Kong, and Singapore), the manufacturing sectors are highly sophisticated, with relatively advanced technology. Many of the products now produced in these countries compete with those from nations such as the United States, Japan, and West Germany.

In less developed countries, manufacturing is concentrated in industries such as textiles, processed food products, wood and leather products, and cosmetics. Also within these countries we are likely to find less capital-intensive industries and smaller, less efficient manufacturing.[3] In Third-World countries, the pattern of manufacturing development has not been even. In the more industrially advanced countries, manufacturing has evolved from the typical consumer-type products to consumer durables, intermediate goods, and metal/machinery equipment. This last category (which includes electrical and construction equipment and machinery, electronic products, and motor vehicles) forms the backbone of the industrial sector in more advanced countries. An examination of two typical manufacturing industries in developing countries highlights these points.

Food-processing industries. Typically, all nations have food-processing industries. However, the level of specialization varies. The beverage industry (especially alcoholic beverages) has advanced more than industries in most countries. While this may have once been a liability for developing countries as exporters to the United States, changing consumer patterns have shifted the scale so that today these basic industries are sources of rising imports into the United States. A case in point: the demand for wine and beer has been growing rapidly in the United States. The increased interest in trying new types of products and desire for variety has made people more likely to try a foreign beer or wine, even though it may not be the traditional French wine. Rising interest in nutrition and strong efforts to discourage drinking of high–alcohol-content beverages such as whiskey, gin, and vodka have increased the consumption of low-alcohol beverages (beer and wine, for example). The preference for domestic beer and French wine has been somewhat diminished as consumers show growing tendencies to try new foreign products (such as Corona beer from Mexico and Concha y Toro wines from Chile). Similarly, consumers are more willing to try new types of canned goods. Eating unfamiliar foods is becoming popular among U.S. consumers. Consumers are more likely to try ethnic canned goods (examples being hearts of palm and black beans) and other unfamiliar delicacies, thus increasing the opportunity for many products.

Textile and apparel industries. These industries still remain among the most protected sectors in international trade. Domestic manufacturers account for about half of apparel and textiles sales in developed countries and about 80 percent in developing nations.[4] Yet, the low labor costs in most developing nations have given these countries a comparative advantage in manufacturing low-cost items. The rapid rise of mass markets for jeans, sweaters, shirts, and the like has made imports of these items an important component of the marketplace. High-fashion apparel, on the contrary, is still produced in the United States as fashion goods are still produced in the nation where they are consumed.[5]

Negotiating the Import Purchase

Flexibility is the key for marketing-oriented importers in financing their import purchases. Preconditional to any order are the sales terms negotiated between exporter and importer, the legal responsibilities of buyer and seller, and other contractual terms, such as delivery price, packing and markings, transportation mode, insurance, delivery location, and scheduled delivery time. A vitally important factor in import purchasing is credit, which the firm should be sure to incorporate in its corporate strategy.

The importer must also be sure to properly gauge the delivery time frame. This must include ordering the merchandise, delivery to point of shipment, documentary compliance, and title transfer at the agreed-upon delivery point. Much will depend, however, on the nature of the imported goods, any necessary product adaptation, availability of various transportation modes from point of production through point of delivery, and the kind, quantity, and complexity of documentation required. It is essential that the delivery time frame, no matter how short or how long, be explicitly determined and incorporated in the sales agreement between importer and exporter.[6]

The Import Order

An import order originates in either of two ways:

through an unsolicited offer from a foreign producer,

the result of scanning sources of supply.

Unsolicited orders come from various sources: foreign exhibitors displaying their goods in trade fairs or via official or private-sector missions to the United States; and foreign catalogs and other promotional materials being sent to the importer. On the other hand, as a result of marketing efforts, an importer can scan sources of supply to serve targeted potential markets. Once the goods are ordered and shipped to the United States, the import firm must develop its own cadre of international representatives or depend on import intermediaries (middlemen) to manage the "mechanics" of importing (such as documentation, tariff compliance, transportation).

Import orders may result from a general request for information about a firm's products, or from soliciting catalogs, brochures, and other materials. These orders may be either general or quite specific; small or large; one-time only, seasonal, or on a regular basis. Whatever the case, careful and prompt attention from the importer is necessary to process the goods through U.S. customs. A quick process from ordering to processing is advisable since negotiations of sales terms, procurement of supply, transportation, and so on can be lengthy. The importer should expedite the process by providing the foreign producer with as much detail as possible about product requirements: complete product description, desired quality assurances (and testing wherever appropriate), quantity, specifications, the nature of packing and shipping and, of course, the time frame for delivery. The earlier this information can be communicated and confirmed, the better.

Early on, the importer needs to do its homework about the full market potential and opportunities for the prospective imported product. This is necessary to determine not only whether the import order should be pursued but also the nature and level of marketing effort required to generate recurring and profitable import sales. Among the information needs of the importer are demand projections, historical trends, market locations, demographics, competition, access factors, distribution channels, domestic transportation, and product design, labeling, and consumption.

Product Adaptation. Very often, foreign producers must modify their products to fit the importer's needs and/or comply with labeling, health, safety, and other regulatory standards and safeguards in the United States. From time to time, the importer must be an educator and carefully and convincingly persuade the foreign producer and/or exporter to make changes in the product's contents (for example, removal of a particular additive) or packaging (size, for instance) in order to satisfy pertinent requirements for selling in the U.S. market. The foreign producer and importer must ascertain which are mandatory adaptations (those required by law) and which are discretionary adaptations (those mandated by cultural, socioeconomic, and usage factors). In the first case, it must be clearly understood that adaptations must be made to comply with customs and other specific regulations. In the second case, a benefit/cost analysis should determine the extent and feasibility of the adaptation required.

Obtaining the Product. Quite often, an importer finds itself in need of a product that the firm's established overseas supplier cannot furnish in the quantity, kind, or time frame requested, or simply does not carry as part of its line. In such a case, the importer has three options:

Find another overseas source of supply,

source from another importer (a temporary measure),

purchase the product wholesale or, if all else fails, retail.

Whatever the case, the importer must find the most economical way to source from suppliers who can provide the best prices consistent with product specifications. It is especially important for the importer to keep records of alternative supply sources, prices paid, comparative prices, goods purchased from alternative supply sources, and the delivery record for each supplier. All these factors impact upon the importer's ability to fill an order.

The Pro-Forma Invoice

The import order signifies a request made to a foreign supplier. A pro-forma invoice is a statement in the form of an invoice for the entry of goods into the United States. It is used when the required commercial or customs invoice is not available at the time of entry. The pro-forma invoice can be used for negotiating the import order and to represent the foreign supplier's offer to sell. In specifying what the foreign supplier presents to sell, the pro-forma invoice relays to the importer and buyer the price and conditions of sale. It is extremely important that a time frame be included, since a period of time will elapse between receipt and acceptance of a price quote. The pro-forma invoice should also indicate agreed-upon changes in the product, labeling requirements, and any other adaptation identified during the order negotiation.

In addition to preparing the pro-forma invoice, the consignee gives a bond promising to fill the required invoice with the district or port director of customs within six months from the date of entry. If the exporter fails to forward the required invoice in time, the U.S. importer will incur a liability under its bond for delinquency in filing the invoice within the specified time.

Once the importer and exporter agree to the terms of sale and any changes or modifications, the import transaction can proceed, the merchandise can be obtained, and its shipment can be expedited to the delivery point.

The Sales Contract

To insure a mutually desired outcome of the transaction, the sales contract should be clearly written, and the merchandise or service to be purchased described precisely. The importer must know exactly what the sales contract involves. No matter how technical the product, both buyer and seller must comprehend each other's contractual responsibilities.

Following the negotiation of an import order, a legally binding agreement should be executed prior to the actual import transaction.[7] This is especially important when the merchandise is a complex product and the specifications, delivery schedule, volume, and/or price of the transaction demand that both the importer and exporter fulfill particular obligations.

In drafting a sound sales contract, the following features should be included:

contract terms

shipment and payment

final sales agreement

legal mechanisms

arbitration

Contract Terms. Fixed-price contracts are the norm in international sales. The contractual terms specify the price of merchandise goods or services at the time of the offering. The price(s) agreed upon are legally valid, regardless of the actual cost to the foreign exporter at the time of contract performance. Therefore, the importer is strongly urged to deal only with those foreign vendors who are careful in specifying the time period for which the set prices are valid, along with delivery terms (CIF, FOB, and so on).

Shipment and Payment. The importer must establish if the foreign exporter has the physical and financial ability to deliver the goods or service. The exporter in turn must determine whether the importer has the financial assets to pay for the goods or service. Orderly shipment and payment schedules should be outlined in detail to assure a satisfactory transaction.

Final Sales Agreement. Central to the final sales agreement is written acceptance from the importer when buyer and seller have come to agreement on contract terms. If representatives or intermediaries are involved, both buyer and seller need to know whether these individuals are authorized to represent them and to obtain certification of this fact.[8]

Legal Mechanisms. Presently, there is no set of laws governing international trade and contracts that is universally recognized. Not surprisingly, importers and exporters will seek their respective nations' laws governing the parties' rights and obligations. Very often exporters and importers turn to the International Chamber of Commerce (ICC) whose Uniform Rules for Contract Guarantees balance the interests of the different parties in a fair and practical manner. The rules are applied to all types of contract guarantee. In determining liability, the guarantor is liable only for the amount mentioned in the guarantee.

Since it is difficult prior to signing a contract to anticipate developments that may affect subsequent performance, the ICC has also developed Rules for the Regulation of Contractual Relations. These rules allow parties to have recourse by arbitration, for example, an agreement arbitrated by an independent third party with the aim of modifying the original contract or filling in gaps.

Arbitration. Import contracts should contain a section that mandates the settlement of disputes under the ICC's Rules of Conciliation and Arbitration. Combining the security and safeguards of institutional arbitration with the flexibility of ad hoc arbitration, the ICC system allows arbitrations to take place anywhere in the world and provides both economy and efficiency in resolving differences arising between exporters and importers in international sales contracts.[9]

Financing the Import Purchase

Initial and subsequent correspondence with the foreign supplier should now address arrangements for payment of the import transaction. Payment procedures must be agreed upon by both buyer and seller. In this regard, there are several alternatives available to the importer to pay for its import purchases.

The importer should seek to be invoiced in U.S. dollars. Frequently, the seller may require payment in the seller's or some other foreign currency. The first situation represents the most common way to pay for imports. However, if the seller requires payment in a currency other than dollars, the importer must make arrangements to do so either through a bank draft drawn in the currency required or via payment on a collection basis (drafts or letters of credit) in that currency.

The basic forms available to the importer to pay for import purchases are

cash in advance,

documentary drafts,

letter of credit,

open-account and consignment sales.

The main aspects of each are summarized in figure 8–2.

Cash in Advance

This is the most secure method to the seller/supplier but the least desirable to the importer. First, cash in advance ties up the importer's capital and can have very high costs if interest rates are high and if goods are delayed. Second, foreign-exchange exposure is high unless payment is done for purchases based on a fixed preagreed price. Shifts in foreign-exchange rates change the cost of imported products. Third, there is a high risk factor due to noncompliance of order, changes in specification, and delays in delivery, transportation, and customs clearance.

Cash in advance is usually done by remitting cash or a bank draft by mail. Payments should be made out to the specific foreign supplier and preferably drawn on the seller's location to avoid further delays (bank clearance). The use of Telex or S.W.I.F.T. (Society for Worldwide Financial Telecommunications) is the fastest means of remitting payment.

Documentary Drafts

This method entails payment on a collection basis, that is, the foreign supplier sends shipping and other commercial and customs-clearance documents that need to be generated in the exporting country through a commercial or other financial institution designated by the importer, accompanied by a draft instructing the importer to pay at sight or at a future date (30, 60, 90, or 120 days usually).

When commercial and political risks are deemed low, exporters usually opt for payments to be collected by way of import drafts. A bank is normally used as a collection agency to secure payments for an import shipment or transaction. Import drafts are less costly than other options and aid the supplier's

Method of Payment	Cash Flow to Exporter	Merchandise Flow to Importer	Risk Factor
Cash in advance	Prior to shipment	After payment	High risk factor due to noncompliance of order specifications or delay time.
Documentary draft	Sight: after shipment	After payment	High risk factor due to noncompliance of order or specifications
	Time: after shipment	Before payment	Lower risk—importer sees goods before payment and has recourse before payment.
Letter of credit	Upon receipt of documents by opening bank	After payment	Importer is protected by conditions of payment—risk of non-compliance is relatively low. However, payment flows before goods are inspected.
Open Account and	After shipment	Before payment	Lowest risk factor to importer. Exporter must fill order as required.
Consignment Sales	After shipment	Before payment	

Source: Adapted from W.A. Grundei, *Servicing World Markets* (Chicago: International Trade Club of Chicago, 1979), p. 43.

Figure 8–2. Import Payments and Importer's Risk Factor

competitive position in overseas markets. The import draft is an order to pay without conditions, drawn by the seller or the buyer. The buyer is obliged to pay an amount specified in the draft either "on sight," for example on presentation or at a future date. The drawee (buyer) is instructed in the draft to pay a specific payee. The payee can be a collection company, another firm or organization, or the drawer (seller).

Drafts provide evidence of a debt to the exporter so that the importer is likely to be more careful in compliance with the import order. The importer pays for goods when the draft and documents are presented, that is, after goods have been shipped and prior to their arrival (sight draft) or after their arrival (time draft) to the United States.

Exhibit 8–1. Export Draft

U.S. $ _____	_____19_____

_____of this *FIRST* of Exchange (Second unpaid)

Pay to the Order of

United States Dollars

for Value received and charge the same to account of

To_____

No._____   Authorized Signature

Date

Gentlemen: ☐ for collection,

We enclose Draft Number_____and documents listed below ☐ for

                                                   ☐ for payment/negotiation under L/C

BILLS OF LADING	B/L COPY	COMM. INV.	INS. CTF.	CTF. ORIG.	CONS. INV.	PKNG. LIST	WGT. CTF.	OTHER DOCUMENTS

Please handle in accordance with instructions marked "X"

☐ Deliver all documents in one mailing.

☐ Deliver documents in two mailings.

☐ Deliver documents against payment if sight draft, or acceptance if time draft.

☐ All charges for account of drawee.

☐ Do not waive charges.

☐ Protest for non-payment / non-acceptance
☐ Do not protest.

☐ Present on arrival of goods.

☐ Advise non-payment / non-acceptance by airmail / cable giving reasons.

☐ Advise payment / acceptance by airmail / cable

IN CASE OF NEED refer to:

Name_____

Address_____

who is empowered by us:

a ☐ To act fully on our behalf, i.e., authorize reductions; extensions; free delivery; waiving of protest, etc.

b ☐ To assist in obtaining acceptance or payment of draft, as drawn, but not to alter its terms in any way.

OTHER INSTRUCTIONS:

Please refer all questions concerning this collection to:
☐ Shipper
☐ Freight Forwarder:

_____

Authorized Signature

Form No. 20-015

Clearly, the risk factor due to noncompliance is reduced as the draft serves as evidence of the transaction. This gives the importer the opportunity to present its case if the obligation cannot be met due to changes in the original contract or order without consent from the importer. The draft is also a flexible, low-cost alternative to a letter of credit and very common in export/import transactions when parties have a long-established relationship. To assure payment by the importer, the exporter usually pays for bank services that include several tracers, for example follow ups by servicing bank.

Letters of Credit

The most common form of financing or credit used in import and export transactions is the letter of credit. Basically, the letter of credit is a documentary promise by which a bank pays a named beneficiary (normally the seller) a specified sum, on behalf of the importer, provided certain conditions are met. The letter of credit protects both exporter and importer in an international deal. The importer is guaranteed that all required paperwork will be presented before payment is made for the merchandise. The exporter is assured of prompt payment when the shipment is made per contractual agreement.

Letters of credit are the most advantageous form of payment in international transactions, especially when the foreign supplier is unfamiliar with the U.S. importer, the importer's credit standing, and trade conditions within the United States. The risk to the importer is relatively low for this term of payment as the exporter cannot collect payment unless it presents evidence of the transaction required by the buyer.

The three main types of letters of credit are:

Irrevocable negotiation letter of credit: This type of letter of credit cannot be canceled or revoked without the agreement of all parties involved. The term *negotiation* means that the letter of credit does not restrict payment to a particular bank. Upon examination and approval of documents by the negotiating bank, the bank will pay the beneficiary and claim reimbursement by the issuing bank.

Irrevocable straight letter of credit: A straight credit is a mechanism that restricts payment to a designated bank—the paying bank—usually in the beneficiary's locale. A straight credit mandates that drafts and documents be delivered on or before the expiration date at the paying bank's office.

Confirmed irrevocable negotiation credit: With this kind of credit, the issuing bank's obligation to pay is backed by a second bank. The second, or confirming, bank obliges payment if the letter of credit terms are met, regardless of whether the issuing bank pays. As with a negotiation letter of credit, a bank in the beneficiary's locale will assure that the documents presented match the requirements and, upon verification of documents, pay the beneficiary.[10]

Exhibit 8–2.   Letter of Credit

SAMPLE
Confirmed Irrevocable Letter of Credit

ANYBANK OF WASHINGTON, D.C.

CABLE: ANYBANK   9600 Louisiana Avenue   TELEX: 000000
Washington, D.C.

DATE: May 1, 1981

An Export Co.
5353 Louisiana Avenue   ADVISED THROUGH: First National
Washington, D.C. 20200   Bank of Arlington, P.O. Box 40,
Arlington, Virginia 22022

Dear Sirs:

Our correspondents, Banque Parisienne de Credit au Commerce et
a l'Industrie, Paris, France
request us to inform you that they have opened with us their irrevocable
credit in your favor for the amount of --Maximum Two Thousand Seven Hundred
Fifty-Seven Dollars and 06/100 ($2,757.06)
by order of An Importing Company, 45 Rue Jean Pierre, 75007 Paris

We are authorized to accept your 60 days sight draft, drawn on us when accompanied by
the following documents which must represent and cover full invoice value of the
merchandise described below:

1) Signed commercial invoice in six (6) copies.
2) Full set of clean ocean bills of lading, dated on board, plus one
   (1) non-negotiable copy if available, issued to the order of
   Banque Parisienne de Credit au Commerce et a l'Industrie,
   notify: An Importing Company, 45 Rue Jean Pierre, 75007 Paris,
   indicating Credit No. 10173.
3) Insurance certificate in duplicate, in negotiable form, covering
   all risks, including war risks, strikes and mines for the value
   of the merchandise plus 10%.

Covering: Perfume No. 337
           As per pro forma invoice dated March 3, 1981
           FOB Baltimore

Merchandise to be forwarded from Baltimore to Le Havre.
Partial shipments prohibited.
The cost of insurance is payable in excess of the credit amount and
reimbursable to you against presentation of justification, when
included in your drawings and added to your invoice.

The above mentioned correspondent engages with you that all drafts drawn under and in
compliance with the terms of this credit will be duly honored on delivery of documents
as specified, if --presented at this office

on or before June 30, 1981   We confirm the credit and thereby undertake that
all drafts drawn and presented as above specified will be duly honored.

R. W. Albert
Authorized Signature

Open-Account and Consignment Sales

The open-account form of payment is an agreement between exporter and importer in which payment is made at a future date, following shipment and delivery of the goods at the destination point or buyer's warehouse facility. With consignment sales, the supplier furnishes the merchandise to the buyer on a deferred payment basis, with no payment made until the goods are sold.

From the importer's perspective, these are the most advantageous and secure forms of payment. However, it may be difficult to obtain credit from foreign suppliers, especially from suppliers in less developed countries due to low capital availability and low levels of working capital. Exporting usually requires some financing from the foreign supplier due to the time lapse between production and shipment. Extending credit involves a significant lengthening of this time period. Unquestionably, this is the lowest risk factor to the importer as the foreign supplier must conform to the order very closely. Nevertheless, the importer's ability to obtain credit or consignment merchandise depends on the importer's ability to generate volume sales of the imported product, credit worthiness, and timely payments.

Summary

When the importer has secured a source of supply, the import order is the initial step in the processing of the import transaction. As soon as the order is issued, the importer must prepare its processing and initiate the import process. This entails a series of steps that are included in the primary flows: the financial flow to pay for the transaction; the physical flow or logistical aspect of the transaction; and the document flow or presentation of adequate documentation to clear the U.S. Customs Service.

Adapting the product for the U.S. market may also be needed. For orders to be processed successfully, the importer must appraise the producer of the item's description and specifications, quality assurances, packing and shipping requirements, and time frame for delivery. The sales contract should also cover contract terms, shipment and payment, the final sales agreement, legal mechanisms, and arbitration.

Payment may be handled by cash in advance, documentary draft, letter of credit (irrevocable negotiation letter of credit, irrevocable straight letter of credit, or confirmed irrevocable negotiation credit), or open-account or consignment sales.

The financial flow is a key component of the import process. The importer needs to evaluate the requirements of the supplier, the market situation, and its own resources in order to determine the most adequate form of financing the import purchase.

Notes

1. See Marta Ortiz-Buonafina, *Profitable Export Marketing,* pp. 165–68.
2. Sidney R. Jumper, Thomas L. Bell, and Bruce A. Ralston, *Economic Growth and Disparities* (Englewood Cliffs, New Jersey: Prentice-Hall, 1980), p. 397.
3. Ibid.
4. Ibid., p. 398.
5. See also Ortiz-Buonafina, *Profitable Export Marketing,* pp. 166–68.
6. For a complete outline of sales contracts, see D. Mark Baker and Glade F. Flake, *Negotiating Sales Contracts* (Washington, D.C.: Small Business Administration, 1975).
7. For more details on this subject, see *Foreign Business Practices* (Washington, D.C.: U.S. Department of Justice), current issue.
8. *Financing Exports and Imports* (New York: Morgan Guaranty Trust, 1977), p. 14.
9. Ortiz-Buonafina, *Profitable Export Marketing,* p. 181.
10. Bank of America N.T.&S.A., *Bank of America International Services,* 1986 ed. (San Francisco: Bank of America N.T.&S.A.[1]), p. 25.

9

Traffic, Customhouse Brokerage, Documentation, and Insurance

This chapter illustrates the factors affecting the mode of transportation chosen in the import process: the role of the customhouse broker; documentation requirements in terms of purpose and use as required by the Customs Service; and the various forms of insurance policies utilized.

Traffic

From the importer's point of view, time, cost, and the safe transportation of goods are essential elements in the import-transaction process. The emphasis lies in the time element: it is crucial in this part of the import-transaction phase due to the complexity and length of the activities involved in processing. It encompasses the import order itself between the parties involved as well as all documentation and activities necessary to clear the goods through customs in both the importing and exporting countries. This includes the actual physical flow of goods from the terminal of departure to the final destination.

Without sacrificing the goods' safety, excess costs and time delays should be avoided in every way to facilitate real savings in the import process. This is why in traffic management it is imperative to understand all issues and needs at hand. Consequently, there should be close contact between the importer and the exporter to expedite the physical flow of goods, to choose the best available mode of transportation, and to insure the provision of all documents and accomplishment of all activities required by customs officials of each respective country.

Time itself is heavily contingent upon distance, speed and mode of transportation, and delays at port as well as customs procedures. The time factor, consequently, affects costs, which can be observed as being explicit or implicit in nature.

Explicit costs are direct, out-of-pocket expenses incurred in the transportation of goods from the exporting country to the importer's warehouse. These include freight charges, packaging, insurance, and storage as well as all shipping-service charges.

Implicit costs can be difficult to estimate ahead of time as they can be unforeseen and might result in more than just cash outlays. They are potential costs (opportunity costs) of using one alternative mode of transportation over the range of alternatives available.[1] These costs are due to delays, losses, damages, and thefts as well as related foreign-exchange losses that occur while goods are in transit. These events result in customer dissatisfaction, not to mention lost sales and profits. Due to their nature, implicit costs are difficult to calculate and are not all completely covered by insurance policies.

Careful evaluation by the importer must be made of the transportation mode chosen to reduce the explicit and implicit costs inherent in the various transportation services.

In the business environment, there are many activities that are taken into account in figuring the cost of transportation. All these activities are performed in a network of facilities and services, be they ports, terminals, and central stations (organizations providing the mode of transportation among other things), as well as the different modes of transportation themselves (water, pipeline, rail, road, and air). In terms of time, cost, and safety, several issues are very important to decision making:

storage and inventory management,

packaging and handling,

landed cost of a product.[2]

Storage and Inventory Management. The importer needs to have a complete understanding of the product and the necessary inventory to maintain the targeted level of sales. Proper storage and inventory management involves the evaluation and close coordination of several factors: the available stock, inventory turnover, storage facilities, and financial abilities of the firm to support such a system. The physical and functional characteristics of the product will dictate the type and size of storage required. Obviously, sales will suffer if inventory is not properly maintained. At the same time, too much inventory will increase the storage, handling, and financial carrying costs. These factors affect the choice of the transportation mode as there is a trade-off involved between time and transportation costs.

Packaging and Handling. The main objective of adequate packaging and handling is the safe delivery of the goods to the final destination in acceptable condition. The packaging involved depends on the product and its susceptibility to damage given the mode of transportation and the handling involved. The package must protect the contents from various elements such as loss, pilferage, and climatic conditions as well as damage from normal handling in the physical flow of goods.

It does not necessarily follow that the safest possible container be used at all times. The most difficult consideration in packing and handling is the trade-off between safety and costs, as freight charges are based on gross weight of both the container and its contents. Tendencies to overpack and economize should be resisted, however, as damages incurred in transit will be noted by the shipping company. Difficulties might then arise in the collection of payment, especially if a letter of credit is involved specifying a "clean" shipping document indicating goods were received in good condition.

Orderly and systematic packaging plus careful invoice preparation detailing the exact quantity of each item in each container along with the proper markings—will facilitate the handling, examination, and release of goods from customs. Unsystematic packaging as well as confusion as to the value and contents of the goods will lead to delays and possible additional duties, as the entire shipment must then be examined by a customs officer at the expense of the importer.[3]

Knowledge of the Uniform Freight Classification and the National Motor Freight Classification systems is essential as certain standards and requirements have to be met based on the goods and type of transportation. Certain goods (such as fragile, hazardous, or perishable products) are required to conform to certain packaging specifications.

The importer can avail itself of the variety of information offered by the manufacturers of shipping materials. Evaluation can then be made as to the different types of containers and packaging materials to enable the importer to lower costs without compromising safety and still conform to packaging requirements.

Landed Cost of the Product. Landed cost of a product entails all costs incurred up to the point of final destination. The level of these costs is important to consider since they are directly added to the final unit price of the goods delivered. These costs are affected by the mode of transportation, distance, and (as discussed in chapter 7) the price escalation of imports. As the product moves from the exporting country to its final destination, it incurs a series of additional costs (such as transportation fees, import duties, forwarding costs, and insurance costs) as well as the markup or profit margins the different channels of distribution add to the product's original factory price. The final figure reflects the *price escalation,* which may contribute to the landed cost of the product being significantly higher than the market price in the exporting country. These factors, consequently, affect the importer's finances and the import demand. Therefore, there are obvious trade-offs in respect to time, cost, and safety that an importer must consider before decisions are made.

The importance of traffic management in the mechanics of the import process must be emphasized. All options and alternatives must be considered as the savings realized from efficient and effective traffic management will positively impact on the importer's future activities and profitable marketing strategy. This in turn should yield a positive approach in balancing time, cost, and safety, not to mention the other considerations such as storage and inventory management, packaging and handling, and landed costs of the product. Essentially, the solution should yield terms-of-sale advantages to all parties involved.

Types of Carriers

Carriers are organizations and companies that make use of vehicles to perform transportation services by rail, air, and water. These services are performed under shipping contracts based on charges known as rates of tariffs. Carriers are classified into various groups for reasons of distinctiveness and simplification.

Most transportation companies have extensive line-haul equipment or over-the-road facilities and can therefore service their clients directly. These are *direct carriers.* On the other hand, some companies are not equipped as extensively and therefore are apt to buy service from other transportation companies. These are *indirect carriers.* Examples of indirect carriers are surface-freight forwarders and airfreight forwarders. The types of carriers most commonly used in international trade are:

  common carriers

  contract carriers

  private carriers

Common carriers must offer their services to any firm or individual who requires it, and cannot refuse except for a reasonable cause.[4] They are regulated by the federal government, although recent legislation has allowed them more opportunities to improve their service and operations. Carriers must publish their rates periodically and must offer them indiscriminately to all customers requesting similar services. Common carriers work within regularly scheduled times between set ports throughout the world, regardless of whether the carriers are full or not.

Contract carriers haul for a selected clientele with whom there is a formal contract for either one or many voyages or shipments. The services provided are scheduled to meet the needs of the clients, and thus the rates vary according to the type of service offered, the product, size of shipment, distance traveled, and so on. The rates are negotiated based on market demand and cost implications. Many common carriers also offer their services under formal contract with the same specialized service as a contract carrier. In this case, the shipment being transported is known as chartered freight. Contract carriers, as opposed to common carriers, offer nonscheduled services to essentially every port in the world, but move only when fully loaded or economically able to do so.

Private carriers are companies or individuals that haul their own goods in their own vehicles. This group makes up 90 percent of the transportation within the United States. However, private carriers do not play a very significant part in international trade due to the restrictive policies of foreign governments. These firms generally own their fleets of transportation such as ships, trucks, and aircraft.

Freight Rates

Freight rates are the rewards payable to carriers—be they private, common, or contract carriers—for the transportation of goods. Cargo freight rates are generally expressed in terms of weight or volume. Weight is usually expressed in weight-ton. There are different weight-ton measurements that are used in international trade. The United States uses the American short ton with an equivalent of 2,000 pounds, and the British use the long-ton equivalent of 2,240 pounds. Measurement by volume uses the long-ton equivalent of 40 cubic feet. With the growing use of the metric system, however, it is becoming more frequent to have rates quoted in terms of 1,000 kilograms metric ton (2,205 pounds). The metric ton's volume measurement is 1,133 cubic meters of 35.33 cubic feet.[5]

The pricing of shipping services is expressed as a freight rate. The charges offered by the shipping companies are greatly affected by competition, market forces of supply and demand, the type of product involved, and the geographic coverage. The final price is a fixed price for a stated period of time, but it is revised regularly. Liner companies are required to file tariff schedules with the Federal Maritime Board (FMB). A tariff is the list of tariff rates filed with the FMB showing a shipping company's rates and rules. Rate quotations are expressed in a weight or measurement basis at ship's option. This means that the rate quoted may apply either per metric ton or per metric volume, whichever produces the greater revenue. This pricing method allows the ship to charge freight rates that will assure a full load at the maximum revenue. Cargo measuring less than 1,133 cubic meters (metric volume) is charged weight-tonnage rates. Cargo measuring more than one metric ton-volume is charged volume rates, which are usually higher than weight charges.

In formulizing the pricing system, importers should recognize certain factors influence the rate structures:

Ship specification, which provides information on the type of vessel being considered (bulk carrier, tanker, or containership),

Type of traffic being conveyed,

General market conditions, which embrace the elements of demand and supply,

Implicit and explicit costs,

The availability of a particular carrier at a particular time at a particular place.

Of all the transportation modes, airfreight is the most expensive in per-ton cost. Even so, airfreight is becoming increasingly important in international trade primarily due to the facts that air transport is by far the fastest mode available and that its capacity has expanded with the wide-body airplanes now in cargo service. It now takes only hours to ship goods that previously would have taken weeks or months on other modes. Recognizably, since air carriers are low-capacity vehicles that require a significant amount of horsepower per ton-mile moved, costs will be high. This mode is best geared to specific markets: fragile goods, perishables, goods of an emergency nature, and, most of all, manufactured goods whose costs are high relative to their mass. Examples are perfume, high tech products, and fashion wear.

By far the best competitive edge in this deregulated business is pricing and service. In pricing, one must pay close attention to air-carrier rates—rates that must be approved by the governments of the trading nations and specified in bilateral agreements. In the United States, rate schedules must be filed with the Civil Aeronautics Board. Freight-rate pricing in the air-cargo industry is far more organized than in the shipping industry. There are four sets of rates used in general:

specific commodity rates, which are applied for commodities using differential weight rates,

general commodity rates, which cover air-cargo charges from export point to destination,

the exemption rates, charges added to shipments that require special handling,

dimensional rates, which are applied when a package is high in volume and low in weight.

The pricing is generally based on the weight scale using per-pound or per-kilogram (1 kilogram = 2.2046 pounds) measurements. There are minimum weight charges along with weight breaks in rates of 100, 500, 1,000, or 66 and 222 pounds. These are called volume spread or weight differentials. All in all, airfreight rates vary according to products transported.

Marking of Imports

The marking of imports is an essential part of packaging because it facilitates shipment and is required by U.S. customs laws. It entails marking all packaged goods on the outside in a legible manner and assuring that the marking will remain from the goods' point of departure to final destination. Marks of identification, dimension of package, destination port, and any other helpful as well as required information are all categorized under this process.

Included in the marking of cargo are several internationally recognized codes that furnish further information on the package, such as handling, nature of cargo, fragility, and climate needs. The importance does not lie only on its informative value but also in requirements. Failure to have proper markings stating the country of origin can lead to a marking duty equal to 10 percent of the customs value of the articles or the goods being destroyed or sent to a bonded warehouse by customs officials at the importer's expense.[6] Markings are also important for insurance purposes. This is due to the natures of the carriers, ports, and handlers alike since they handle goods according to the markings (or as they see fit in the event of inadequate or absent markings). Therefore, if anything is damaged due to negligence of markings on the part of the contracted carrier, one may consider insurance procedures. If adequate markings are not present or obvious, then it is the fault of the party involved in shipping the goods.

Factors Affecting the Choice
of Transportation Mode

Every choice of transportation mode is derived from the particular characteristics and requirements of each import order. The various factors affecting the choice of transportation mode are:

cost

speed

geographic location

type of product

reliability (See chapter 5 for a detailed discussion of transportation.)

Cost. Airplanes and trucks are relatively low-volume–capacity vehicles and offer faster service at higher costs per ton-mile than trains, ships, pipelines and barges. In addition, airplane and truck transportation require more crew per unit of cargo and horsepower to overcome inertia, thus justifying a higher price. As mentioned earlier, air and truck transportation are most valuable for manufactured goods whose costs are high relative to their volume.

Ships, railroads, and pipelines offer lower-cost alternatives, though they are much slower than air and truck. These modes employ smaller crews and lower horsepower, and their high volumes permit costs to be amortized over a greater number of units. The importance of cost when related to choice lies in the landed cost of the product, which affects the terms of sale, since all the costs are inevitably tagged on to the final cost of the goods.

Speed. The speed of different modes of transportation varies greatly within a range of 15 miles per hour for cargo vessels to 600 for air cargo. Speed should be considered in terms of such issues as cost, reliability, the goods to be transported, and the demand and need on the part of the importer.

Geographic Location. When choosing a transportation mode, an importer must evaluate carefully the geographic location and accessibility of the goods being shipped. These evaluations are important in assisting the importer in estimating the costs involved, since difficulties may arise in shipping goods from one location to another. Such evaluations also aid in finding viable modes that are time- and cost-efficient, in the hope of expediting orders. This need for evaluating geographic location arises in some cases where a particular transportation mode does not reach the destination or even where only one airport or port can be reached. These situations call for intermodal transportation as well as possibly using neighboring facilities, as Bolivia uses Peru for port facilities.

Within the United States, the waterways are a highly important mode of transportation. The barging system along the Mississippi River and all its tributary rivers penetrates the heartland of America, reaching from New Orleans to Pittsburgh, Chicago, and St. Louis, to mention some of the prime markets for merchandise trade. This waterway system is one of the most economical in the country, and it moves millions of tons a year. However, few foreign manufacturers know the importance of this system, and many importers do not take advantage of its potential due to lack of knowledge.

Type of Product. A number of factors are essential in the choice of mode, even to the point of disregarding costs over time and safety such as dangerous cargo and cargo of an emergency nature. These factors involve weight, volume, nature of product, value relative to mass, the degree of urgency on the part of the importer, and accessibility.

Reliability. This issue of reliability is very important to the importer in terms of cost, time, and safety. An importer can estimate costs very well, but must depend on the implicit costs being reliable as well. That is, the importer hopes that no unforeseen event will boost costs. This also applies to time, since regular and dependable service is of the utmost importance in making estimates. The safety factor involves packaging and handling as well as any activity during transport or voyage. The different modes of transportation offer different levels of risk factors that can affect liability—air cargo being low-risk and shipping having a high-risk level.

The Customhouse Broker

There are over two hundred laws that the Customs Service must implement and enforce dealing with the importation of goods to the United States. The complexity of the various customs regulations and requirements can lead to cumbersome details and costly mistakes on the part of the importer. Although customs officers can supply helpful information, they are prohibited by law to serve as agents. A competent Customhouse Broker (CHB) can facilitate importation by efficiently guiding the goods through the customs channels.

These brokers are well informed about import procedures and requirements and maintain close coordination between importers and their suppliers to assure the efficient entry of goods into this country and avert costly delays and penalties at the port of entry.

Customhouse brokers are licensed by the U.S. Treasury Department after an extensive examination by customs officials. The applicant is tested for proficient knowledge of customs regulations as well as moral character. Corporations, partnerships, or sole proprietorships can qualify to be licensed as a CHB.[7] In the case of a corporation or partnership, at least two officers must hold licenses, while sole proprietorships are required to have only one license holder. Licenses are subject to revocation at any time for just and sufficient cause, such as malpractice.

Larger CHBs are also freight forwarders. This helps to coordinate the entry of goods through customs and the transportation procedures between ports and the final destinations.

The broker works under a certified power of attorney signed by the importer, which legally appoints the broker as its agent. The importer can then assign all shipping papers to the CHB to facilitate and expedite customs-related entry papers. Importers are allowed five days excluding Sundays and holidays to present the necessary papers and secure the release of the goods. Extensions of this general order time can be requested by the broker if necessary. However, if these papers are not presented after the time allowed, the shipment is sent by the customhouse to a bonded warehouse at the risk and expense of the buyer. If after one year, the goods are not claimed and do not properly clear through customs, the merchandise can be placed for sale by the U.S. government.

Services provided by the CHB include:

Preparing the customs entry form and assuring that all the necessary documentation is in order for proper processing through customs channels.

Calculating the amount of duty according to the Tariff Act.

If necessary, requesting extensions of the general order time from the collector of customs.

Providing the surety bond required by the customhouse, which guarantees full payment of all duties.

Arranging for the goods to be transferred under bond from the port of entry to an interior destination for customs clearance (Immediate Transportation Entry Form).

Obtaining special permits for immediate delivery of perishable goods or special merchandise (Immediate Delivery Form).

Preparing the warehouse entry bond and arranging for goods to be transferred to the bonded warehouse.

Arranging for the withdrawal of goods from the bonded warehouse in part or completely. Payment of duties will be made according to the amount of goods withdrawn.

Pursuing appropriate administrative channels if disagreements occur with customs over rate or value of appraised goods.

The value of an experienced CHB can be immeasurable, especially to the importer located away from U.S. ports of entry. Charges vary depending on the complexity and amount of activity required. Great care should be given to the selection of a customhouse broker. The importer's bank can serve as reference for competent, financially sound CHBs. Several other sources are available to facilitate the selection:

Custom House Guide and the monthly magazine *American Import & Export Management,* published by Import Publications, Inc., in New York. A list of customhouse brokers is published annually by geographic areas.

Customs Brokers and Forwarders Association of America, Inc., in New York publishes a list of national CHBs.

Customhouse brokers play a vital and essential role in facilitating the entry, clearance, and movement of import cargo. Their services will be needed as long as there are complex regulations pertaining to the movement of merchandise.

Documentation

It is important that there be an understanding of the nature and requirements of all documents in the import process. The need for documentation in the entire trade process is important, due to the rise in trade, regulations, and need for formal control in the entry as well as departure of trade goods between nations. It is thus imperative that the importer be well informed of the required documents and their basic functions for the proper and timely clearance of the imported goods. In this section we shall discuss the most commonly used import documents that the importer or broker needs to prepare to clear the goods through customs:

power of attorney

surety bond

commercial invoice

informal entries

consumption entries

transportation entries

temporary importation

drawback entries

Power of Attorney. A nonresident individual, partnership, or foreign corporation may issue a power of attorney to a regular employee, partner, corporate officer or customhouse broker to transact customs business in the United States. The person to whom this power is entrusted must be a resident of the United States, so he or she may represent the issuer of the power of attorney in matters related to the particular business in question. The most important requirement customs expects is proof of the authority of the said issuer to issue the power of attorney. See exhibit 9–1 for the power-of-attorney form.

Surety Bond. Goods when entered through customs must be accompanied by a surety bond secured from a U.S. surety company. This bond must at least equal all duty and charges for the import shipment. When an importer employs the services of a customhouse broker, the broker's bond is used to provide the required coverage. In the event that goods move out of the control of customs before duty is paid, the broker is required to enter into a bond with customs, whereby the amount of duty is guaranteed to be paid.

Since the Customs Service announced on October 19, 1984, that the preexisting myriad of bond forms would be consolidated, there is presently one general-purpose bond form for all import activation, except the Air Carrier Blanket Form.

Commercial Invoice. Beginning March 1, 1982, the commercial invoice can be provided to replace the special customs invoice previously required. The invoice—signed by the seller, shipper, or its agent—must provide a detailed listing of the goods, prices, weights, and particular markings of each shipment. The currency used and all charges and costs (including freight, insurance, and commission) incurred in bringing the merchandise to the U.S. port must be stated. The invoice must be in English or an accurate English translation must be attached. See exhibit 9–2 for an example.

Exhibit 9–1. Power of Attorney

Department of the Treasury
U. S. Customs Service
141.32, C.R.

POWER OF ATTORNEY

Check appropriate box:
☐ Individual
☐ Partnership
☐ Corporation
☐ Sole Proprietorship

KNOW ALL MEN BY THESE PRESENTS: That, _____

(Full Name of person, partnership, or corporation, or sole proprietorship (Identify)

a corporation doing business under the laws of the State of _____ or a

doing business as _____ residing at

having an office and place of business at _____, hereby constitutes and appoints each of the following persons

(Give full name of each agent designated)

as a true and lawful agent and attorney of the grantor named above for and in the name, place, and stead of said grantor from this date and in Customs District ____-____, and in no other name, to make, endorse, sign, declare, or swear to any entry, withdrawal, declaration, certificate, bill of lading, or other document required by law or regulation in connection with the importation, transportation, or exportation of any merchandise shipped or consigned by or to said grantor; to perform any act or condition which may be required by law or regulation in connection with such merchandise; to receive any merchandise deliverable to said grantor;

To make endorsements on bills of lading conferring authority to make entry and collect drawback, and to make, sign, declare, or swear to any statement, supplemental statement, schedule, supplemental schedule, certificate of delivery, certificate of manufacture, certificate of manufacture and delivery, abstract of manufacturing records, declaration of proprietor on drawback entry, declaration of exporter on drawback entry, or any other affidavit or document which may be required by law or regulation for drawback purposes, regardless of whether such bill of lading, sworn statement, schedule, certificate, abstract, declaration, or other affidavit or document is intended for filling in said district or in any other customs district;

voluntarily given and accepted under applicable laws and regulations, consignee's and owner's declarations provided for in section 485, Tariff Act of 1930, as amended, or affidavits in connection with the entry of merchandise;

To sign and swear to any document and to perform any act that may be necessary or required by law or regulation in connection with the entering, clearing, lading, unlading, or operation of any vessel or other means of conveyance owned or operated by said grantor;

And generally to transact at the customhouses in said district any and all customs business, including making, signing, and filing of protests under section 514 of the Tariff Act of 1930, in which said grantor is or may be concerned or interested and which may properly be transacted or performed by an agent and attorney, giving to said agent and attorney full power and authority to do anything whatever requisite and necessary to be done in the premises as fully as said grantor could do if present and acting, hereby ratifying and confirming all that the said agent and attorney shall lawfully do by virtue of these presents; the foregoing power of attorney to remain in full force and effect until the _____ day of _____, 19____, or until notice of revocation in writing is duly given to and received by the District Director of Customs of the district aforesaid. If the donor of this power of attorney is a partnership, and said the power shall in no case have any force or effect after the expiration of 2 years from the date of its receipt in the office of the district director of customs of the said district.

IN WITNESS WHEREOF, the said _____

has caused these presents to be sealed and signed: (Signature) _____

(Capacity) _____

WITNESS: _____

_____ (Date)

(Corporate seal) *(Optional)

(SEE OVER)

Customs Form 5291 (10-07-80)

INDIVIDUAL OR PARTNERSHIP CERTIFICATION *(Optional)

CITY _____

COUNTY _____ } ss:

STATE _____

On this _____ day of _____, 19___, personally appeared before me _____, personally known or sufficiently identified to me, who certifies that

residing at _____ free act and deed.

_____(is)(are) the individual(s) who executed the foregoing instrument and acknowledge it to be _____

_____

(Notary Public)

CORPORATE CERTIFICATION *(Optional)

(To be made by an officer other than the one who executes the power of attorney)

I, _____, certify that I am the _____

of _____, organized under the laws of the State of _____

that _____, who signed this power of attorney on behalf of the donor, is the _____

of said corporation; and that said power of attorney was duly signed, sealed, and attested for and behalf of said corporation by authority of its governing body as the

same appears in a resolution of the Board of Directors passed at a regular meeting held on the _____ day of _____, now in my possession or custody. I

further certify that the resolution is in accordance with the articles of incorporation and bylaws of said corporation.

IN WITNESS WHEREOF, I have hereunto set my hand and affixed the seal of said corporation, at the City of _____ this _____ day of

_____, 19 _____

_____

(Signature)

_____

(Date)

If the corporation has no corporate seal, the fact shall be stated, in which case a scroll or adhesive shall appear in the appropriate, designated place.

Customs powers of attorney of residents (including resident corporations) shall be without power of substitution except for the purpose of executing shipper's export declarations. However, a power of attorney executed in favor of a licensed customhouse broker may specify that the power of attorney is granted to the customhouse broker to act through any of its licensed officers or any employee specifically authorized to act for such customhouse broker by power of attorney.

*NOTE: The corporate seal may be omitted. Customs does not require completion of a certification. The grantor has the option of executing the certification or omitting it.

★ U.S.GPO:1987-0-542-156/61066

Exhibit 9–2. Factura Comercial (Commercial Invoice)

Sold to / Vendido a.

Shipped to / Consignado a.

FACTURA COMERCIAL

DATE FECHA	YOUR ORDER/SU PEDIDO:	TERMS/FORMA DE PAGO.	SALESMAN	INVOICE/FACTURA
QUANTITY CANTIDAD	DESCRIPTION. DESCRIPCION		UNIT PRICE PRECIO UNID.	TOTAL U.S. DOLLARS

CERTIFICAMOS QUE ESTA FACTURA ESTA CORRECTA Y QUE LOS PRODUCTOS OFRECIDOS SON DE FABRICACIÓN DE LOS ESTADOS UNIDOS DE AMÉRICA.

THESE COMMODITIES LICENSED BY U.S. FOR FINAL DESTINATION

POR _____

DIVERSION CONTRARY TO U.S. LAW PROHIBITED

Informal Entries. This form is used for entries valued at under $1,250.00 if commercial or for entries of personal dutiable merchandise under $500.00. It is a simplified entry and does not require as much detail as a consumption entry. This entry is not appraised by the commodity specialist at customs; it is usually liquidated (or paid) at entry.

Consumption Entries. A consumption entry (CF7501) must be prepared when merchandise is imported to be used by the importer or sold in the United States. In such an event, duty must be paid. (See figure 9–1.) This entry is also required to provide customs with a full description of all the goods and units involved. Included in the requirements is provision of proof of surety duties and the particular importer. All of the required information serves two purposes:

A customs formality and measure of control,

A means to obtain data for useful statistics on all merchandise.

Even when the merchandise is duty-free, the importer is still required to provide the consumption entry to serve the two purposes.

Transportation Entries. This form, an *Immediate Transportation Entry* (CF7512), is specifically used to transfer merchandise "in bond" to another port in the United States where customs clearance finally takes place. Therefore, full description, duty rates, and exact values are not required on this entry. It is important however that the shipment travel common carrier and under bond until it reaches its final destination.

Temporary Importation. This entry is made for goods imported into the United States that are not for sale and are of temporary nature. These goods pay no duty, yet they are required to be under bond for their exportation within one year from the date of entry. In some cases, with approval of the director of port, the one-year limit may be extended up to three years. Usually the bonds involved are double the value of the estimated duties. The Temporary Importation Bond Entry is prepared on the CF7501 Entry Summary.

Drawback Entries. These entries are made by the importer under two conditions in order to receive duty refunds.

1. If the imported shipment does not conform to order and/or specifications, as long as customs has inspected the shipment and agreed, the order may be exported within ninety days and the importer will receive a refund of 99 percent of the duties originally charged. The remaining 1 percent is retained by customs as an administration fee.

Exhibit 9–3. Informal Entry

INFORMAL ENTRY
DEPARTMENT OF THE TREASURY
UNITED STATES CUSTOMS SERVICE

INFORMAL ENTRY

6.7, 10.71, 141.68, 142.13, 143.23 -
143.26, 145.4, 145.12, C.R.

Form approved
O.M.B. No. 48-R0236

ORIGINAL

IMPORTER			PORT		
ADDRESS OF IMPORTER (Show Zip Code)					

MARKS & NOS.; AWB OR B/L NO.	DESCRIPTION OF MERCHANDISE AND/OR T.S.U.S. ANNO. REPORTING NUMBER	VALUE	RATE	DUTY
	QUANTITY			
	07 TOTAL DUTY			
	TOTAL I.R. TAX			
	TOTAL COLLECTION	$		

I.T. NO.	DATE OF IMPORTATION	COUNTRY OF EXPORTATION	IMPORTING CARRIER	G.O. NO.
I.T. FROM PORT OF:				

I declare that the information above set forth is accurate to the best of my knowledge and belief and that I have not received and do not know of any other invoice than that attached.

SIGNATURE OF IMPORTER OR AGENT

Validation shows location, date and amount of payment.

Customs Form 5119-A (10-27-77)

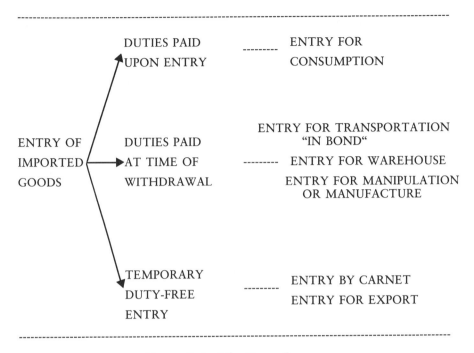

Figure 9–1. The Entry Process

2. Under the same condition, if the shipment is exported within three years without substantial transformation to the shipment and verified by customs, the importer may receive a full refund of duties.

Import Procedure Forms. Within five days of a shipment arriving in the United States, the importer or customhouse broker must file with customs an original bill of lading, carrier's certificate, or any authorized proof of title, such as a commercial or customs invoice. This is accompanied with a signed entry manifest. If the merchandise arrives by air, the airway bill may be used. If a customs or commercial invoice is not presented at the time of entry, customs will accept a pro-forma landed invoice to guarantee submission of the required invoice within six months.

If the importer wishes to take immediate possession of the goods, a *Special Permit for Immediate Delivery* (exhibit 9–7) may be applied for prior to the arrival of the merchandise. Approval of the application is given for certain perishable goods and special articles. Goods that are for the use of the importer or to be sold in the United States may be entered under the Consumption Entry. These goods then proceed to be appraised or appraisal can be delayed by filing an *Immediate Transportation Entry* (CF7512) described previously).

Exhibit 9–4. Consumption Entry

☆ U.S.GPO:1984-0-450-820

ENTRY SUMMARY

Form Approved OMB No. 1515-0065

DEPARTMENT OF THE TREASURY
UNITED STATES CUSTOMS SERVICE

(1.) Entry No.	(2.) Entry Type Code	3. Entry Summary Date
4. Entry Date	(5.) Port Code	
6. Bond No.	7. Bond Type Code	8. Broker/Importer File No.

9. Ultimate Consignee Name and Address

10. Consignee No.

(11) Importer of Record Name and Address

(12) Importer No.

(13) Exporting Country — 14. Export Date

(15) Country of Origin — 16. Missing Documents

State

(17) I.T. No. — (18) I.T. Date

(19) B/L or AWB No. — 20. Mode of Transportation — 21. Manufacturer I.D. — 22. Reference No.

(23) Importing Carrier — 24. Foreign Port of Lading — 25. Location of Goods/G.O. No.

26. U.S. Port of Unlading — (27) Import Date

(28) Line No.	30. (A) T.S.U.S.A. No. (B) ADA/CVD Case No.	31. (A) Gross Weight (B) Manifest Qty.	(32) Net Quantity in T.S.U.S.A. Units	33. (A) Entered Value (B) CHGS (C) Relationship	34. (A) T.S.U.S.A. Rate (B) ADA/CVD Rate (C) I.R.C. Rate (D) Visa No.	(35) Duty and I.R. Tax

(29) Description of Merchandise

Dollars | Cents

(36) Declaration of Importer of Record (Owner or Purchaser) or Authorized Agent

I declare that I am the importer of record and that the actual owner, purchaser, or consignee for customs purposes is as shown above. **OR** owner or purchaser or agent thereof.

I further declare that the merchandise was obtained pursuant to a purchase or agreement to purchase and that the prices set forth in the invoice are true. **OR** was not obtained pursuant to a purchase or agreement to purchase and the statements in the invoice as to value or price are true to the best of my knowledge and belief.

I also declare that the statements in the documents herein filed fully disclose to the best of my knowledge and belief the true prices, values, quantities, rebates, drawbacks, fees, commissions, and royalties and are true and correct, and that all goods or services provided to the seller of the merchandise either free or at reduced cost are fully disclosed. I will immediately furnish to the appropriate customs officer any information showing a different state of facts.

Notice required by Paperwork Reduction Act of 1980: This information is needed to ensure that importers/exporters are complying with U.S. customs laws, to allow us to compute and collect the right amount of money, to enforce other agency requirements, and to collect accurate statistical information on imports. Your response is mandatory.

↓ U.S. CUSTOMS USE ↓

A. Liq. Code	B. Ascertained Duty
	C. Ascertained Tax
	D. Ascertained Other
	E. Ascertained Total

(41) Signature of Declarant, Title, and Date

TOTALS

(37) Duty	
(38) Tax	
(39) Other	
(40) Total	

Customs Form 7501 (030984)

Exhibit 9–5. Transportation Entry

TRANSPORTATION ENTRY AND MANIFEST OF GOODS
SUBJECT TO CUSTOMS INSPECTION AND PERMIT (IN-TRANSIT ENTRY)

CUSTOMS   FORM   7512
      10-2-73

Form Approved
O.M.B. No. 48-R0212

**TRANSPORTATION ENTRY AND MANIFEST OF
GOODS SUBJECT TO CUSTOMS INSPECTION
AND PERMIT**

UNITED STATES CUSTOMS SERVICE

.... Entry No ....

Port ....

Date ....

Entry No ....

Class of Entry ....
(I.T.)(Wd.T.)(Wd.Ex.)(T.E.)(Drawback, etc.)

Dist.   Port   First U. S. Port
No...............   Code No.................... of Unlading ....

Port of ....   Date ....

Entered or imported by .... to be shipped

in bond via .... consigned to
          (C.H.L. number)   (Vessel or carrier)   (Car number and initial)   (Pier or station)
District Director of Customs .... Final foreign destination ....
                                                          (For exportations only)

Consignee ....
                 (At customs port of exit or destination)

Foreign port of lading .... B/L No. .... Date of sailing ....
            (Above information to be furnished only when merchandise is imported by vessel)

Imported on the .... Flag ... . on .... via ....
        (Name of vessel or carrier and motive power)   (Date imported)   (Last foreign port)

Exported from .... on .... Goods now at ....
         (Country)   (Date)   (Name of warehouse, station, pier, etc.)

Marks and Numbers of Packages	DESCRIPTION AND QUANTITY OF MERCHANDISE NUMBER AND KIND OF PACKAGES (Describe fully as per shipping papers)	GROSS WEIGHT IN POUNDS	VALUE (Dollars only)	RATE	DUTY

G. O. No. ....

**CERTIFICATE OF LADING FOR TRANSPORTATION IN BOND
AND/OR LADING FOR EXPORTATION FOR**

.... (Port)

WITH THE EXCEPTIONS NOTED ABOVE, THE WITHIN-
DESCRIBED GOODS WERE:
Delivered to the Carrier
named above, for delivery to
the District Director of
Customs at destination sealed
with Customs seals

Laden on the—

.... (Vessel, vehicle, or aircraft)
which cleared for —

Nos....................................
or the packages (were) (were
not) labeled, or corded and
sealed.

on .... (Date)

as verified by export records.

.... (Inspector or warehouse officer)

.... (Date)

.... (Inspector)

.... (Date)

I truly declare that the statements contained herein are true and
correct to the best of my knowledge and belief.

Entered or withdrawn by ....

....

....

To the Inspector or Warehouse Officer: The above-described
goods shall be disposed of as specified herein.

.... *For the District Director of Customs*

Received from the district director of customs of above district the
merchandise described in this manifest for transportation and delivery
into the custody of the customs officers at the port named above, all
packages in apparent good order except as noted hereon.

....

.... *Attorney or Agent of Carrier*

Exhibit 9–6. Drawback Entry

	DEPARTMENT OF THE TREASURY UNITED STATES CUSTOMS SERVICE **DRAWBACK ENTRY COVERING SAME CONDITION MERCHANDISE** 19 CFR 191.2, 191.4, 191.141, 191.156, 191.165	**J**	OMB. NO. 1515-0020

				OMB. NO. 1515-0020

Form layout:

DEPARTMENT OF THE TREASURY / UNITED STATES CUSTOMS SERVICE
DRAWBACK ENTRY COVERING SAME CONDITION MERCHANDISE
19 CFR 191.2, 191.4, 191.141, 191.156, 191.165

OMB. NO. 1515-0020
1. Drawback Entry No.
2. Drawback Entry Date

3. Location of Merchandise (Pier, etc.)
4. Exporting Carrier
5. Port of Exportation (Code)
6. Ultimate Port of Destination

7. Name of Person or Business Paying Duty
8. Importer of Record Name
9. Imp. of Rec. ID No.
10. Processing District/Port (Code)

11. Importing Carrier
12. Port of Importation
13. Date of Importation
14. Date Released by Customs

✱	15. MARKS AND NUMBERS OF PACKAGES	16. QUANTITY	17. DESCRIPTION OF MERCHANDISE	18. VALUE	19. DUTY PAID
IMP.					
EXP.					

20. In Compliance with 19 USC 1313 (J) I declare that the merchandise was not used and that it was or will be: ☐ Exported in the same condition as when imported. OR ☐ Destroyed under Customs supervision.

I declare that the indicated duty was paid on the merchandise described in this entry, that it is to be or was exported to the country indicated, and that it is not to be consumed or relanded within the limits of the United States or its possessions. I further declare that, to the best of my knowledge and belief, the said merchandise is the same in quantity, quality, value, package, pieces, etc. (except as noted on Affidavit) as specified in this document, that no allowance or reduction of duties has been made, and that no part of the duties paid has been refunded by way of drawback or otherwise

21. Signature of Declarant
22. Date
23. Name and Address of Declarant

24. Name of Firm/Address

25. Check any that apply:
☐ Accelerated Payment Requested
☐ Filed Under Exporter's Summary Procedure
☐ Proof of Exportation Attached

We hereby authorize the below named person to make entry and collect drawback on the goods described above:

26. Name of Person Authorized to Collect Drawback (if other than exporter)
27. Address

28. Signature of Exporter
29. Date
30. Name and Address of Exporter

31. AFFIDAVIT

The undersigned hereby certifies that the merchandise herein described is the same and in the same condition as that merchandise imported under Consumption Entry No._____ at_____ on_____, and the undersigned further certifies that this merchandise was not subjected to any process of manufacture or other operation except the following allowable incidental operations: _____

The subject merchandise will be destroyed under Customs supervision or exported at_____ on or about_____. The undersigned consents and agrees to keep open its factory and/or place of business and to keep records relative to this transaction available for examination at all reasonable hours by authorized Government officers, for a period of 3 years from the date of payment of the drawback claim. The undersigned is fully aware of the sanctions provided in 18 U.S.C. 1001 and 18 U.S.C. 550.

32. Date
33. Signature/Title/Company Name

ENTRY RECORD

34. Claimant ID No.
35. Reference No.
36. Duty Drawback (Acc.)
37. I.R. Drawback (Acc.)
38. TYPE CODES Entry 42 Bond
39. Bond No.
40. Port Code

41. Import Entry No.(s)
Date(s)
42. Import Entry Liq. Date(s), If Known

CUSTOMS USE ONLY

STATEMENT OF EXAMINING OFFICER

43 ☐ Prior notice of intent to export is hereby waived.
44 ☐ Customs has decided not to examine the merchandise and it may now be exported.
45 ☐ CF 3499 attached

46 ☐ Customs examination is required:
47. Location of Examination
48. Date of Examination
49. Location of Goods if to be destroyed

50 ☐ I have examined the merchandise and found it to be the same merchandise described above, in the same condition as imported, or changed in condition as allowed by law.
52. Title of Examining Officer

51 ☐ Same condition drawback cannot be authorized for the following reason(s):
53. Signature of Examining Officer and Date

LADING REPORT

54. Date Laden
55. Port Code
56. Carrier

57. Destination
58. Exceptions

I certify that the packages described above were laden for export.

59. Signature of Lading Officer
60. Date

LIQUIDATION DATA

61. Duty Paid $
62. I.R. Tax Paid $
63. Liq. Date

	ACCELERATED	NOT ACCELERATED	
64. Gross Drawback	$	$	68 ☐ REFUND
65. Less 1%	$	$	69 ☐ INCREASE
66. Less Acc. Drawback Refund	$		70 ☐ NO CHANGE
67. Net Drawback	$	$	71. Liq. Code/Initials

✱Attach Additional Sheets, If Necessary

"J" Side

Customs Form 7539 (032384)

Exhibit 9–6. Drawback Entry *(continued)*

OMB. NO. 1515-0020

DEPARTMENT OF THE TREASURY
UNITED STATES CUSTOMS SERVICE

DRAWBACK ENTRY COVERING REJECTED MERCHANDISE

C

19 CFR 191.2, 191.4, 191.142, 191.165

1. Drawback Entry No.	
2. Drawback Entry Date	

3. Location of Merchandise (Pier, etc.)	4. Exporting Carrier	5. Port of Exportation (Code)	6. Ultimate Port of Destination
7. Name of Person or Business Paying Duty	8. Importer of Record Name	9. Imp. of Rec. ID No.	10. Processing District/Port (Code)
11. Importing Carrier	12. Port of Importation	13. Date of Importation	14. Date Released by Customs

	15. MARKS AND NUMBERS OF PACKAGES	16. QUANTITY	17. DESCRIPTION OF MERCHANDISE	18. VALUE	19. DUTY PAID
IMPORTED					
EXPORTED					

20. The merchandise does not conform to sample or specifications in the following particulars (Submit samples or specifications if available).

21. The merchandise was shipped without consent of the consignee.

I declare that duty (as specified above) was paid on the merchandise described in this entry and that the merchandise is to be exported to the country indicated; and is not to be consumed or relanded within the limits of the United States or its possessions. I further declare that, to the best of my knowledge and belief, the said merchandise is the same in quantity, quality, value and package, as specified in this entry; that no allowance nor reduction of duties has been made; and that no part of the duties paid has been refunded by way of drawback or otherwise.

22. Signature of Declarant	23. Date	24. Name and Address of Declarant
25. Name of Firm/Address		26. Import Entry Liq. Date, If Known

We hereby authorize the below-named person to make entry and collect drawback on the goods described above:

27. Name of Person Authorized to Collect Drawback (if other than exporter)	28. Address
29. Signature of Exporter	30. Date	31. Name and Address of Exporter

Entry Record

32. Claimant's Name	33. Claimant's ID No.	34. Ref. No. (If Applicable)	35. Import Entry No.	36. Entry Date	37. Codes
					Entry 43 / Bond / Port

CUSTOMS USE ONLY

PACKAGES DESCRIBED ABOVE RECEIVED IN CUSTOMS CUSTODY.

40. Exceptions

EXAMINATION

38. Date received in Customs	39. District and Port

41. I found that the merchandise [ ] does [ ] does not bear evidence of deterioration; and [ ] does [ ] does not bear evidence of having been in use since release from Customs custody. I have examined the merchandise and found it to be identical to the merchandise described above, except as follows: (Item 40) →

42. The merchandise [ ] does [ ] does not conform to sample or specifications for which the order was placed. (This item to be completed only when claim is made of failure to conform to sample or specifications).

43. Date	44. Signature of Examining Officer/Title

LADING REPORT

45. Date Laden	46. Port Code	47. Port of Destination	48. Exceptions

49. Carrier

I certify that the packages described above were laden for export.

50. Signature of Lading Officer	51. Date

LIQUIDATION

Liquidation Data		Net Drawback	
52. Liq. Date	53. Gross Drawback $	54. If Manual, Issued To	
55. Reliq. Date	56. Less 1% $		
57. Liq. Code/Initials	58. Net Drawback $	59. [ ] Refund [ ] No Change	

Paperwork Reduction Act of 1980—Notice. We request the information on this form to enforce the laws of the United States, to fulfill the Customs Regulations, to ensure that the claimant is entitled to drawback, and to have the necessary information which permits Customs to calculate and refund (or increase) the correct amount of duty and/or tax. Your response is mandatory and to your benefit.

RETURN THIS FORM TO THE DISTRICT NAMED ABOVE.

*Attach Additional Sheets, If Necessary.   "C" Side   Customs Form 7539 (032384)

Exhibit 9–7. Special Permit for Immediate Delivery

DEPARTMENT OF THE TREASURY
UNITED STATES CUSTOMS SERVICE

Form Approved
OMB No. 1515-0069

ENTRY/IMMEDIATE DELIVERY

19 CFR 142.3, 142.16, 142.22, 142.24

1. ARRIVAL DATE	2. ELECTED ENTRY DATE	3. ENTRY TYPE CODE/NAME	4. ENTRY NUMBER
5. PORT	6. SINGLE TRANS. BOND	7. BROKER/IMPORTER FILE NUMBER	
	8. CONSIGNEE NUMBER		9. IMPORTER NUMBER
10. ULTIMATE CONSIGNEE NAME		11. IMPORTER OF RECORD NAME	
12. CARRIER CODE	13. VOYAGE/FLIGHT/TRIP	14. LOCATION OF GOODS—CODE(S)/NAME(S)	
15. VESSEL CODE/NAME			
16. U.S. PORT OF UNLADING	17. MANIFEST NUMBER	18. G.O. NUMBER	19. TOTAL VALUE
20. DESCRIPTION OF MERCHANDISE			

21. IT/BL/AWB CODE	22. IT/BL/AWB NO.	23. MANIFEST QUANTITY	24. TSUSA NUMBER	25. COUNTRY OF ORIGIN	26. MANUFACTURER NO.

27. CERTIFICATION

I hereby make application for entry/immediate delivery. I certify that the above information is accurate, the bond is sufficient, valid, and current, and that all requirements of 19 CFR Part 142 have been met.

SIGNATURE OF APPLICANT

X

PHONE NO.	DATE

29. BROKER OR OTHER GOVT. AGENCY USE

28. CUSTOMS USE ONLY

☐ OTHER AGENCY ACTION REQUIRED, NAMELY:

☐ CUSTOMS EXAMINATION REQUIRED.

☐ ENTRY REJECTED, BECAUSE:

DELIVERY AUTHORIZED:	SIGNATURE	DATE

Paperwork Reduction Act Notice: This information is needed to determine the admissibility of imports into the United States and to provide the necessary information for the examination of the cargo and to establish the liability for payment of duties and taxes. Your response is necessary.

Customs Form 3461 (112085)

This entry allows the goods to be transferred under bond to a warehouse to be stored until withdrawn partially or fully by filing the *Warehouse Withdrawal for Consumption Entry* (exhibit 9–8). Duty is then paid as goods are released. Ships that hold goods destined for another country can serve as bonded warehouses.

Appraisement. After the entry form, along with the necessary papers, has been filed, the invoice is sent to the appraisers. The shipment is examined by customs samplers supported by a team of import specialists. Further examination, if necessary, is conducted at the "appraiser stores." These stores include laboratories in which substances are analyzed to ascertain their properties and true value.

Liquidation. Once appraisal is completed and the rate and amount of duty are assessed, the importer or CHB can liquidate the entry. Or, if disagreements occur, a protest is then filed. The import-specialist team reevaluates the shipment, agreeing with the claim or forwarding the protest to the U.S. Customs Court for a final decision.

Insurance

Insurance is a real transportation-related cost as well. The importer needs to be insured and protected from losses arising during the transportation of goods from their point of departure to their final destination. This need to be insured is due to the hazards and risks involved but not covered by the carriers in freight claims. In the transportation business, both nationally and internationally, virtually all carriers carry liability insurance of their own. The problem of insurance on the part of the importer arises from all exemptions allotted to the carriers by the American Carriage of Goods by Sea Act of 1936 and the Federal Aviation Act. Even though the air-cargo industry is not formally regulated as other modes, there are accepted guidelines that the industry follows, such as the limit of liability (which is usually stated as a value per shipment or per pound), filed tariffs as conclusive evidence of the contract of carriage, and the carrier liability on loss and damage due to their negligence.

There are several insurance policies from which an importer may choose. The choice rests upon several key variables: the needs of the insured, the volume of business transactions conducted, and the frequency of use for a particular insurance policy. The insurance policy chosen must meet all the requirements of the shipper and the consignee and thus be appropriate for the goods involved.[8] An importer can choose among the following types of policy:

Specific policy: Such a policy is issued to cover one particular shipment.

Open or floating policy: Most cargo insurance is written under this type of policy, which insures all shipments while in transit within a specific

Exhibit 9–8. Warehouse Withdrawal for Consumption Entry

DUTY PAID

WAREHOUSE WITHDRAWAL FOR CONSUMPTION

Form Approved
O.M.B. No. 1515-0004

This Space for Census Use Only	U.S. CUSTOMS SERVICE	This Space for Customs Use Only
BLOCK AND FILE NO.		WITHDRAWAL NO. AND DATE
	10.64; 19.11; 19.15; 19.16; 125.31; 125.33; 141.61; 141.68; 146.46, C.R.	
Port of Entry Name	Dist. and Port Code	Whse. Bond No. and Date
Importing Vessel (Name) or Carrier		Date of Importation
Merchandise Entered By		

MARKS & NUMBERS OF PACKAGES COUNTRY OF ORIGIN OF MERCHANDISE (1)	DESCRIPTION OF MERCHANDISE IN TERMS OF T.S.U.S. ANNO., NO. AND KIND OF PACKAGES (2)	NET QUANTITY IN T.S.U.S. ANNO. UNITS (2a)	ENTERED VALUE IN U.S. DOLLARS (3)	T.S.U.S. ANNO. REPORTING NO. (4)	TARIFF OR I.R.C. RATE (5)	DUTY AND I.R. TAX (6)	
						Dollars	Cents
Bond							
Withdrawal							
Balance							
Warehouse							
Withdrawer					(Date)		

Withdrawer hereby authorized to withdraw the above-described merchandise.

_____
(Importer)

_____
(Withdrawer)

For sale by district directors of customs.

GPO 946-351

Customs Form 7505 (04-07-81)

geographic area. The amount of the policy and the name of the vessel are declared when shipment of the goods is undertaken. This open policy is individually adaptable to the shipping behavior of the trader and offers additional protection as the goods are still insured even if the policyholder fails to notify the insurer of the shipment. This policy enables the insured to calculate the explicit insurance costs of the particular shipment by the rate schedule provided with the policy, which lists the premium charged various commodities to ports throughout the world.

Blanket policy: In contrast to the open or floating policy, the blanket policy requires one fixed lump sum with the coverage amount set for the length of the contract term and covering the firm's shipments within a particular trade area.

One cannot overstate the importance of insurance in the import process. In the case of claims in particular, the importer should protect its position by appointing competent surveyors and by performing personal inspections. These inspections for clues that indicate problems should be made both before and at the time of unloading. Careful observation can lead to a successful claim.

The insurance business does not end for the importer at the point of entry. The material has to remain insured at the warehouse for all possible risks. Flood and liability insurance are both needed here. This is followed by the domestic inland-, river-, or air-transportation insurance to final destination until the importer legally passes title to the final buyer. At this point, inventory is transformed into accounts receivable, which in turn requires insurance up to payment. All this is important because it has a direct impact in the process of building the appropriate price structure with the minimum of risks to the importer.

Summary

In the arrangements for moving goods both safely and rapidly from the exporter, critical factors must be noted. Choice of a particular mode of transportation (waterways, airways, roadways, railways, pipelines) is affected by many factors such as cost, speed, reliability, geographic location, the nature of the product, and, in turn, national and/or international government requirements. Storage and inventory management, packaging and handling, and landed cost of the product are also significant. The proper preparation of documentation is also critical. It must be accurate and specific in terms of use and intent in order to generate the fastest possible flow of goods. Careful selection of a customhouse broker and insurance policy (specific, open or floating, or blanket) are advisable.

Exhibit 9-9. Sample Marine Insurance Policy

ORIGINAL MARINE INSURANCE POLICY

[X] ORIGINAL AND DUPLICATE ISSUED, THE ONE BEING ACCOMPLISHED, THE OTHER TO STAND NULL AND VOID.
[ ] ISSUED IN ORIGINAL ONLY.

Insurer: Hartford Insurance Company of the Southeast
Orlando, Florida 32801

THE HARTFORD

Cable Address: **HARTFIRE**

The Insurance Company (hereinafter called The Company) shall be designated herein by Co. Code:

CoCode **J**

Policy No. XXXXXXXXXXXXX **000201**

Policy No. X2XXXXXXXXXX3

000201

This is a Marine Insurance Policy, including all the terms and conditions of the agreement between the Company and the Insured or the Party(ies) to which he may assign the policy. The Company, in consideration of premium as agreed, hereby insures the Party(ies) specified below, lost or not lost, for account of whom it may concern, in accordance with the terms and conditions as specified hereafter. Warranted free from any liability for unpaid premiums as respects purchasers or pledgees of the goods insured. All shipments subject to the conditions on the reverse side hereof.

1. **DESCRIPTION OF SHIPMENT**

   (a) **Insured** XXXX SUPERIOR ENTERPRISES CORPORATION X XXX
   Key Biscayne, FL

   (b) **Route:** Shipped via

   At and from

   Sailing or B/L date

   To

   Check if "On Deck" Bill of Lading issued [ ]

   (c) **Property shipped (Description):**

   SPECIMEN

   Marks and Numbers

   (d) **Valued at and insured for**

   (e) **Loss payable to Insured or order.**

2. **ENDORSEMENT — This Policy is Transferred by Endorsement as Follows:**...
   ....*by*..
   (Authorized Signature)

3. **PERILS INSURED AND SPECIAL CONDITIONS — Shipments under deck are insured:**

   Covering against all risks of direct physical loss or damage from any external cause but excepting those risks excluded by the F. C. & S. and S. R. & C. C . warranties herein; also warranted free from any claims arising out of the inherent vice of the goods insured or consequent upon loss of time and/or market.

   SPECIMEN

4. **STANDARD CLAUSES.** The following clauses of American Institute of Marine Underwriters (April 1, 1966) are hereby included: Warehouse to Warehouse Transit Clause; Craft, & c., Clause; F. P. A. Clause; G/A Clause; Both to Blame Clause; Shore Clause; Explosion Clause; Warehousing & Forwarding Clause; Inchmaree Clause; Bill of Lading & c., Clause; Labels Clause; Machine Clause; Constructive Total Loss Clause; Duty of Insured; Carrier Clause; F. C. & S. Warranty; S. R. & C. C. Warranty; Delay Warranty.

   Shipments subject to an "On Deck" Bill of Lading are insured and warranted free of particular average unless caused by the vessel being stranded, sunk, burnt, on fire or in collision; but losses by jettison and washing overboard shall be paid irrespective of percentage.

   WAR RISKS AND STRIKES, RIOTS AND CIVIL COMMOTION covered, per latest form of American Institute of Marine Underwriters on date of attachment of risk.

   In Witness Whereof, the Company designated herein as insurer has caused this policy to be signed by its President and a Secretary, but the same shall not be binding unless countersigned by the Insured or his duly authorized representative or a duly authorized agent of the Company.

Michael S. Wilder, *Secretary*

Donald R. Frahm, *President*

SPECIMEN

Form PPO-101-8 Printed in U.S.A.

1

Authorized Signature

Date

Exhibit 9–9. Sample Marine Insurance Policy *(continued)*

SPECIAL CONDITIONS

1. a. Except as may be otherwise provided herein or endorsed hereon; Insured property is covered against the perils of the seas, fires, assailing thieves, jettisons, barratry of the master and mariners and all other like perils.
   b. Insured property shipped by air (and connecting conveyances) and by mail (ordinary or registered and including parcel post) is covered against all risks of direct physical loss or damage from any external cause except those risks excluded by the F.C. & S. and S.R. & C.C. warranties herein; shipments by air, however, are not covered against loss or damage due to cold or to changes in atmospheric pressure.
2. Warranted by the Insured free of claim for damage or injury from dampness, change of flavor, or being spotted, discolored, musty or mouldy unless caused by actual contact of sea water with articles damaged occasioned by sea perils.
3. Including transit by craft and/or ligher to and from the vessel. Each craft and/or lighter to be deemed a separate insurance. The insured are not to be prejudiced by any agreement exempting lightermen from liability.
4. In all cases of damage caused by perils insured against the extent of loss shall, so far as practicable, be ascertained by a separation of the damaged goods from the sound and a sale or appraisement (by survey) of the damaged goods only.
5. The Company shall be liable for only such proportion of General Average and Salvage Charges as the sum hereby insured (less Particular Average for which the Company is liable hereunder, if any) bears to the Contributory Value of the property hereby insured.
6. Covered losses hereunder shall be paid or made good in thirty (30) days after proofs of loss and proofs of interest are filed with the Company, the amount of any outstanding premium due the Company being first deducted if required by the Company.
7. Proofs of loss to be authenticated by an approved Claim Agent of the Company, if there be one at or near the place where such proofs are taken, or if there be none in the vicinity, by a Correspondent of the American Institute of Marine Underwriters, or Lloyd's Agent and such agent or correspondent must be represented on all surveys. It is agreed that claim agents or correspondents are to intervene only for the purpose of ascertaining and reporting the nature, cause and extent of the loss or damage and that they shall not be cited in any legal proceedings.
8. In case of any loss or misfortune it shall be lawful and necessary for the insured, his or their factors, servants and assigns to sue, labor and travel for, in and about the defense, safeguard and recovery of the property or interests insured herein, or any part thereof without prejudice to this insurance, to the charges whereof the Company will contribute in proportion as the sum insured bears to the whole sum at risk. It is agreed that the acts of the insured or of the Company, or its agents, in recovering, saving and preserving the property insured in case of disaster shall not be considered a waiver or an acceptance of abandonment nor as affirming or denying any liability under this policy.
9. It is a condition of this insurance that upon payment of any loss the Company shall be subrogated to all rights and claims against the third parties arising out of such loss. It is a further condition of this insurance that if the Insured or his or their assigns have entered or shall enter into any special agreement whereby any carrier or bailee is released from its common law or statutory liability for any loss, or have or shall have waived, compromised, settled or otherwise impaired any right of claim against a third party to which the Company would be subrogated upon payment of a loss without prior agreement of the Company and endorsement hereon, the Company shall be free from liability with respect to such loss but its right to retain or recover the premium shall not be affected.
10. The Company will indemnify the Insured for loss or damage to the insured property directly resulting from fumigation of the carrying vessel while the insured goods are on board.
11. Other Insurance — In case the Insured or others shall have effected any other ocean marine insurance directly or indirectly upon the property insured, prior in day of date to the time of attachment of any specific risk hereunder, then the Company shall be liable only for so much as the amount of such prior insurance may be deficient toward fully covering the property hereby insured, and in this event shall return the premium upon so much of the sum by them insured as they shall be exonerated by such prior insurance. In case of any other ocean marine insurance upon the said property subsequent in day of date to the time of attachment of any specific risk hereunder, the Company shall nevertheless be liable for the full extent of the sum by them insured upon the said risk without right to claim contribution from such subseqent insurance.
12. No suit or action on this policy shall be sustainable in any court of Law or Equity unless the Insured shall have complied in full with all the terms and conditions of this insurance, nor unless same shall be commenced within twelve (12) months next after the happening of the loss, provided that where such limitation of time is prohibited by the laws of the State wherein this policy is issued, then no such suit or action shall be sustainable unless commenced within the shortest limitation of time permitted by the laws of such State.

INSTRUCTIONS FOR FILING CLAIMS

In the event of loss, or expected loss or damage, to goods or merchandise insured under a Marine policy, the procedures below must be followed immediately. THESE INSTRUCTIONS ARE VERY IMPORTANT. FAILURE TO COMPLY WITH THEM MAY INVALIDATE CLAIM AGAINST THE COMPANY.

1. If shipment is tendered by carrier or other parties in whose custody the loss or damage may have occurred, exceptions must be noted upon the delivery receipt. If the carrier declines to deliver goods unless a clean receipt is signed, file immediate written protest with the carrier or party tendering delivery protesting against such action and describe the actual condition of the goods as received as well as holding them responsible for any loss which may be determined by survey.
2. Details of the loss or damage, must be reported immediately to the nearest Claims Agent of the Company listed herein. If no representative is listed for your locality, report must be made to the nearest Representative of the following:
   (a) Correspondent of the American Institute of Marine Underwriters
   (b) Lloyds' Agent

In the event none of the foregoing representatives are available, report must be made to a licensed or registered surveyor or recognized insurance authority.

The Claim Agent, correspondent or representative should be requested to hold survey of the goods IMMEDIATELY and issue a Certificate of Survey stating the cause, nature and extent of the loss or damage. The cost of such survey is to be paid by the party requesting survey and the cost thereof will be included in any valid claim against the Company.

3. The carrier should be invited to attend survey in company with surveyor appointed by the Claims Agent or above representatives. PLEASE NOTE: Claims against carriers may become disallowed by law if prompt notices are not given within the prescribed time designated in the shipping documents. The timely limit under Ocean Bills of Lading is three days and shipments by Air within seven days after delivery of goods.
4. Goods in shipping containers must be preserved in the condition received until completion of survey.
5. To facilitate adjustment of any claim recoverable under the terms and conditions of the policy the following documents should be promptly presented to the Company at either the office at Hartford Plaza, Hartford, Connecticut 06115, U.S.A., or at the Company address appearing on the face of the policy, or to the nearest Settling Agent (Settling Agents are designated in this list by an asterisk):
   a. Survey Report
   b. Original or Duplicate Policy, properly endorsed by the payee.
   c. Complete Set of Commercial Invoice(s)
   d. Certified copy of specification and/or packing list and/or weight and/or gauge certificate
   e. Bill(s) of Lading
   f. Copy of written claim filed with the carrier(s), with reply, if available.
   g. Any other information or documents relating to the claim or consignment.

"**Note:** In case of total loss of vessel and cargo, it is essential and necessary that all negotiable (original) Bills of Lading under which goods were shipped and both original and duplicate policies of insurance be surrendered. In addition, it is required that you furnish the Company with the original letter from the steamship company certifying that the goods as described in the Bill of Lading were actually on board the vessel at the time she became a total loss."

6. It is understood and agreed by the insured, that Claim Agents of this Company are only authorized to certify as to the cause, nature and extent of damage and that they cannot be cited in any proceedings.
7. In case of General Average, and in order to avoid delay in the prompt delivery of shipment it is advisable that immediate notice be given to Company's Claim Agent and request they arrange to tender appropriate General Average Guarantee to the vessel's agent and if you are required, by the Agent of the vessel, to post a cash deposit to cover General Average contribution and/or salvage charges, refund of such deposit customarily will be made by Underwriters upon surrender of the original deposit receipt, endorsed in blank by the party whose name appears thereon as depositor. In addition to this receipt Underwriters require surrender of evidence of insurance such as the original policy of insurance, together with copy of Bill of Lading and Commercial Invoice.

NOTICE

In order to collect a valid claim it is required in many countries to conform with Revenue Laws, Stamp Act or similar legislation requiring policies to be stamped upon receipt or within a specific time.

LIST OF CLAIMS AGENTS (JUNE 1985)
(SETTLING AGENTS DESIGNATED BY*)

EUROPE

*Amsterdam	DeVos & Zoon
Antwerp	VanPeborgh & Co.
Athens	Macrymichalos Brothers, S.A.
Barcelona	MacAndrews & Company, Ltd.
Belfast	W. McCalla & Co., Ltd.
Bergen	Johan Martens
Bordeaux	Andre Pierron
*Bremen	F. Reck & Company
Cadiz	Daniel Mac-Pherson & Company
Cologne	Peter Reschop
Copenhagen	Jansen & Company
Dublin	George Bell & Co., Ltd.
Duisburg	Peter Reschop
Dusseldorf	Breffka & Hehnke
Gydnia	Average Agents' Office
Genoa	Amministrazione Mackenzie
Gibraltar	Prescott, Ltd
Glasgow	McLeod & McAllister
Gothenburg	Lindahl & Collins, A/B
Hamburg	Burmester, Duncker & Jolly
Helsinki	Henrik Krause
Leghorn	Ditta Vincenzo Capanna
LeHavre	Jacques Durand-Viel
Lisbon	James Rawes & Company, Ltd.
Liverpool	Liverpool & Glasgow Salvage Assn.
*London	W. K. Webster & Co.
Madrid	MacAndrews & Co. Ltd.
Malmo	Frick & Frick, Ltd.
Marseilles	Gellatly Hankey & Co. (France) S.A.R.L.
Naples	Gastaldi & C, SPA
Neuchatel	Commissariat D'Avaries (Transport) S.A.
Oporto	Rawes (Pertiagen) Lda.
Oslo	Wesmans Havaribureau A/S
*Paris	Toplis & Harding, S.A.
*Rome	Gastaldi International S.R.L.
Rotterdam	John Hudig & Son
Stockholm	A.B. Olson & Wright
Union of Socialist Republic	USSR Foreign Insurance Dept. Ingosstrakh
Venice	G. Radonicich and C.S.A.S.
Vienna	Gellatly Hankey Marine Services

MIDDLE EAST AND ASIA

Amman	Spinney's (1948) Ltd.
Bangkok	The Borneo Co. (Thailand) Ltd.
Beijing	The People's Insurance Co. of China
*Beirut	Weber & Co.
*Bombay	F.E. Hardcastle & Co., Pvt., Ltd.
Busan	Hyopsung Shipping Corp.
*Calcutta	Gladstone Agencies Ltd.
Chittagong	James Finlay & Co., Ltd.
Colombo	Delmege Forsyth & Co., Ltd.
Dammam	Arabian Inspection & Survey Co.
Dubai	Maritime & Mercantile Internat'l
Guam	Atkins Kroll (Guam), Ltd.
Haifa	Jona Kuebler, Ltd.
*Hong Kong	Gilman & Co., Ltd.
Honolulu	Pacific Insurance Co., Ltd.
Istanbul	Vitsan Mumessilik
Jakarta	Superintending Company of Indonesia, Ltd.
Jeddah	Arabian Inspection & Survey Co. (A.E.T. Lloyds)
*Karachi	James Finlay & Co.. Ltd.
Kobe	Cornes & Co., Ltd.
Kuala Lumpur	Harper Wira Sdn, Berhad
Kuwait	Kuwait Marine & Mercantile Co., K.S.C.
Lattakia	Syrian Maritime & Transport
Madras	Wilson & Co., (Private) Ltd. Chordia Mansion
Mangalore	Peirce, Leslie (India) Pvt., Ltd.
*Manila	Jardine Davies/E.E. Elser Inc.
Naha	Connell Bros. Co. Ltd.
Penang	Sandilands Claims & Settlements Sdn., Bhd.
Rangoon	Burma Ports Corp.
*Singapore	Boustead Services Pte. Ltd.
Taipei	Tait & Co., Ltd.
Yokohama	Cornes & Co., Inc.

AUSTRALIA AND NEW ZEALAND

Adelaide	Danzas Wills Pty. Ltd.
Brisbane	Macdonald Hamilton & Co.
*Melbourne	P&O Australia Ltd.
*Sydney	H.C.T.A. Pty. Ltd.
Auckland	C.B. Thomas (Marine) Ltd.
Christchurch	Thomas Macky & Co. Ltd.
*Wellington	Blueport A.C.T. (N.Z.) Ltd.

AMERICAS AND WEST INDIES

Arica	Marto Huerta H
Asuncion	Ernesto S. Reuter
Balboa	Associated Steamship Agents, Ltd.
Belem	Agencies Mundiaia S.A.
Bogota	Houston, Ltda.
Bridgetown	Gardiner Austin & Company, Ltd.
Buenos Aires	James P. Browne & Co.
Callao	See Lima, Peru
Caracas	W. Moller, C.A.
Corinto	Adan Boza & Cia
Curacao (Willemstad)	Maduro & Curiel Bank N.V.
Georgetown	Guyana National Shipping Corp. Ltd.
Guatemala City	Agencies Unidas De Guatemala, S.A.
Guayaquil	S.A. Commercial Anglo Ecuatoriana
Hamilton	Harnett & Richardson, Ltd.
Kingston	R.S. Gamble & Son, Ltd.
Kingston, St. V	Hazells, Ltd.
La Paz	La Britanica S.A.
Lima	Denis M. Pilkington
Managua	Adan Boza & Cia
Mexico City	Watson Phillips y Cia Sucs S.A.
*Montevideo	John R. Ayling & Son
Nassau	Nassau Survey Agency Ltd.
Panama City	Pacific — Ford S.A.
Port au Prince	J. B. Vital & Co., Sucrs
Port of Spain	N.J. Gransaull & Co., Ltd.
Recife	Thom & Cia Ltd.
Rio De Janeiro	Expresso Mercantile Agencia
San Jose	H.T. Purdy, Inc.
San Juan	Francis B. Crocco, Inc.
San Pedro Sula	Adan Boza & Cia
*Santiago	Gibbs & Cia. S.A.C.
San Salvador	Gibson y Co., Suc.
Santo Domingo	Frederic Schad C. por A.
Tampico	Pulford S.A.
Vera Cruz	Castro Hermanos De Veracruz S.A.

AFRICA

Accra	Caleb Brett (Ghana) Ltd.
Addis Ababa	Gellatly, Hankey & Co.
Alexandria	Cargo Supervision & Surveying Office
Algiers	Societe Algerienne Establissement
Apapa (Lagos)	Intercotra, Ltd.
Capetown	Rennie Murray & Co. (Pty), Ltd.
Casablanca	Marbar S.A.
Dakar	Cie. des Experts Maritimes
Dar-Es-Salaam	General Agricultural Products
Durban	Rennie Murray & Co. (Pty), Ltd.
*Johannesburg	Rennie Murray & Co. (Pty), Ltd.
Kenitra	E.M. Allegre & Cie.
Khartoum	Gezira Trade & Service Co., Ltd.
Maputo	Rennies Shipping Ltda.
Mombasa	Toplis & Harding (Kenya) Ltd.
Monrovia	Denco Shipping Lines, Inc.
Nairobi	Toplis & Harding (Kenya) Ltd.
Port Elizabeth	Rennie Murray & Co. (Pty), Ltd.
Port Louis	Scott & Co., Ltd.
Port Said	El Menia Shipping Agency
Port Sudan	Gezire Trade & Services Co. Ltd.
Tangier	See Casablanca
Tunis	Societe Commerciale Tunisienne

Form PPO-101-8

Notes

1. For further discussion of explicit and implicit costs, see Marta Ortiz-Buonafina, *Profitable Export Marketing,* pp. 194–97.

2. The following section is summarized from ibid., p. 195–96.

3. *Importing into the United States* (Washington, D.C.: U.S. Customs Service, 1986), p. 13.

4. Paul T. MacElhiney, *Transportation for Marketing and Business Students* (Totowa, New Jersey: Littlefield, Adams, 1975), pp. 6–7.

5. See also Ortiz-Buonafina, pp. 201–2.

6. *Importing into the United States,* p. 39.

7. Alfred Murr, *Export/Import Traffic Management and Forwarding,* 6th ed. (Centreville, Maryland: Cornell Maritime Press, 1979), p. 261.

8. For a more complete discussion of insurance policies, see op. cit., pp. 177–80.

10
Import Procedures

Customs-Clearance Procedures

All goods to be imported into the customs territory of the United States (which includes the fifty states, the District of Columbia, and Puerto Rico), whether duty-free or dutiable and regardless of value, require a Customs Entry and, often, fulfillment of specific procedures. The importer bears the liability of compliance with all such procedures and, unless otherwise relieved by laws and regulations, for all duties accrued. Such liability can only be discharged by payment.[1]

All charges relating to an import constitute a personal debt of the importer and take precedence over any other debt, even in case of death or insolvency. The U.S. government's claim against the estate for unpaid duties has priority over other obligations to any creditor(s).[2]

Entry Procedures

Entry of goods requires that documentation has been presented to a customs officer to release goods imported from customs custody. The documents (such as the bill of lading) are evidence of ownership. In addition, necessary invoices with other documents (packing slips and so on) will accompany the document package. These documents will assist customs in assessing duties, gathering statistical data on imported goods, and ascertaining that all laws and regulations are being obeyed. This process is commonly referred to as submission.

The entry must have in place a surety bond or customs bond, except if valued under $250, and payment of all duties and taxes must be complete. With payment/deposit of all duties and taxes completed, filing is complete. Numerous types of entries that can be made, such as entered for consumption, entered for warehouse, and entered temporarily under bond. *Entered for consumption* means that entry has been made with appropriate documentation to customs with estimated duties as marked. *Entered for warehouse* means that documents are entered for customs' assessment, statistical data collection, and application of laws and regulations. *Entered temporarily under bond* implies that supporting documents under bond have been filed with customs in proper form.

Merchandise can be entered only by the owner, purchaser, or a licensed customhouse broker. If the merchandise is consigned "to order," entry can be made by a person who has possession of the bill of lading endorsed by the consignor. An airway bill of lading is commonly used for goods transported by air. For customs purposes, common procedures call for entry to be made by a person or firm certified as the owner of the merchandise by the carrier transporting it to the port of entry. The carrier issues a "carrier's certificate"; however, a shipping receipt or duplicate bill of lading are permissible for entry.[3]

Marking of Imported Goods. Section 304 of the Tariff Act of 1930 outlines the markings required on all goods imported. This includes the containers or packages in which goods are transported. The basic requirement for the marking is that it be permanent, legible, and conspicuous. All goods (including packaging) that originate in a foreign country must be marked in such a manner that the ultimate purchaser in the United States can recognize the country of origin of this good. The term *United States* here includes all of its territories and possessions except the Virgin Islands, American Samoa, Wake Islands, Kingman Reef, Johnston Island, and Guam. Goods not meeting these marking specifications will be subject to an additional duty of 10 percent on the final appraised value of the goods. Items exempt from marking regulations include:

Goods that cannot be marked,

Goods that would be injured if marked prior to shipment,

Goods that cannot be marked prior to shipment except at an expense economically prohibitive of its importation,

Goods made of a crude substance,

Goods whose container substantially indicates the country of origin,

Goods imported for the use of the importer and not intended for sale in its present form or any other form,

Goods to be processed in the United States by the importer or for the importer's account other than for the purpose of concealing the origin of such articles and in such manner that any marks contemplated would necessarily be obliterated, destroyed, or permanently concealed,

Goods whose ultimate purchaser will recognize their origin because of the character of the good or from the circumstances of the importation, even though they are not marked to indicate their origin,

Goods that are produced twenty years prior to being imported,

Goods that cannot be marked after importation except at a prohibitive expense and for which the negligence of not marking overseas prior to importation was not based on the importer, producer, seller, or shipper's disregard of the regulations.

Should the goods meet the preceding specific requirements and not need to be marked, the container that contains the goods must show the country of origin in English with abbreviations permitted. Common practice dictates that when the words *United States*, the letters *U.S.* or *U.S.A.*, or names of any cities in the United States are used on a good of foreign origin or its container, that the name of the country of origin preceded by "product of" or "made in" be marked in close proximity. The intent of this requirement is to not mislead the public that the good was manufactured in the United States. For souvenirs and goods marked with trademarks or trade names, similar requirements must be met.

Declaration of Entry by Agent. Entry of merchandise can be done through an agent who has full knowledge of the facts. The agent is given power of attorney to declare documents; however, no bond to produce declaration of the consignee is required. Neither the declaration of the actual owner nor the bond will be accepted unless executed by the actual owner or an authorized agent, and filed by the consignee or the authorized agent. Should the owner be a nonresident, the actual owner's declaration is unacceptable unless filed with the owner's bond and resident corporate surety.[4]

Power of Attorney. Limited or general power of attorney may be executed for the transaction by an agent or attorney for a portion of or all customs business of the principal.

For example, an individual that is not a regular importer may appoint another individual as his or her unpaid agent for customs purposes by executing a power of attorney applicable to a single noncommercial shipment. Such power of attorney may be written, printed, or stamped on the invoice, or it may appear on a separate paper attached to such invoice. The said power authorizes an agent to execute the owner's import declaration and to enter on his or her behalf or account the goods described in the invoice. The duration of a power of attorney issued by a partnership does not exceed two years from the date of execution.

Other power of attorneys have an unlimited time frame. Revocation can take place at any time with the appropriate documentation submitted to customs district director. The holder of a power of attorney for a resident principal can appoint a subagent only for the purpose of executing shippers' export declarations. The designated subagent is not permitted to further delegate authority.

Authority given to a customhouse broker permits delegation of that authority to any of its licensed officers or authorized officers or employees.

The power of attorney will specify the districts in which the agent has authority to represent the principal. Prior to representing the principal, the customhouse broker must obtain a power of attorney document that is kept in file should the Treasury Department request review of files.[5]

Presentation of Entries. Entry documents must be prepared in a legible, indelible manner and shall be endorsed by the importer. The required forms according to regulation must be filled out with all necessary information. The endorsement of the consignee's declaration on the documentation for goods entered for consumption, for warehouse, or for temporary importation under bond shall be regarded as the signing of the entry required by the Tariff Act of 1930. The Department of Commerce's International Trade Administration allocates an identifying number for goods subject to an antidumping or countervailing-duty order. Entries that include such merchandise and do not have the identifying number will be rejected.

Separate Entries. It is common for various elements of a single shipment of merchandise to be entered separately. The shipment must be addressed to one consignee. Merchandise that does not exceed $250 in value and is free of duty need not be entered. The consignee must keep in mind that:

Different portions will be entered under different entries for different ports of entry.

Each entry will be appraised according to its class as such and will be processed by different customs commodity-specialist teams.

The separate entries are handled with separate bills of lading.

When separate entries for one consignment are made, the following procedures shall apply:

The entries shall be presented simultaneously when practicable.

A separate consignee's declaration shall be filed for each entry.

Each entry shall cover whole packages or not less than one ton of bulk merchandise, except when a portion of the merchandise is entered under a temporary importation bond.

The U.S. government collects statistical information concerning imports for each class of merchandise subject to separate statistical reporting numbers. The applicable information is required by the General Statistics Headnotes, Tariff Schedules of the United States Annotated (TSUSA).

Place and Time of Filing. An application for immediate delivery and entry, entry summary, or withdrawal documentation shall be filed at the customhouse or at any other customs location approved by the district director in the district where the merchandise is to be or has been released. Filing of documents is to be done during normal business hours.[6]

Liability of Duties

The liability for duties is incurred when imported merchandise arrives within a customs territory of the United States. Goods that are imported and subsequently exported will be subject to duty on each ensuing import in addition to duty on the first importation. This regulation does not generally apply to personal and household effects taken abroad and returned to the United States, such as items brought along on vacation. In addition to liability for duties, all taxes due to the Internal Revenue Service are owed as provided by law or regulation. With importation, the importer has a personal debt to the United States that can be discharged by payment in full of all duties unless exempted by law or regulation. Payment can be made to the broker, who subsequently pays the U.S. Customs Service. Should the broker not forward these funds on behalf of the importer, the liability is still due from the importer. This payment would constitute one check or bank draft payable to the broker, which would include both duties and the broker's fees and charges. The broker submits the duties to customs on behalf of the importer. An alternative method would be to use two negotiable instruments, one payable to the U.S. Customs Service and the other compensating the broker for its services. The duties check to the Customs Service will be forwarded by the broker.

It is common practice to deposit estimated duties with the customs officer authorized to receive duties when filing import documentation. There are numerous exceptions to this practice. If entry has been for warehouse, the deposit of estimated duties shall occur when the withdrawal for consumption is provided. Under an informal mail entry, payment is made by the addressee at the time of delivery. When merchandise has not as yet been appraised for value, deposit of estimated duties will be made upon determination of value by the customs officer. An entry for transportation or under bond also does not require a deposit of estimated duties. When under bond, the merchandise may be for permanent exhibition, a trade fair, or comparable reasons. Deposit of estimated duties is not required on entry or withdrawal for consumption of cigars and cigarettes and bulk distilled spirits transferred to the bonded premises of a distilled-spirits plant. The requirement of the Bureau of Alcohol, Tobacco and Firearms is that by regulation, an approved original copy of the Alcohol, Tobacco and Firearms Form must be completed and accompany the entry or withdrawal for consumption.

Liquidation of Duties

Liquidation means the final calculation or determination of the duties/drawback accrued on an entry. All entries pertaining to imported merchandise will be liquidated. Excluded from this category is merchandise for temporary-importation-bond entries and that for transportation in bond or for immediate exportation. In the duties calculation, value is rounded to the nearest dollar. In the event of a discrepancy of under $10 between liquidated duties and estimated duties, the difference is generally disregarded and the entry is endorsed as entered. Merchandise entered and not liquidated within one year shall be deemed liquidated by operation of law at the rate of duty, value, quantity, and amount of duties asserted by the importer at the time of filing an entry summary for consumption in proper form. This regulation applies to entries of merchandise for consumption or withdrawals of merchandise for consumption made on or after April 1, 1979.[7]

Classification of Merchandise under the Tariff Schedules of the United States

Merchandise is classified using the Tariff Schedules of the United States (TSUS) as a guideline. Interpretation of the TSUS is conducted by the administrative and judicial bodies. The applicable rates of duty will be those in effect on the date of entry or withdrawal for consumption. The exception is merchandise covered by an entry for immediate transportation or shipped but returned to the port of entry.

In the event that the merchandise is discoverd to be commingled (that is, merchandise of different rates is put together), the district director will notify the importer of such findings and the commingled articles will be subject to the highest rate of duty applicable to any portion. This ruling will not apply if the quantity and value of each of the product types can be readily determined employing customs' methods.

Determining Value. The value applied to merchandise determines the duty assessed to imported goods. Goods that are not specified on the final list shall be appraised in accordance with Section 402 of the Tariff Act of 1930 as amended. For goods specified on the final list, appraisement will be ruled by Section 402a of the act, as redesignated and amended. For merchandise that is included on the final list and has been allotted a unit value, the value will be confirmed in accordance with Section 402a, as amended, to determine that the goods are included on the list. In calculating the value, if it is within a reasonable range of the final list, the goods will be appraised in accordance with Section 402a and classified at the rate applicable to such appraised value.

If the value calculated is outside the reasonable range of the final list, appraisal will be done under Section 402 as amended and shall be classified at the rate applicable to that appraised value. The district director has the authority to decide the amount of dutiable charges that are included in the appraised value of the merchandise. The tariff classification, rate of duty, value, and estimated duties must meet the approval of the district director. The preceding information shall appear on the invoice next to the applicable articles. The item number and rate of duty shall be noted in the left-hand portion of the invoice. All calculations of deductions and additions to invoice value must appear on the invoice. Also, if there are any discrepancies between the entered unit value per article and the invoiced unit value, the entered unit value must be indicated. Finally, all notations by importers must appear in blue or black ink.

New Harmonized System. The new harmonized system is an international commodity-classification system that was implemented in the United States in 1987. The Harmonized System is a method to classify products for customs tariff, statistical, and transport-documentation purpose. The system is based on the current Customs Cooperation Council Nomenclature. The detailed classification contains about 5,000 headings and subheadings outlined in 96 chapters and 20 sections. In addition, there are interpretation rules and legal notes to the chapters and sections that provide the legal text. By incorporating this system, countries can better label goods for tariff or statistical purposes.[8]

The Entry Process

Upon arrival of merchandise into the United States, entry of documents is required within five working days (unless a longer time is authorized by law or regulation, or by the district director in writing). If documents are presented prior to arrival, the port of entry and time will be specified. For merchandise to be released from customs, entry documentation must include the following:

1. Customs Entry Form 3461 or Form 7533 as required,
2. Evidence of permission to enter goods,
3. A commercial invoice, pro-forma invoice, or acceptable documentation in place of the commercial invoice,
4. Packing list where required,
5. Specific documents as required by customs, federal, state, or local agencies for a particular shipment,
6. Additional copies of documentation for the district director of customs.

Merchandise that has entered customs will not be released at the time customs receives entry documentation. Release of goods will take place if a bond and Customs Form 301 are filed, a corporate surety is executed, or secured by cash deposits or obligations of the U.S. have been filed.

Kinds of Entries

Entry for Consumption. Goods entered for immediate consumption are the most common type of entry. If not held for examination, they can be forwarded with a bond. Merchandise is inspected to ascertain that invoicing has been accurately processed. Prior to entering the market of the United States, the merchandise must meet all regulations or laws that govern the import of this product.

Entry for Warehouse. Goods that qualify for duty may be entered into a bonded warehouse with the expense and risk incurred by the importer. Upon entry of the merchandise, a warehouse-entry–summary Customs Form 7501 must be filed. Duties are paid when goods are taken out of the warehouse and prepared for consumption. This alleviates the need to deposit an estimate of duties upon entry. If the merchandise was entered under another form of entry and has remained under continuous customs duty, a substitute entry will be processed. If the previous entry required a deposit for estimated duties, these funds will be refunded.

It is the responsibility of the importer to include on the entry form its selection of a bonded warehouse. Should the merchandise require inspection by customs, then upon satisfaction of customs regulations, the merchandise will be moved to the designated warehouse. The time limit for bonded merchandise is five years from date of importation. To remove all or part of the goods requires endorsement of the withdrawal form along with the filing of the appropriate bond. There are limits on who can remove merchandise from a bonded warehouse. Those eligible include the person with financial responsibility for duties being withdrawn, the importer on file for warehouse entry, and the actual owner or the individual the title has been transferred to.

Goods can be taken from one warehouse and forwarded to another port of entry, provided that withdrawal for consumption is processed at the port of destination prior to the expiration of the warehousing time limit. The merchandise is entered at the new port of entry for rewarehousing by the consignee named on the withdrawal form.

The duty rate applicable to warehoused merchandise is the rate in effect at the time of withdrawal from warehouse for consumption. More specifically, it is the rate at the time of filing withdrawal documentation. With the permission of the Secretary of Treasury, merchandise may be withdrawn from warehouse for consumption and payment for duty may not be applicable.

Entry for Transportation "in Bond." Merchandise that is entered at a port in the United States can be entered for transportation in bond without appraisement to any other port of entry designated by the importer, and by a designated bonded carrier. Goods that are entered under immediate transportation with no appraisement entry can be entered for that purpose, for transportation and exportation, or for an alternate form of entry. There is a time limit in this case also: one year. If more than a year has passed from the original importation date, an entry for consumption is the only acceptable entry form.

The other entries eligible for transportation under bond are:

Warehouse/rewarehouse withdrawal for transportation,

Warehouse/rewarehouse withdrawal for exportation or transportation and exportation,

Transportation and exportation,

Exportation.

Entry for Manipulation or Manufacture. Merchandise entered into a bonded warehouse may be manipulated or further manufactured without payment of duty. There are approximately fifteen hundred such warehouses dispersed through the United States and broken down to eight categories defined by the type of operation. In warehouses established for merchandise manipulation, the good may be cleaned, sorted, repacked, or changed in some other cosmetic manner. Manufacturing is not permitted in a manipulation warehouse. The warehouse is monitored by customs, and expenses to manipulate merchandise are paid by the proprietor. When the product has been refined, it can be withdrawn for exportation to other countries or certain U.S. insular possessions without payment of duties. If the duty is paid, then the merchandise may be withdrawn for consumption.

Buildings or parts thereof may be classified as bonded manufacturing warehouses if they meet the requirements of location, construction, and administration of operations as outlined by customs. These warehouses must be used only for manufacture or assembly of imported goods/materials that are subject to internal revenue tax and will be exported when completed. This makes the finished product exempt from duty.

Entry by Carnet. Merchandise may be entered temporarily duty-free using a carnet, an international customs document authorized by U.S. customs regulations. Acceptable carnets are ATA (*Admissions Temporaire* or Temporary Admissions) carnet is insured by the U.S. Council of the International Chamber of Commerce. This organization has been designated by the U.S. Customs Service as the issuing and guaranteeing organization of ATA carnets in the United States.

This entry applies to temporary duty-free entry of professional equipment, commercial samples, and advertising material. With the ATA carnet, documents can be processed in advance and merchandise can pass through numerous countries without delay. The time limit for an ATA carnet is one year.

TIR (*Transport International Routier* or International Road Transport) carnets give the green light to vehicles traveling by road, containers with their contents to cross territory without inspection and little delays of an administrative nature. The tractor trailers cross the entire country with containers that have been sealed by customs at port of entry and remain so until the final destination. At the point of final destination, the merchandise can be inspected when the customs seal is broken. The carnet is terminated at the end of the transit. In the United States, the Equipment Interchange Association has been authorized by the Customs Service to be the issuing and guaranteeing association for TIR carnets.[9]

Duty Assessment

Valuation of Merchandise. It is the responsibility of U.S. customs officers to allocate a value for imported goods. In the majority of cases, the customs value of goods exported to the United States on or after July 1, 1980 is the transaction value. If this method is not applicable, then a subsequent sequence of valuation methods is utilized.[10] The sequence is:

> transaction value
> deductive value
> computed value
> other value

If the first alternative valuation method (transaction value) is not applicable, the next method in the sequence (deductive value) is applied.

Transaction Value. The transaction value of goods imported into the United States is the price paid or payable. There is no concern as to how this price was arrived at. The price paid/payable may include an amount for assembly of imported goods in which the seller has no interest other than as the assembler. The value added would be the components and required adjustments. In addition, the following items must be added into the price paid/payable if not previously included in the price of the imported merchandise:

1. Packing costs incurred by the buyer (cost of containers, coverings, labor, and materials used in packing for transport).
2. Selling commission incurred by the buyer and paid to the seller's agent.

3. Costs incurred for any assistance provided by the buyer of imported merchandise (for example, components, parts, tools, molds, or design work) that is used in the production or sale of merchandise.

4. Fees for royalty or license related to the imported goods that the buyer has paid as a condition of sale. However this will vary depending on the circumstances of the sale.

5. Proceeds for a subsequent resale, disposal, or use of the goods that should be allocated to the seller and that are subject to duty.

If it is deemed that insufficient information is available for any of the preceding items, the transaction value cannot be determined.

Deductive Value. The deductive value (the next appraisement method in the sequence of merchandise valuation) is calculated when the transaction value of identical or similar merchandise cannot be determined. Generally, deductive value is the resale value of the imported merchandise in the United States. This value has additions and deductions that massage the value. If the goods are sold in the same condition as when imported, the unit price is the unit price at which the merchandise concerned is sold in the greatest aggregate quantity at or about such date of importation. However, if the goods are sold in the imported condition but not at or close to the date of importation of appraised merchandise, the price is the unit price at which the merchandise concerned is sold in the greatest aggregate quantity after the date of importation of the merchandise being appraised but before the close of the ninetieth day after the date of such importation.

Deductions from the unit price include:

commissions paid/payable and additions for profit and general expenses, actual and associated insurance, and transportation costs incurred for shipment of merchandise,

federal taxes and customs duties payable on merchandise imported and any federal excise tax,

value added to the processing of merchandise after importation when information is available to substantiate the cost incurred.

Computed Value. The next basis for appraisal of goods is computed value. Computed value includes the total of the following items:

The cost of value of the materials, the fabrication, and other processing used in the production of goods imported.

Profit and general expenses (which should be compared with those for products comparable to the imported merchandise for consistency).

Assistance in producing the goods (materials, fabrication, or general expenses) if not previously included by the producer. (Care should be taken to not double account for this item.)

Other Value. If the value of the imported goods cannot be determined, the goods will be appraised using one of the methods just discussed with minor modifications to arrive at a value. The methods can be reasonably adjusted by valuing identical merchandise exported at a similar time to the merchandise being appraised. Customs values for identical goods previously determined under the deductive value and computed value could be applied. Finally, the ninety-day requirement could be extended to assist in arriving at a value.

Penalties for Civil and Criminal Fraud. The Tariff Act of 1930 generally applies to any person who commits fraud, gross negligence, or negligence when entering goods into the United States by some form of misrepresentation. The person will be subject to a monetary penalty, and goods may be seized to insure that the penalty is paid. More specifically, civil fraud is enforced by the Customs Service upon individuals and corporations that have been negligent in their documentation by error of either omission or commission. The same applies to criminal fraud, where false documentation costs $5,000 in fine, two years imprisonment, or both for each importation or potential importation. These statutes are enforced by government agents to prevent evasion of duty payment.[11]

Special Provisions

Mail Entries. The U.S. mail is another form of importation of merchandise into the United States. Goods using the mail system are subject to customs inspection if the contents of the package appear to contain more than correspondence. Goods can be imported under either formal or informal entry depending upon whether the value of the shipment exceeds $1,000. The Customs Service and Postal Service have joint regulations that require customs-declaration forms to be affixed to the package. Pertinent information includes the nature of the contents and their value.

If the value of the shipment is less than $1,000, the entry is prepared by a customs officer, and the Postal Service will deliver the goods to the destination upon payment of duty. The Postal Service charges a fee for its service. In the case where the shipment is valued at more than $1,000, the addressee is contacted to process documents for entry at the nearest port of entry.

There are advantages to using the U.S. Postal Service to import merchandise:

For goods that are valued under $1,000, duty will be collected by the delivery person at the point of delivery.

For goods that are small in size and low in value, the Postal Service provides a very inexpensive means of shipment.

Documentation for duty-free goods is not required if the value is not in excess of $1,000.

It is not necessary to clear shipments personally if the value is under $1,000.[12]

Drawback. By definition, a drawback is a refund that is (in whole or in part) a customs duty, internal revenue tax, or fee lawfully assessed or collected because of a particular use made of the goods on which the duty, tax, or fee, was assessed or collected. To be eligible for this drawback, documentation (a proposal) must be filed. Executed by the producer or manufacturer, it should request treatment under the drawback regulations. Official acceptance of this request will be forwarded from customs upon approval or rejection of the drawback proposal. By definition, merchandise classified as a drawback product is a finished or partially completed product that has been manufactured in the United States under a drawback contract. A drawback product may be exported, at which point a claim for drawback would be made. If the product requires further manufacturing with other drawback contracts, then the drawback would be sought upon final completion and exportation of the drawback product.

The actual drawback entry is documentation that contains all pertinent information that applies to the claim for a drawback payment. The duties that are subject to drawback include all ordinary customs duties, dumping duties assessed, countervailing duties assessed, and marking duties assessed. Refunds of duties and taxes are ordinarily made upon the exportation of goods manufactured in the United States in whole or in part with the use of imported merchandise. Also, if imported duty-paid merchandise and domestic or duty-free goods of a comparable type and quality are used to manufacture goods within three years of receiving the imported goods, then drawback is available.

The refund of all duties paid is provided when:

goods that have been imported are exported from a customs warehouse,

imported goods are destroyed or exported by customs.

Goods that are warehoused in a customs bonded warehouse and later abandoned to the U.S. government may result in a refund in duties.[13]

Generalized System of Preference (GSP). This program provides duty-free treatment of specific merchandise categories (identified in chapter 7) imported directly from designated beneficiary countries. The purpose is to stimulate economic growth in less developed countries. To qualify for eligible merchandise status and be entered duty-free or to be eligible for preferred reduced duties, the goods must meet regulations outlined in the Tariff Schedules of the United States. Imported goods must be produced in the developing country and the cost or value of materials or direct costs of processing from the developing country must make up at least 35 percent of the estimated value of the merchandise. Beneficiary developing countries and articles eligible for duty-free treatment are designated by the president by executive order in accordance with Sections 502(a)(1) and 503(a) of the Trade Act of 1974. The definition of *country* includes any foreign country, any overseas dependent territory or possession of a foreign country, or the Trust Territory of the Pacific Islands. See exhibit 10–1.

For merchandise to enter duty-free and be eligible for GSP treatment, certain requirements apply. First, duty-free treatment is claimed during entry by submitting a written claim and including the prefix *A* to the Tariff Schedules of the United States. However, should duty-free treatment be applied for after the goods have been entered, the Certificate of Origin may be submitted as the claim.

For merchandise whose value exceeds $250, the (GSP) Certificate of Origin Form A must be filed. This form provides evidence as to the country of origin. Form A must be properly completed and endorsed by the exporter in the country from which it is directly imported. Certification by an appropriate government authority in that country is also required. Should the original Form A be destroyed or misplaced, a duplicate is acceptable provided that the appropriate government body in the country of origin issues and endorses said document with the word *duplicate* in box 4. The duplicate form must also provide the original date of issue of the Certificate of Origin. With regards to goods valued at $250 or less, the filing of a Certificate of Origin is waived. The district director may require evidence to substantiate the country of origin. If there is insufficient evidence to satisfy the district director as to the country of origin, then the merchandise shall not be deemed to have originated in a beneficiary developing country. These requirements are established by the director.

In arriving at a cost or value of merchandise, the following items must be included:

Producer's actual cost for materials;

Freight, insurance, packing, and all other costs incurred in transporting goods/materials (if not included in producer's actual cost);

The actual cost of wastage less any revenue from its sale;

Taxes and/or duties paid on materials by the beneficiary developing country;

For material received without charge, at less than fair market value: material and its manufacture including general expenses, built-in profit margin, and freight, insurance, packing, and all other costs incurred in transporting materials to the manufacturer's plant.

If data are not available to ascertain the value of the goods, then the appraising officer shall employ reasonable methods to arrive at a value.[14]

Should additional information be required in regards to the administrative and operational aspects of the GSP, questions should be addressed to the Director, Duty Assessment Division, U.S.Customs Service, Washington, D.C. 20229.

Caribbean Basin Initiative (CBI). The Caribbean Basin Recovery Act, referred to as the Caribbean Basin Initiative, authorizes the president to proclaim duty-free treatment for all eligible articles from any beneficiary country. Goods are classified as "eligible articles" when they are imported directly from a beneficiary country. The country-of-origin criterion must also be met. There is however a list of goods that may not be considered eligible articles and thus are not eligible to duty-free treatment under the CBI:

Textile and apparel articles that are subject to textile agreements.

Footwear, handbags, luggage, flat goods, work gloves, and leather wearing apparel not designated on August 5, 1983, as eligible articles for the purpose of the Generalized System of Preferences under Title V, Trade Act of 1974, as amended.

Tuna, prepared or preserved in any manner, in air-tight containers.

Petroleum, or any product derived from petroleum, provided for in Part 10, Schedule 4, Tariff Schedules of the United States (TSUS).

Watches and watch parts (including cases, bracelets, and straps) of whatever type including, but not limited to, mechanical, quartz digital, and quartz analog, if such watches or watch parts contain any material that is the product of any country with respect to which TSUS column-2 rates of duty apply.

Sugars, syrups, and molasses, subject to specified restrictions found in the TSUS.

As was the case with GSP countries, CBI countries must meet the criteria, while the good must either be wholly the growth, product, or manufacture of a beneficiary country or else be a new or different article of commerce that has been grown, produced, or manufactured in a beneficiary country. All materials incorporated into the goods must come from a beneficiary country (though not all materials have to be from the same beneficiary country). Should any materials from a nonbeneficiary country be included, the goods would not be classified as "eligible articles." In order to be exempt from duty under the CBI, the district director must be satisfied that all requirements have been met. The claim for duty-free treatment can be filed at entry by entering the prefix

Exhibit 10–1.   Generalised System of Preferences

1. Goods consigned from (Exporter's business name, address, country)	Reference No
	GENERALISED SYSTEM OF PREFERENCES **CERTIFICATE OF ORIGIN** (Combined declaration and certificate) **FORM A**
2. Goods consigned to (Consignee's name, address, country)	Issued in _____ (country) See Notes overleaf
3. Means of transport and route (as far as known)	4. For official use.

5. Item number	6. Marks and numbers of packages	7. Number and kind of packages; description of goods	8. Origin criterion (see Notes overleaf)	9. Gross weight or other quantity	10. Number and date of invoices

11. Certification	12. Declaration by the exporter
It is hereby certified, on the basis of control carried out, that the declaration by the exporter is correct.	The undersigned hereby declares that the above details and statements are correct; that all the goods were produced in _____ (country) and that they comply with the origin requirements specified for those goods in the Generalised System of Preferences for goods exported to _____ (importing country)
Place and date, signature and stamp of certifying authority	Place and date, signature of authorised signatory

Exhibit 10–1. Generalised System of Preferences *(continued)*

APPLICATION FOR CERTIFICATE OF ORIGIN
Form B

The undersigned, being the exporter of the goods described overleaf, DECLARES that these goods were produced in. . . . . (country)
SPECIFIES as follows the grounds on which the goods are claimed to comply with GSP origin requirements)

. . . .
. . . .
. . . .

SUBMITS the following supporting documents²)

. . . .
. . . .
. . . .

UNDERTKES to submit, at the request of the appropriate authorities of the exporting country, any additional supporting evidence which these authorities may require for the purpose of issuing a certificate of origin, and undertakes, if required, to agree to any inspection of his accounts and any check on the processes of manufacture of the above goods, carried out by the said authorities. REQUESTS the issue of a certificate of origin for these goods.

Place and date . . . .

. . . .
(signature of authorized signatory)

¹) To be completed if materials or components originating in another country have been used in the manufacture of the goods in question. Indicate the materials or components used, their Brussels Nomenclature tariff heading, theri country of origin and, where appropriate, the manufacturing processes qualifying the goods as originating in the country of manufacture (application of List B or of the special conditions laid down in List A), the goods produce and their Brussels Nomenclature tariff heading.
Where the origin criteria involve a percentage value, give information enabling this percentage to be verified — for example the value of imported materials and components and those of undetermined origin and the ex factory price of the exported goods, where applicable.

²) For example, import documents, invoices, etc., relating to the materials or components used.

NOTES

A. **Procedure for claiming preference.** A declaration on the certificate of origin form must be prepared by the exporter of the goods and submitted in duplicate, together with a GSP application form, to the certifying authority of the country of exportation which will, if satisfied, certify the top copy of the certificate of origin and return it to the exporter for transmission to the importer in the country of destination. The certifying authority will at the same time return to the exporter for his retention the duplicate copy of the certificate of origin, but will itself retain the GSP application form duly completed and signed by the exporter.

B. **Sanctions.** Persons who furnish, or cause to be furnished, information which relates to origin or consignment, and which is untrue in a material particular are liable to legal penalties and to the suspension of facilities for their goods to obtain preference.

"C" in front of the TSUS item number for each article for which such treatment is applicable. Should the claim be filed after the goods have been entered, the filing of the Certificate of Origin shall constitute the written claim. See exhibit 10–2.

Duty-free entry under the CBI is available if the sum of the cost/value of the material produced in a beneficiary country/countries is not less than 35 percent of the estimated value of the merchandise at the time of entry. In estimating the value/cost of the merchandise, the regulations are comparable to those applicable to GSP.

To be eligible for duty-free treatment, the goods must be transported directly from the beneficiary country to the U.S. customs territory. By *direct*, the regulations specify that the goods must not pass through the territory of a nonbeneficiary country. Should the goods go through a nonbeneficiary country, provided the goods do not enter the commerce of that country, the regulation has not been broken. Evidence of the transport is documented on the bill of lading and invoices accompanying the shipment. The destination on the bill of lading must be the United States. In the event that the destination is not the United States and a nonbeneficiary country is passed through, the goods will be imported into the U.S. only if:

the goods remained in the control of the customs authority of the nonbeneficiary country,

the goods did not enter into the commerce of the nonbeneficiary country and meet the approval of the district director, and

operations included only loading and unloading, and activities to insure the good condition of the merchandise.

The Certificate of Origin should be filed with the district director when CBI treatment is requested. This evidence pertains to the country of origin of the shipment and should be filed with the entry summary. Form A must be accurately completed and the Caribbean Basin Initiative must replace the General System of Preferences. As required by the GSP, proper endorsement will hasten the processing of this document. The requirement of certification by government officials is waived for the CBI.[15]

Summary

Importation of merchandise into the United States is a meticulous process in terms of the documentation that must be submitted to customs to allow for smooth entry. Prior to movement of any merchandise, goods must be marked, the appropriate documents must be processed, approval of entry must be obtained, and

Exhibit 10–2. Certificate of Origin

CERTIFICATE OF ORIGIN   I   № 12791

(ORIGINAL)

THE CHAMBER OF COMMERCE OF GUATEMALA, Certifies: a) that Mr.
, who declared to act on behalf of
, a businessman domiciled in
Guatemala City, presented himself in the Offices of the Chamber of Commerce
today to request that this Certificate be Issued.

declared under oath that the

merchandise indicated below, shipped by   air
in   , which sailed (will sail) from   Airport "La Aurora"

Guatemala Guatemala   on   destination
, consigned to
has originated or been produced in

Trade Marks	Quantity	Description of Merchandise	Gross weight	Net	Value

b) that the goods described above are the product of
, as appears from the documentation
submitted for the purpose and analyzed by this Chamber.

IN FAITH WHEREOF, this Certificate is signed by the Applicant and by the Manager of the
Chamber of Commerce of Guatemala, in the City of Guatemala, on

APLICANT

multicrops, s. a.

THE CHAMBER OF COMMERCE OF GUATEMALA

CHAMBER OF COMMERCE OF GUATEMALA

2 SET. 1988

MANAGEMENT

MANAGER

Delgado Impresos & Cía. Ltda. Tels.: 23-7-92, 51-80-47

duties and taxes on the merchandise must be paid. Under some conditions, components of a shipment of merchandise may be entered separately.

The sequence of evaluation methods comprises transaction value, deductive value, computed value, and other value. Special provisions exist for mail entries, drawbacks, and goods coming into the United States under the General System of Preferences or Caribbean Basin Initiative.

Due to the complex nature of the regulations and the various types of entries (for consumption, for warehouse, for transportation "in bond," for manipulation or manufacture, and by carnet), precise knowledge is needed to accurately assess classification and any tax or duty liability. Here a specialist may be valuable to an importer.

Notes

1. In accordance with the Tariff Act of 1930, importations are subject to the process of entry unless otherwise exempted. The Tariff Act of 1930 was amended, 19 U.S.C. 1484, 1484a, 1498.
2. Customs Regulations, 19 CR 141.
3. 19 CR 141.0 to 141.3.
4. 19 CR 141-5.
5. 19 CR 141-5 to 141.7.
6. 19 CR 141-8 to 141.10.
7. 19 CR 141-2, 141.3, 141.20, 159-1 to 159.4.
8. 19 CR 152-2.
9. For more details on customs regulations covering entries, see 19 CR 142-1/ CR 145-6.
10. 19 CR 152-6 to 152.15.
11. *Importing into the United States*, p. 63.
12. Eugene T. Rossides, *U.S. Import Trade Regulation*, pp. 24–25.
13. 19 CR 191-2, 191-3.
14. 19 CR 10-54 to CR 10-56.
15. 19 CR 10-60 to CR 10-61.

Epilogue

lobal interdependence is a present fact and a future trend. Bilateral
and multilateral flows of direct investment, goods and services, capital,
and technology are increasing; and few nations can survive, let alone
compete, in a mercantilist vacuum.

Indicative of what the future holds for major trading nations such as the
United States is the machine-tool industry. Companies purchase, sell, and exchange technologies with little attention to national boundaries. Interestingly,
importing plays a major role in the competitive strategies of U.S. machine-tool
companies. While battling foreign competition, firms are tapping foreign
technology. The majority import low-cost parts and some completed machines,
and a number of companies have become the licensees of foreign firms to assemble and sell machines designed abroad. Some U.S. firms are entering into
agreements with foreign manufacturers to produce U.S.-designed machines and
then import some of the equipment into the United States.

In spite of all the protectionist saber-rattling among industrialized nations
as well as between advanced and developing countries, the future looks bright
for imports. For the United States, imported goods and services are continually
expanding and currently exceed 12.5 percent of U.S. spending, a post–World
War II high according to 1987 U.S. Department of Commerce Statistics. This
dependency on imports is expected to continue.

There are six reasons for the continued trend in importing:

1. Many products that industrial and consumer buyers need or desire are
not made in the United States. For example, Amana's highly competitive
microwave oven, made in the United States, cannot function without its electronic core, the magnetron, which is not produced here. Other products made
exclusively offshore come to mind: 35-mm cameras, videocassette recorders,
and compact-disk players. Therefore, the competition that exists is among
foreign exporters. Moreover, a weakened dollar has virtually no effect on these
kinds of imports, but merely *increases* the dollar value of foreign products entering the United States.

2. Many imported products have a better reputation than domestic ones. Consequently, American consumers have developed loyalties to foreign brands for reasons of quality, reliability, service, style, or stature. Here, too, price fluctuations and differential exchange rates are not very meaningful. Witness the successes of Toyota, Gucci, Louis Vuitton, and Benetton.

3. Foreign exporters of capital goods often have a financial advantage in competing with domestic firms in the U.S. market. Even when quality is equal and the quoted import price is higher, U.S. industrial buyers often choose the foreign import due to extremely favorable seller-arranged financing.

4. The dual transformation of the U.S. economy—toward services and the renewal of manufacturing in selected industries—bodes well for imports. In the first instance, the shift to a services economy means that imports will fill the gap in America's manufacturing base. In the second, U.S. manufacturing firms will source components and subassembled products from abroad to improve their cost-efficiency.

5. Newly industrializing nations continually seek foreign markets for their goods. High-debt ones in particular (such as Brazil and Mexico) are under great pressure to export to earn foreign exchange to service their external debt. Many have made tremendous inroads, winning over once reluctant American consumers, in shoes, textiles, apparel, automotive parts, furniture, and machine parts.

6. Imports will continue to be strong mainly because the U.S. economy is so large and relatively healthy. The United States, for example, comprises half the world market for consumer electronics and purchases almost one-third of the world supply of auto parts. Moreover, as the U.S. economy continues to expand faster than those of Europe and the Third World, export-oriented economies will continue to target the American market.

Essentially, the question no longer is whether the United States should import. Instead, it is how to develop more efficient and effective import management and marketing.

Bibliography

American Bar Association. *Current Legal Aspects of International Trade Law*, Chicago: American Bar Associaton, 1982.

Andres, William A. *Protectionism: The Hidden Pricetag*, Vital Speeches (October 15, 1984), p. 13(4).

Andres, William A. *The Case for Open Trade: Speaking out for the Consumer*, Vital Speeches (August 1, 1985), pp. 623–26.

Anjana, S.J., et al. *Developments in International Trade Policy*. Washington, D.C.: International Monetary Fund, 1982.

Arndt, Sven W., et al. *Exchange Rates, Trade & the U.S. Economy*. Cambridge, Massachusetts: Ballinger, 1985.

Balassa, Bela. *Changing Patterns in Foreign Trade & Payments*. New York: W.W. Norton, 1978.

Balassa, Bela. *World Trade: Constraints & Opportunities in the 80's*. Allanheld, France: Atlantic Institute. 1979.

Baldwin, Robert E., and Richardson, David J. *International Trade and Finance Readings*, 2nd ed. Boston: Little, Brown, 1981.

Batchelor, R.A., et al. *Industrialization and the Basis for Trade*. New York: Cambridge University Press, 1980.

Bhagwati, Jagdish. *Foreign Trade Regimes and Economic Development: Anatomy and Consequences of Exchange Regimes,* Vol II. Cambridge, Massachusetts: Ballinger, 1978.

Branch, Allen E. *Elements of Exports Practice*. London: Chapman and Hall Publishing Co., 1977.

Carlson, Jack, and Graham, Hugh. *The Economic Importance of Exports to the United States*, Georgetown University Center for Strategic and International Studies, Washington, D.C.: Significant Issues Series, vol. 5 (5), 1980.

Cavusgil, S.T., and Nevin, John R. *International Marketing: An Annotated Bibliography*, 8th ed. Chicago: American Marketing Association, 1983.

Clark, M. "The Free Trade Fight (Canada-United States Trade)," *Macleans* (May 12, 1986), p. 20.

Cline, William R. *Reciprocity: A New Approach to World Trade Policy?* Cambridge, Massachusetts: MIT Institute of Economics, 1982.

Cline, William R., et al. *Trade Negotiations in the Tokyo Round: A Quantitative Assessment*. Washington, D.C.: Brookings Institution, 1978.

Crandall, Robert W. "Import Quotas and the Automobile Industry: the Cost of Protectionism," *Brookings Review* (Summer 1984), p. 8–17.

Customs Regulations. Washington, D.C. U.S. Treasury Department, Customs Service, 1985 reprint.

Daily News Record, "Rift's Wide as Gall Launches MFA Discussion" (July 24, 1985), p. 7.

Dam, Kenneth W. *The GATT Law—The International Economic Organization*. Chicago: University of Chicago Press, 1970.

De La Torre, Jose, Jr. *Exports of Manufactured Goods from Developing Countries: Marketing Factors and the Role of the Foreign Enterprise*, Salem, N.H.: Ayer, 1976.

Department of State Bulletin. *U.S.–Japan Joint Report on Sectoral Discussions (transcript)*(March 1986), p. 32.

Eason, Henry. *Keeping Afloat in the Import Flood*, Nations Business, 1985, pp. 42–44. September, Vol. 73, No. 9.

Ellsworth, P.T., and Leith, J. Clark. *The International Economy*, 6th ed. New York: Macmillan, 1984.

Eltringham, D.P. *Imports and Exports*. Elmsford, New York: Pergamon, 1977.

Ericson, H. *Tighter Curbs on Textiles Debated*, Journal of Commerce, p. A1, March 20, 1985.

Feder, Gershon. *On Exports and Economic Growth*. Washington, D.C.: World Bank, 1982.

Felber, John E. *Guide for the Prospective American Importer*, Newark: International Intertrade, 1960.

Gibbs, I., and Konovalov, V. *Volume Quotas with Heterogeneous Product Categories*. Economic Record, p. 294 (303), Vol. 60 #170, September 1984.

Goldsmith, Howard R. *How to Make a Fortune in Import-Export*. Englewood Cliffs, New Jersey: Reston, 1981.

Hamilton, Carl. *Effects of Non-Tariff Barriers to Trade on Prices, Employment and Imports: The Case of the Swedish Textile Clothing Industry*. Washington, D.C.: World Bank, 1980.

Holtzman, Jay M. *Imports: The Growing Problem*, Hardware Age (August 1984), p. 9 (1).

Ikeda, Yoshizo. *Trends in World Trade and Finance: A Business View*, Japan: Management (Spring 1986), pp. 6–8.

Importing into the United States. Washington, D.C.: U.S. Customs Service, 1986.

Ingham, Barbara. *Tropical Exports and Economic Development: New Perspectives on Producer Response in Three Low-Income Countries*. New York: St. Martin's 1980.

International Trade Center. *Standard Practices for Import & Export Restrictions & Exchange Controls*. Unpublished.

Journal of Commerce, *Half of International Trade Bound by Non-Tariff Barriers* (February 1, 1983), p. 23 B.

Journal of Maritime Law and Commerce.

Jumper, S.R., et al. *Economic Growth and Disparities*. Englewood Cliffs, New Jersey: Prentice-Hall, 1980.

Kahn, Helen, and Geoff Sundstrom. *Protection Is Bad for Automakers, Economist Says*, Automotive News, pp. 1–2, (July 2, 1984).

Kiam, Victor. *United States Trade Policy: Who's Managing the Oars?* Industry Week (February 3, 1980), p. 14.

Kinnear, T.C., and Bernhardt, K.L. *Principles of Marketing.* Glenview, Illinois: Scott, Foresman, 1983.

Kotler, Philip. *Marketing Management,* 5th ed. Englewood Cliffs, New Jersey: Prentice-Hall, 1984.

Lary, Hal B. *Imports from Manufacturers of Less Developed Countries.* Studies in International Economic Relations, no. 4. Cambridge, Massachusetts: National Bureau of Economic Research. 1968.

Lawrence, Robert, and Culbertson, John. *Is Free Trade Good or Bad for U.S.,* U.S. News & World Report (September 23, 1985), p. 53 (1).

Lovell, Malcolm R., Jr., *An Antidote for Protectionism,* Brookings Review (fall 1984), p. 23 (6).

MacElhiney, Paul T. *Transportation for Marketing and Business Students.* Totowa, New Jersey: Littlefield, Adams, 1975.

Marcy, Steve. *Fair Market Test for Product Imports Is Criticized,* Oil Daily (May 15, 1985), p. 10.

Matzels, Alfred. *Exports and Economic Growth of Developing Countries.* New York: Cambridge University Press, 1969.

McCarthy, E.J., and Perreault, W.D. *Basic Marketing,* 8th ed., Homewood, Illinois: Richard D. Irwin, 1984.

McLaughlin, John. *Protectionist Strategies,* National Review (August 9, 1985), p. 22 (1).

Murr, Alfred. *Export/Import Traffic Management and Forwarding,* 6th ed., Centreville, Maryland: Cornell Maritime Press, 1979.

O'Reilly, A. Koffman. *Countertrade: Dilemma for Administration,* Journal of Commerce (March 8, 1984), p. 3 A.

Orley, Tom. *Flexibility, Key to Trade with Comecom,* European Chemical News (October 28, 1985), p. 15.

Ortiz-Buonafina, Marta. *Profitable Export Marketing: A Strategy for U.S. Business.* Englewood Cliffs, New Jersey: Prentice-Hall, 1984.

Perkins, Elizabeth. *Results of the Tokyo Round: Proceedings of the Multilateral Trade Negotiations.* Washington, D.C.: Chamber of Commerce, 1979.

Rathmell, J.M. *Managing the Marketing Function.* New York: John Wiley & Sons, 1969.

Revzin, Phillip. *U.S. Quotas Irk Turkish Textile Exporters.* Wall Street Journal, April, 1986, p. 36.

Rossides, Eugene T. *Customs, Tariffs & Trade.* London: Graham & Trotman, 1977.

Rossides, Eugene T. *U.S. Import Trade Regulation.* Washington, D.C.: Bureau of National Affairs, 1985.

Root, William A. *Trade Controls That Work,* Foreign Policy, (fall 1984), pp. 61–(80).

Siposs, Allan J. *Importing: Practical Tips and Ideas for Entrepreneurs and Managers.* Irvine, California: International Commercial Services, Division of ICS Group, 1983.

Stern, L.W., and El Ansary, A.I. *Marketing Channels.* Englewood Cliffs, New Jersey: Prentice-Hall, 1982.

Tariff Schedule of the United States 1987. Washington, D.C.: U.S. International Trade Commission, 1986.

Taussig, Frank W. *Some Aspects of the Tariff Questions: An Examination of the Development of American Industries under Protection.* AMS Pr. New York: 1931 (sic).

Trade: U.S. Policy since 1945. Washington, D.C.: Congressional Quarterly, 1984.

U.S. Bureau of the Census, *Statistical Abstract of the U.S.: 1988* (108th edition) (Washington, D.C.: U.S. Department of Commerce, 1988).

U.S. Bureau of the Census, *Statistical Abstract of the U.S.: 1987* (107th edition) (Washington, D.C.: U.S. Department of Commerce, 1987).

U.S. Bureau of the Census, *Statistical Abstract of the U.S.: 1986* (106th edition) (Washington, D.C.: U.S. Department of Commerce, 1985).

United States Chamber of Commerce, *Foreign Commerce Handbook.* Washington, D.C.: United States Chamber of Commerce, 1981.

U.S. Treasury Department, Customs Service. *Customs Regulations of the United States.* Washington, D.C.: U.S. Government Printing Office, 1981.

U.S. Treasury Department, Customs Service, Office of Regulations and Rulings. *Customs Regulations of the United States.* Washington, D.C.: U.S. Government Printing Office, 1984.

U.S. Treasury Department, Customs Service, Office of Commercial Operations. *Customs Valuations Rulings under the Trade Agreement Act of 1979.* Washington, D.C.: U.S. Government Printing Office, 1984.

U.S. Treasury Department, Customs Service. *Drawback: A Duty Refund on Certain Exports.* Washignton, D.C.: U.S. Government Printing Office, 1984.

U.S. Treasury Department, Customs Service. *Free Ports and Zones: U.S. Customs Procedures and Requirements.* Washington, D.C.: U.S. Government Printing Office, 1984.

U.S. Treasury Department, Customs Service. *Miscellaneous Tariffs and Customs Amendments.* Washington, D.C.: U.S. Govrnment Printing Office, 1984.

U.S. Treasury Department, Customs Service. *T.I.R. Temporary Importation under Bond.* Washington, D.C.: U.S. Government Printing Office, 1983.

U.S. Treasury Department, Customs Service. *U.S. Customs: International Mail Imports.* Washington, D.C.: U.S. Government Printing Office, 1983.

U.S. Treasury Department, Customs Service. *United States Import Requirements.* Washington, D.C.: U.S. Government Printing Office, 1981.

United States Trade: Performance in 1987 and Outlook. Washington, D.C.: U.S. Department of Commerce, 1988.

Walsh, James L. *Countertrade: Not Just for East–West Anymore,* World Trade Journal (January-February 1983), pp. 3–11.

Weidenbaum, Murray L. *The Assault on International Trade,* National Review (December 28, 1984), pp. 29–31.

Wightman, Richard. *If Textile Bill Created, What Will It Mean?* Daily News Record (August 6, 1986), p. 1.

Wightman, R. *U.S. Textile Execs Talk Tough on Import at ITME Meeting,* Daily News Record, pp. 2-7, v. 14, (October 11, 1984).

Index

About the Authors

Jerry Haar is Associate Professor of Business, Florida International University, and Adjunct Scholar at the American Enterprise Institute, Washington, D.C. Dr. Haar is also a principal in Hayden Haar, Inc., a business development and management consulting firm, and Vice President of the World Trade Center, Miami. Previously, Dr. Haar was Director of Programs in the Washington office of the Council of the Americas, a business association of over 200 U.S. corporations comprising approximately 90 percent of U.S. private investment in Latin America, the Caribbean, and Canada.

Dr. Haar received his B.A. cum laude from the School of International Service, The American University; his master's from Johns Hopkins; and his Ph.D. from Columbia University. He is also a graduate of Harvard University's Executive Program in Management and Health Finance. From 1972 to 1973 Dr. Haar was a Fulbright Scholar at the Fundação Getúlio Vargas in Brazil. Dr. Haar has authored three books and a number of articles and has been a consultant to companies in the United States and abroad in the areas of importing and exporting, strategic planning, management evaluation, market research, and training.

Marta Ortiz-Buonafina is Associate Professor of Marketing at Florida International University. She holds a Ph.D. in International Affairs. She is the author of *The Impact of Import Substitution Industrialization on Marketing Activities: A Case Study of the Guatemalan Commercial Sector* (University Press of America, 1981) and *Profitable Export Marketing: A Strategy for U.S. Business* (Prentice-Hall, 1984). She has also written articles for *Akron Business and Economic Review* and *Journal of Macromarketing*. She received a Fulbright Lecturing Award, Master's Program, Universidad Francisco Marroquin, Guatemala in the summer of 1987.

Dr. Ortiz-Buonafina is listed in *Who's Who and Why of Successful Florida Women* and *Who's Who in Florida's Latin Community (1986), The World's Who's Who of Women* (1987), and *Who's Who in Florida* (1988).